The Astro-Geology of Earthquakes and Volcanoes

Lind Weber

Copyright 1994 by Lind Weber
All rights reserved.

No part of this book may be reproduced or transmitted in any form or by any means, electronic or mechanical, including photocopying or recording, or by any information storage and retrieval system, without written permission from the author and publisher. Requests and inquiries may be mailed to: American Federation of Astrologers, Inc., 6535 S. Rural Road, Tempe, AZ 85283.

First Printing: 1994
Current Printing: 2011

ISBN-10: 0-86690-446-8
ISBN-13: 978-0-86690-446-9

Cover Design: Jack Cipolla

Published by:
American Federation of Astrologers, Inc.
6535 S. Rural Road
Tempe, AZ 85285-2040

Printed in the United States of America

Dedication

This book is dedicated to Mary Kay Kemble, wife and friend.

She lived with it from the beginning.

I thank her for her patience and encouragement and for always being there.

Acknowledgements

Somewhere in the text I noted that you really don't get the job done alone.

Very special thanks to triple Sagittarius Carole Arbour who dashed into the typing breech. learning as she went along astrologese, geologese and the astrological symbols as well as my handwriting. It was undaunted courage unto foolhardiness, like that of another triple Sagittarian, George Armstrong Custer.

Special thanks to Martha E. Ramsey of the AFA who in true Aquarian fashion ``winged'' it on acceptance, time and final editing. She also came up with the title.

Thanks to Denise Tapp, who over the years has done research and supplied pre-20th century charts and encouragement.

Thanks to my mother Marion Rehill Weber who in tough times has given both financial and moral support.

Finally, I wish to thank some of my astrologer friends who have helped in this, each one in his or her own way, some inadvertently or unawares; Carole Griffin, Danuta Miller, Anna Mattera, John Goode, Michael Smith, T. Stan Riddle, Jo Anne Stover, Eleanor Cermak, Jan Snodgrass Shirley Chenoweth and Sophia Mason.

Thank you to everyone who ever helped with this book. Thank you, God. It took a full Jupiter cycle.

Preface

March 26, 1993 began nondescript and continued that way. No job, no money. Stayed at home to save money. I deliberately refused to check a one-day construction job and paid a bill.

The day wasted, I decided to stoke my mind. With no desire to write, I read of Atlantis and great quakes of Mu and gas belts, of disappeared lands and men who searched for them and believed in them.

I left the house and bought a can of coffee. I came back and lay down, switched on the country music television. And began to read *The Mystery of Atlantis* by Charles Berlitz.

"In six minutes 60,000 people perished. A great concourse of people had collected for safety upon a new quay built entirely of marble, but suddenly it sank down with all the people on it, and not one of the dead bodies floated to the surface. . . . The water where the quay went down is now 600 feet deep. The area covered by this earthquake was very great. Humboldt says that a portion of `the earth's surface four times as great as the size of Europe was simultaneously shaken."

It extended from Canada to Algiers. At eight leagues from Morocco the ground opened and swallowed a village of 10,000 inhabitants and closed again over them. "I have that chart," I said, and left the bed.

It was exactly 4:30 p.m. AST, St. Thomas, U.S. Virgin Islands and by 6:00 p.m. the work of 13 years had fallen into place. I understood the process of vulcanism from Sun to Earth to elimination. The missing pieces of the timing mechanism and the vulcanistic process moved into place like watch gears. I'll refer to the day in the text, for it took me to the beginning and end of the process.

The true gift of the amateur is unfettered confidence. I didn't know how to erect a chart when I began this. I hadn't read a text on geology. I'd worked 15 years as a stone mason and I'd just reached astrology across the occult and lost lands and pyramids, led there by a knowledge of stone masonry. I'd glanced at a book on the Great Pyramid, said, "No you can't build it that way . . . all the masons in one place. . . ."

When Mt. St. Helen erupted, I began to place volcanoes and quakes in a wheel taking the data directly from the ephemeris.

Charts from some locales had recurring patterns and these were different from those of other locales whose charts also had recurring patterns. And the charts of quakes as compared to volcanoes...well you see.

I was off and running and very close then. Amazing how long it takes to cover a short distance.

I don't drink anymore, but I lit a cigar that had waited on the bookshelf for years.

Astrologers have a mechanism in the ephemeris that can time the past, present and future. This mechanism of planetary observation offers correlations to recurring events.

Geologists have a machine that tells you where quakes just happened and how much energy they produce in terms of vibrations. Neither side does much in the way of forecasting and they aren't speaking to each other much either, lost in jargon, wandering the halls of credentials, fleeing dragons of thought and possible error.

My first move was based on the decision to try and find a means of locating a quake in a forecast. I'd noticed differences in charts for different locales after my first batch of EM (Earth motion—quake or volcano, the all-American acronym which the reader will come to appreciate) charts so it offered a starting point. As I amassed charts, all collected randomly, all hand copied, I soon noticed a distinction between quake and volcano eruption charts as well. Inadvertently I'd stumbled on the process of vulcanism and the means of establishing an overall cyclical timing method. Heretofore astrologers worked from a previous quake or eclipse, say to a period of intense planetary energy, but in terms of time it could not tell how far the quake energy or potential had developed and energy intensity was only a partial picture of the quake chart. There was, in fact, another energy measure, planetary separation, that was not being used. Timing mechanisms were hit and miss and the locale signature was by and large undeveloped, often through false approaches such as locale charts, e.g. the founding of a state or country.

In fits and bursts it all came together on March 26, 1993 after some 13 years I had correlated the beginning and the vulcanism process in the same hour, bringing process, time and local together.

What follows is a text on EM forecasting that provides an integrated use of astrology and geology. For various reasons including some practical personal ones, I've chosen to present it in succinct sections, more on the level of a manual than either a specialized text or a literary work. I believe some great ideas get lost in these two genres.

Whether a position is put froward assertively or a priori noted as hypothesis, I believe the overall viewpoint deserves consideration and I invite examination of the parts. The overall methodology will be discussed in its own chapter.

Contents

Section I
Earthquakes and Vulcanism—The Geological Overview

Chapter 1—The Solar Timer of Vulcanism	3
Chapter 2—The Gas Belts of James Churchward	7
Chapter 3—The New Madrid Quake and the Appalachian Gas Belt	11
Chapter 4—Anatomy of the Gas Belts	13
Chapter 5—Catastrophism: An Overview	17
Chapter 6—Catastrophism: The Key to Major EM	19
Chapter 7—Chandler Wobble	21
Chapter 8—Why Geology and Astrology Should Cooperate	25
Chapter 9—Evacuation	27
Chapter 10—The True Tragedy of Future Em	29

Section II
Earthquakes and Vulcanism—The Astrological Overview

Chapter 11—Planetary Overview	33
Chapter 12—On the Sun	35
Chapter 13—On the Moon	37
Chapter 14—The Other Planets	41
Chapter 15—Planetary Groups in EM	47
Chapter 16—A List of Simultaneous Events	49
Chapter 17—Drawing the EM Event Chart	51
Chapter 18—Signs and Aspect Complexes	53
Chapter 19—What the Ancients Can Teach Us	55

Chapter 20—Why I Do Not Use Ascendant Charts in EM	57
Chapter 21—Why I Don't Use Locality Charts	59
Chapter 22—Midpoints in EM	61
Chapter 23—The Rolling Signature	63
Chapter 24—Stored Energy	65
Chapter 25—Outer Planet Aspect Intensity	67
Chapter 26—Planetary Patterns Forming the Signature	69
Chapter 27—The Use of Aspects in EM Forecasting	71
Chapter 28—Simultaneous Events	73
Chapter 29—An Astro-Geological Overview	75
Chapter 30—Cairo 1992	79
Chapter 31—Geological Timing for EM: A Method	83
Chapter 32—EM Degrees	85
Chapter 33—Significance of Minor EM	87
Chapter 34—EM Weather	89
Chapter 35—Forecasting the EM Event: The Difficult Made Succinct	91
Chapter 36—Final Timing: The Hour	93
Chapter 37—Approaching and Separating Aspects	95

Section III
Location Signatures

Chapter 38—The Location Signature	99
Chapter 39—Methodology of EM Sample	101
Chapter 40—Lunar Enhancement	103
Chapter 41—The Signature of Alaska, Aleutians, Katchamka, Kuril Islands and the Bering Sea	105
Chapter 42—The Signature of Japan	109
Chapter 43—Philippine Islands Signature	117
Chapter 44—The Signature of the Celebes	121
Chapter 45—The Signature of Eastern Indonesia	125
Chapter 46—The Signature of Indonesia	127
Chapter 47—The Signature of the Marianas and the Caroline Islands and Bonin	129
Chapter 48—The Signature of the Solomon Islands	131
Chapter 49—The Signature of Australia	133
Chapter 50—The Signature of Macquerie Island	135
Chapter 51—The Signature of Antarctica	137

Chapter 52—The Signature of New Caledonia and the Loylaty Islands — 139

Chapter 53—The Signature of the New Hebrides Islands — 141

Chapter 54—The Signature of Fiji Island — 143

Chapter 55—The Signature of Polynesia — 145

Chapter 56—The Signature of Samoa and Tonga — 147

Chapter 57—The Signature of New Zeland — 149

Chapter 58—The Signature of Chile — 155

Chapter 59—The Signature of Peru — 159

Chapter 60—The Signature of Ecuador and Colombia — 161

Chapter 61—The Signature of Central America — 163

Chapter 62—The Signature of Mexico — 165

Chapter 63—The Signature of California — 169

Chapter 64—The Signature of New Madrid — 177

Chapter 65—The Caribbean Signature — 183

Chapter 66—The Signature of France — 189

Chapter 67—The Signature of Italy — 191

Chapter 68—The Signature of Greece — 193

Chapter 69—The Signature of Turkey — 195

Chapter 70—The Signature of Iran — 197

Chapter 71—The Signature of Tblisi — 199

Chapter 72—The Signature of Afghanistan, Hindu Kush and India — 201

Chapter 73—The Signature of Assam India — 203

Chapter 74—The Signature of China and Russia — 205

Chapter 75—An Overview on Vulcanism — 207

Chapter 76—Forecasting the Volcanic Eruption — 211

Appendices and Comments

Appendix I—Simultaneous Events as Related to Lunar Enhancement and the Universal Signature — 217

Appendix II—The Cancer-Capricorn Axis — 223

Appendix III—Grand Trine Water Quakes — 227

Appendix IV—French Earthquakes — 233

Appendix V—Grand Trine Water Volcanoes — 235

Appendix VI—Volcanoes: Grand Trine Fire, Saturn in Pisces, Jupiter in Pisces, Jupiter in Scorpio — 237

Appendix VII—The Semantics of Prediction — 241

Appendix VIII—Full Circle — 245

Section I

Earthquakes and Vulcanism: The Geological Overview

1

The Solar Timer of Vulcanism

In 1946, John Henry Nelson undertook a study of the Sun. He worked for RCA. Radio was growing but periodically it encountered transmission problems—static in a word. Nelson was neither an astronomer nor an astrologer, untrained in the first and never having considered the second. He did not know the universal symbols of the planets used by both.

He observed the sun and quickly noted that instances of solar activity coincided with periods of poor transmission and began correlating all this with planetary angles and positions. Simply, he began to practice astrology—as does the *Farmer's Almanac*. Nelson fell into solar astrology using the sun as center, since that was his interest. He noticed that 60° and 120° angles produced smooth reception and 0°, 90° and 180° static.

Guy L. Playfair and Scott Hill, authors of the *Cycles of Heaven*, one of many books telling the story of Nelson, claim he was "the first to show beyond reasonable doubt that there was any connection between terrestrial phenomenon. We cannot help wondering why it was left to a non-astrologer and non-professional astronomer to make this discovery."

This is not the only incident involving the profound ignorance and even more profound arrogance of Playfair and Hill regarding astrology. Later in the book one of them judges a horoscope bought from a machine, basically using ignorance as his credentials. I am amazed to find how annoying these two remain after a dozen years. Inadvertently, they did pay homage to the unfettered mind of another amateur, Nelson. The book as a whole is excellent.

Back to the matter at hand, solar activity, Nelson's charts were formed using exact (partile) aspects. Nelson also used 15° aspect multiples as weather astrologers had for centuries. In short, Nelson produced by observation the same astrology as was in general use, but he produced it in regard to solar activity.

Geology has no time reference in regard to EM (Earth Motion), whether this be a cyclical, linear or ongoing sense of timing. Astrology has all these senses of timing by correlating planetary positions and EM events in the ephemeris.

Throughout history mankind has paid special note to the spring solstice, the entry of the sun into 00:00 Aries, known as the beginning of spring. Astrologically speaking this is the beginning of the year in terms of seasons.

The budding and seeding. In the zodiac of 360° this degree has a connotation of beginning. Each of the cardinal signs, Aries, Cancer, Libra, and Capricorn also have a connotation of beginning under their own steam, a dynamic, Martian tone of doing things. Mars is the ruler of Aries and the Sun is a special guest there, exalted in astrologese.

Somewhere along the line I began to chart solar events as well, storms, flares, high sun spot activity. Whatever the nature of the event and /or terminology, the charts produced are similar. Solar events have a signature chart.

Let's return to Nelson. For the observer of EM he made an important observation. He showed through the painful reality of radio static that these solar events showed up on earth as static virtually simultaneously. A cause/effect relationship was observed, if not proven and it was enough to work with for functional results of 85 percent (Nelson). The fact that solar energy from a distance is able to effect Earth forthwith is important in the EM time scheme as it allows the laying out of a time continuum.

What follows is a premise on the process of vulcanism itself with an ongoing timing mechanism integrated.

Major solar activity often occurs with some or all of the following conditions as noted through the ephemeris. The solar activity and the ephemeris positions constitute agreed on realities. Solar activity often has present planets in very early cardinal degrees, let us say zero to four, Venus-Pluto interactions, usually approaching closely, partile, or just separating.

Finally on March 23, 1993, it became obvious. There were the partile major aspects as opposed to the widely separated aspects, or those falling at 15° of the major quake, and the moderate separation involved in volcanic eruptions and moderate quakes. Here was a beginning. Early cardinal, partile aspects, not separating aspects. This means an earlier time.

Everything begins with the Sun. After all it is the center of our planetary system. The Sun itself marks the overall rhythm of EM.

- Early cardinal 0-4°—Solar activity and inner earth vulcanism.
- Cardinal first decanate 0-9°59"—Earth vulcanism and volcanic eruptions.
- Cardinal second decanate 10-19°59"—Major volcanic eruptions (separation) Moderate quakes. Shallow quakes. Quakes nearest active vulcanism etc.

Overlapping occurs and at times very early cardinal will produce a major quake or eruption. Here it indicates a new infusion of solar energy, the balloon bursts. Finally all three cardinal decanates together indicate a sustained period of energizing. Major EM occurs. If a quake, strong vulcanism is involved.

Overlapping also occurs because ongoing multiple processes are involved. Furthermore in terms of location, EM energy build up is initiated, continued, or completed (major EM event). By major, I mean to exclude the minor quakes of a vulcanistic location, or the shallow quakes near a magma chamber.

Thus by reading the degrees, for they are sequential, we note:

Solar events initiate an increase in inner earth (core and mantle) vulcanism. Heat increases with subsequent increases in flow (inner earth convection). As convection rises volcanic eruptions and quakes increase in locations sensitive to the planetary signature of the moment meeting those conditions astrological and geological outlined elsewhere in this text. Vulcanism itself has a universal signature based on an early cardinal emphasis which is the common point, whatever the rest of the planetary disbursement may be.

Apparently inner vulcanism occurs through the earth as a whole. When it reaches the limits of the outer mantle it has already differentiated routes as it passes through the mantle, but this is possibly not the only heat source. At the limits of the outer mantle some of this heat and deep magma is channeled into the gas belts, themselves mainly fueled by superheated steam. These ``belts'' are roughly horizontal and lay at the Moho between the mantle and the crust. (Gas Belts, Chapter 2). From the gas belts magma generated at various levels is driven upward by the snorkel principle. This vertical distribution ends in areas of surface vulcanism, plate juncture, volcanoes, blowhole system (fumaroles) as in the Alaska Valley of 10,000 Smokes. A similar area was found by naval geologists on the Pacific Ocean floor in early 1993.

When vulcanism is considered as the driving force, and all quakes either directly or secondarily the result of it, a simple picture emerges of a living earth renewing itself through a solar switch turned on periodically. While there may be variations in the solar switch, it must be fairly orderly or the earth would die if inert or explode if overheated.

Here the times of early cardinal degree position, as well as the switch regulators Mercury and Jupiter, come into play. Mercury and Jupiter are involved in initiating and transmitting the vulcanistic energy throughout the process within both the Sun and Earth themselves.

Above I sketched an outline of a timing continuum and a process. Actually they exist together for all practical purposes.

Sun, Mercury and Jupiter in suitable aspect turn on solar activity, itself in part vulcanistic, at the appropriate times, early cardinal with suitable Venus-Pluto energizing and partile aspects between other planets—further energizing. Again, given that the planets themselves as a group never occupy exactly the same positions as a group, the timing and output of these regularly recurring solar events varies. Planetary cycles lend stability as a whole, but overlapping cycles also cause time variations and event aberrations.

Thus in planetary strong periods and patterns extra energy is produced. This vents itself as usual in quakes and surface vulcanism. A strong increase in energy may overload, block, or rupture a system and at that time and location, major EM occurs.

Over simplifying, major EM is the result of failure to equitably distribute the earth's inner heat, or through damage to the distribution system itself.

Major EM is a reflection of breakdown, itself a natural result of the vulcanistic process which renews, reuses, and relocates the very crust of the earth itself—sometimes on a grand scale.

2

The Gas Belts of James Churchward

Vulcanism is the process and timer of EM and the basic nature of major EM—breakdown in the vulcanistic distribution system is a natural eventuality, but acyclical.

In this chapter I'll attempt to lay out a possible distribution system and describe it before moving on to some additional comments on catastrophism. In the geology of catastrophism lay the answers to major EM, both volcanoes and quakes, as simple or simultaneous events outside of the everyday range, but still part of an ongoing process.

Aristotle felt that quakes and volcanoes were the results of gas, and modern geology dismissed him. The gas is super-heated steam, ever more pressurized. This is not the propellant power of a steam boiler turning a ships prop or train's wheel. This steam cuts through rock like a laser and drives rivers of magma before it. I've read quite a few texts on both quakes and volcanoes in the last dozen years but not much about this process. Both volcanoes and quakes seem to have little in the way of background, appearing suddenly, at one's door step like remittance men who failed to keep their end of the bargain.

Obviously steam is the main propellant force for vulcanism. It functions both in the production of magma and the propulsion. This is not to deny heat vectors arising from the mantle and frictively produced magma heat, as where two tectonic plates collide or one dives under another in subduction.

What probably occurs is an interaction of heating sources. Ocean water leaks in at rift sites, principally around mid-oceanic rift sites. A rift separates and here heat is not frictively produced. This is the source of most of the super heated steam. Some is immediately returned to drive continental drift, in the creation of pillow lava and to keep the ocean from leaking into the inner earth.

The gas belts utilize basic plumbing and physics, the snorkel principle and the sink trap, here reversed since gas rises, and converted into a compression chamber. The notion of lighter molten rock flowing up does not contradict this. It is lighter because it is super charged with steam bubbles. Near the surface of the earth or crust, its rate of rise would increase as compressed steam expanding increases propellant force. The belt distribution system lies along the Moho. Finally, vertically rising magma to a volcano probably rises from the belt and may or may not involve magma chambers.

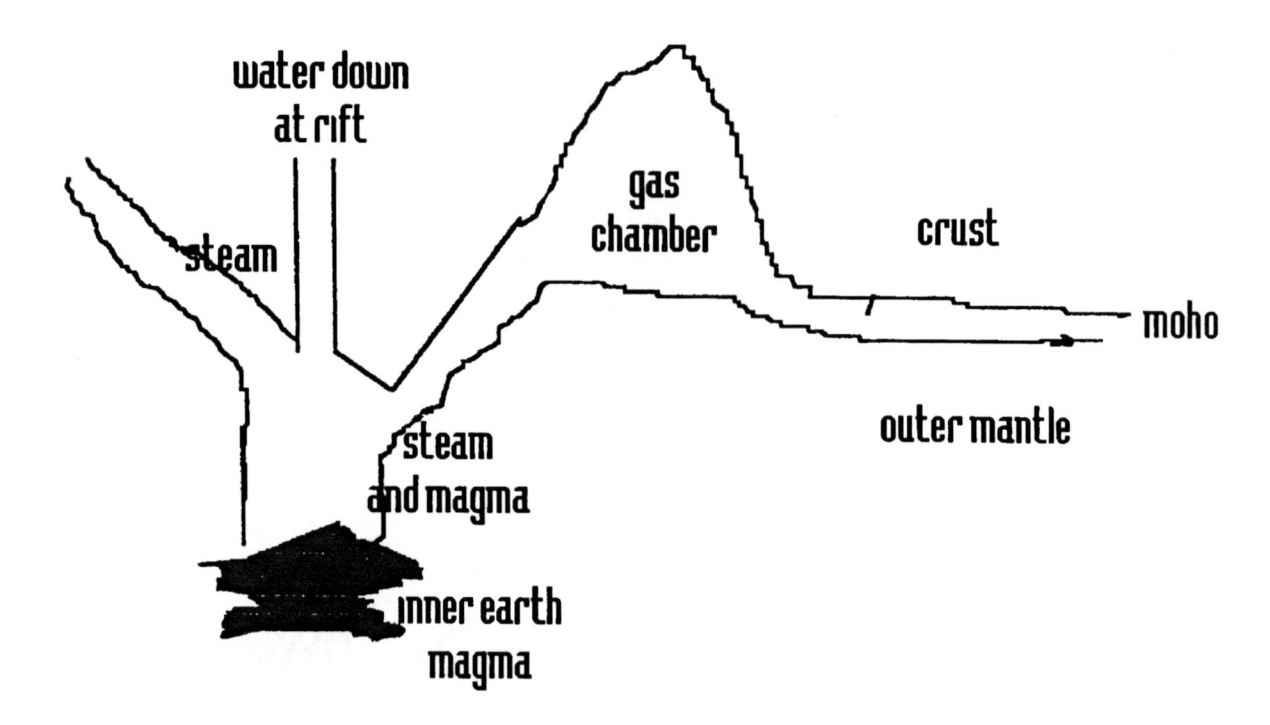

Diagram labels: water down at rift; steam; gas chamber; crust; moho; outer mantle; steam and magma; inner earth magma

In 1931, Colonel James Churchward published a series of books on Mu or Lemuria, the Pacific counterpart of Atlantis whose break up and sinking purportedly preceded that of Atlantis. The series would probably come under the index of anthropology—radical. But you can't lose a civilization under the sea without talking about it and that involves quite a few thoughts on geology. This was a continent that sank, larger by far than the Titanic.

According to Churchward, he found the information about the gas belts in Tibet from old maps found in a monastery. A man of no small ego, his documentation is sketchy, but I intuitively trust him. He was too ornery to waste time in dishonesty. Churchward sensed that the gas belts were very large—mind boggling as it were—through his belief or knowledge of their destructive power. He made no attempt to measure them, but merely noted their position and one other interesting point, the southern branch of the Great Central Belt is deeper. The Great Central Belt circles the globe in the equatorial regions. Here to the south, there to the north. It is referred to as the Pacific Cross Belt in that Ocean.

Another situation involving an eye or almond shaped loop also appears. Usually this is noted, but I may have also noted it as a branch. The belt system is contained in James Churchward series on Mu *The Children of Mu Volume 2*, 1931, republished in 1968.

The second great belt is the Great Pacific Circuit Belt more or less following the Ring of Fire. Three parallel belts run along the coast of Western South America and inland, the middle one also running beneath Central America. A division divides, remaining one side in the sea the other beneath Central America. A second division, the one beneath Central America runs beneath Nevada and does not branch but in Idaho turns at 45° into Montana. The third division divides and runs beneath Arizona, Utah and Idaho on its western side and New Mexico, Colorado, Wyoming, and Montana on it's eastern side.

The Appalachian Belt starts approximately at the mouth of the Mississippi River, moving more or less in a line to Lake Ontario. In Virginia, a branch moves seaward along the East Coast. Both branches meet at the Southern tip of Greenland crossing the Atlantic in an arc entering Norway and the Gulf of Bothnia, midway, and continuing on into Russia.

Parts of Europe are covered by branches from the Central Cross Belt North. Branches from the South Division move into Asia Minor, and Africa.

James Churchward's belts tend to follow the action spots of the earth. The skeptic might say he drew them after the fact, but several problems arise with the position of the skeptic. Some of the belt detail, particularly in the western U.S., passes through dormant zones, but zones with future potential. And he does not write from a geological standpoint. I note again my first impression, perhaps a crank, but not deceitful. Geology is vague on the causes of quakes in the area radiating out from New Madrid. It is noteworthy that this belt ends up near the St. Lawrence Seaway, a sensitive area.

The Gas Belts need examination by astrologers and geologists. Similarity of charts for quakes in locations along their course, as well as the documentation of simultaneous events, would go a long way toward corroborating their existence. The notion that all heat is generated from within the earth or by subduction is reasonable, but the matter of propellant still has to be considered. The explosive force behind a volcano can only come from steam. The same goes for quake uplift in certain instances. Rock tilt and rock lava effects account for others.

The continued efforts to avoid dealing with a magma propellant are absurd. If it flies in the face of gradualism, the fault is with gradualism. If it flies in the face of computer soundings well, the fault is with the computer. There is no agreement in geological computer simulated models. What in fact exists are semi-official positions which keep disagreement more or less under wraps. Further understanding is available with the concepts of vulcanism and gas belts—the horizontal conduit system providing the means for delivery of a propellant and unknown amounts of magma. The gas belts also have other gas chambers along their length, all based on principles of physics, heat moving upward. This system must be huge, in terms that we don't think of or even want to contemplate.

Did Mu or Atlantis exist? Many who have considered the matter judiciously believe so. The literature is available, some noted throughout this book. I'll just say that fitting the pieces together of Gotwanda or Pangaea is no final proof. It is interesting that the Dolphin Ridge itself is parallel to Europe and North America. The geology of the Caribbean and the North Sea deserves a closer look as well.

The only stone that could be generated down there would be alluvial in nature or pillow lava now. Other rock present would include some carried by icebergs. This would be evident by random groupings of several types of rock and random dispersion since the icebergs drifted in certain directions on winds and ocean currents. As they melted stones broke loose—this an extremely random dispersion.

Now if the camera sees land-type formation down there or can track an outline of beach sand, or coastal formations, what is the nature of the North-South division and rises?

Finally if angular stone formations are found, they may be somewhat rounded by dissolving, but pillow lava cannot square itself. Stone can only erode from square to round.

Personally, I don't see mountain peaks as being alluvial in the middle of the ocean or being pillow lava. And those north/south hills and valleys? Why this walk on the wild side? One can understand major EM thorough catastrophism, but not through gradualism.

Returning to the gas belts, in the gas chamber, with increased earth heat and the rising of loose molten magma, the pressure would begin to push the magma in horizontal directions. Moving towards the rift, the magma would meet the trap and plug it. Some might drive through it and be dealt with through the rift. This would theoretically function in a continental drift fashion and would hit the sea floor as pillow lava.

The gas chamber near the rifts is the gathering point for both magma and superheated steam. It must also provide a horizontal conduit, the belt. Pressurized magma moving into the superheated pressurized steam of the gas chamber is pushed forward horizontally. Along it's path through the belt, heat may induce quakes at certain points. Ultimately the magma will reach a surface magma chamber beneath a volcano. This chamber, one way or another, represents a dead end and the propellant pressure forces it out, whether in flow or explosive *nuee ardiente* eruption. As it nears the earth's surface the expansion of compressed steam further abets and accelerates the process. And fumaroles—these are pressure vents, safety valves as it were, present here and there along rifts, in Alaska's Valley of 10,000 Smokes, here and there on the Pacific floor and elsewhere, the steaming volcano. In the presence of major vulcanism, these end up blocked or overloaded.

I've now shown a possible means, process and timing mechanism for vulcanism. Inevitable and factored into the living earth it is nevertheless, a break down and again for this reason somewhat acyclical. Let's examine the gas chamber in the Gas Belt. Using available knowledge, what might be inferred about it?

From its position on a tube it functions as a storage chamber, but it also has another potential, that of a stone aneurysm that can blow out. This occurs in a magma chamber—this last gas chamber is usually the cause of a super chamber which is nearest the earth's surface. This was probably the process at Thera and Krakatoa, mini versions of some of the Atlantean and Muvian disasters, if indeed they happened. Churchward, not a geologist and not inclined to psychic geology, notes simply that the gas chambers collapsed and the continents sank.

If one places a molten liquid against its solid counterpart, there will not be major melting without additional outside heat. Clearly the gas belts were cut by super heated steam and a direction was achieved by least resistance, exactly like a river. Like a river it would have a direction, the heat moving it along, in search of vertical tributaries, ultimately the magma must reach an end chamber or magma chamber, so as not to block the belt.

Super heated gas rises upward. Slowly it cuts stone off the belt sides, melting it off as magma and granitic aggregate. Arriving at a chamber, superheated steam melts the chamber even larger and higher. If a chamber were large enough it would bring about its own collapse, notably when one of it's sides moved outside of vertical support for whatever land mass lay above it, or became too thin for that land mass at arch center.

In the case of Atlantis, this would be a possibility for two reasons. The land mass would be narrow, a strip parallel to both Europe and North America. Tradition also notes that in fact it was or became a series of islands. The major sinking covering thousands of years with individual sinkings having both gradual and abrupt phases. Another detail of the legend is the concurrence of quakes and volcanic activities.

As a feasible scenario whose major premise depends on whether these chambers exist, I say, explain Krakotoa on the basis of there not being an extremely large chamber as an explosive source.

Atlantis legends are also very clear. It disappeared north to south, all accounts agree. This is another inferred proof for the gas belts. The Great Central Gas Belt according to Churchward, runs in two belts from the Pacific through Central America, ending up with it's North and South divisions on each side of the Mediterranean, Iberia and North Africa respectively. Churchward writes that the South sections are newer and deeper. Inadvertently Churchward corroborated his gas belts with Atlantis.

Working with this legend or history, we may infer a branch belt running north towards Iceland and Greenland but stopping well short of them because the Appalachian Belt runs through Iceland in an east/west direction. As the end chamber (north) would be the most stressed, heated, carved, it would be the first to collapse. The branch belt would carve another end chamber at the new, shortened, more southerly end, created by the collapse. The sequence repeated itself several times. Finally, a collapse occurred that also effected the Great Central Circuit Belt. At this time we may assume the south division was created ("deeper" and "later"—Churchward).

According to legend, we also know that Atlantis had active volcanoes. The end chamber would have to vent, erupt, as it carved itself out to the point of collapse. Legend tells of their cities of red, white and black stone. The black stone was probably of volcanic origin.

This illustrates a process of vulcanism that probably brought down the Atlantean Islands and Krakatoa. The story of the gas belts fits the legend of Atlantis. The belts have the same physics as giant plumbing systems and boilers. Astrology notes that there are periodic increases and decreases in the earth's inner vulcanism through solar activity. Lastly, the regularity of this solar activity and the absence of knowable cyclical dates covering thousands of years—Atlantis sank at irregular intervals infers that major EM is the result of a breakdown.

3

The New Madrid Quake and the Appalachian Gas Belt

If Atlantis is a much noted possibility, New Madrid remains an obscure actuality. On December 16, 1811 at 2:00 a.m. LMT, according to one diarist, perhaps the greatest quake since Columbus' arrival ripped through the center of the continent. Uplift and subsidence could be measured in dozens of feet. The course of the Mississippi River was altered—I've never read how much. Forests were damaged and Reelfoot Lake was created. The coordinates for New Madrid are 89W32 and 36N35.

By some combination of Richter power and geology, it was strongly felt over thousands of square miles. It may have been 9R+. It is not known, in fact, if New Madrid was the epicenter. In the early spring there were two or three more major events, though smaller than New Madrid I.

The event remains little noticed because only a few trappers were there at the time, and there was little or no loss of life. Economic damage was non-existent, there being no economy. I'm sure some trap lines were lost but.... This was not San Francisco 1906, with a dazed Caruso wandering the streets and fires breaking out in a glamorous port creating a panorama of confusion and economic destruction. There were only trees without the perspective of man or camera. As America developed it became a footnote, not a legend.

The Appalachian Gas Belt, as noted by Colonel James Churchward, runs from the Mississsippi Delta in a line to Lake Ontario and up the St. Lawrence Seaway, arcing to the southern tip of Greenland. It passes through Iceland, Norway and into the former Soviet Union. At New Madrid, the belt lies halfway between New Madrid and the Atlantic coast. The actual epicenter may be unknown. New Madrid and other damaged areas may represent receptive geology—that is one which is more susceptible to quake damages. Mexico City 1985, was such a quake. With its epicenter offshore, it passed inland with little damage until it hit the filled lands of Mexico City.

The Richmond Virginia quake of August 31, 1886 represents another area of apparent susceptibility. In this instance it would be to the seaward side of the Gas Belt. If perpendicular lines are drawn through the gas belt from New Madrid and Richmond, the possibility exists that the next "New Madrid" quake may be in New York.

Now an interesting question arises, which direction is the gas belt moving?

In Atlantis, legends state the destruction occurred from North to South, as the gas and magma moving from South to North blocked its own tunnel in collapses.

Let us say the belt area perpendicular to New Madrid was blocked and then the belt area perpendicular to Richmond, we might infer that the gas moved from North to South. A power source is necessary. I would say the North Sea vulcanism, rampant and ongoing also furnishes the energy for the eastward Appalachian belt extending through mid Norway into Russia.

The St. Lawrence Seaway represents an obvious fault, like Baja, California. Its system leads back into Lake Ontario and the belt probably passes somewhere between Buffalo and Syracuse, New York. It could also function as a safety valve system. Small quakes in this area are relatively common.

The hypothesis is extremely simple. Watch for increased North Sea activity. Note quakes and vulcanism together. The reason that there are relatively few quakes in the high North Sea is that it functions as a shunting system to the east and west, besides its main dispersion of magma to lower latitudes.

4

Anatomy of the Gas Belts

The gas belts of Churchward tantalize with their richness of explanatory possibility regarding EM. They provide connection and process through the means of a horizontal system of distribution for the earth's lifeforce process of vulcanism. This overall distribution system is indicative of the general nature of vulcanism, which is also corroborated astrologically by its common signature. Volcano charts are pretty much the same everywhere.

The equatorial bulge, may be in part the accumulated magma shunted from higher latitudes. Blockage of belts and chambers in higher latitudes may be the prime cause of the Chandler Wobble increase, as magma fails to move towards the equator. The effect of liquids in a "solid" spinning object is demonstrable through eggs or other models as principles of everyday physics. The Belts may at once enhance both the stability and instability of the earth.

Churchward notes the depths of the belts as from 3 to 15 miles below the earth's surface. While some may run through the crust, it is evident by inference that they exist at the Moho where there is at once a constant source of heat and a point of joining between viscous and solid rock. Where two surfaces join, a point of weakness exists, here equivalent to point-of-least-resistance for water flow.

The belts, as I see them, visualized in terms of heat and stone, resemble upside down rivers whose beds are in large part carved vertically by the rising of heat as opposed to the horizontal carving of a river bed by water flow. When circumstances permit, magma may also figure in the carving.

A stone mason by profession, I've burned stone to break it. A single stone or boulder when burned duplicates in miniature the geological process of larger bodies under vulcanism.

The point being that fire and heat destroy rock by cleaving, sharding and pulverizing as well as melting. The stone bottom of the Moho, here a ceiling under heat, drops its stone into the magma below, the river bed or belt being on the semi-viscous level of the outer mantle top. The ceiling thus rises higher and higher. This is the formation of the gas chamber. A magma chamber is only a gas chamber at the momentary end of the line. Here it may figure in a surface eruption. As it empties, it also may collapse.

As the chamber grows wider and higher, sculpted by heat, hot gas is trapped, thus accelerating the cutting process.

Now the main dynamic purpose of the gas chamber in vulcanism operates. Trapped, the gas super-heated steam from sea water is now a propellant and under the snorkel principle, compression now forces magma horizontally through the belts. Momentum soon gains over inertia.

Under certain conditions this pressure will force magma in two directions. Magma reaching a sea rift will figure in the creation of new gas which at some point will move back up the belt and reload the chamber. The compressed gas is primarily steam, ever accessible, ever renewable. While no one has yet been to the Moho and computer generated models are not indisputable, at the process level, the basic physics involved are fairly obvious.

Returning to the astrology, these heat-vector increases within the earth occur when planets fall in the first $10°$ of the cardinal signs. Since this is a regularly recurring phenomenon in terms of the faster planets, Sun, Moon, Mercury, Venus, Mars it may be conceptualized as the thermostat having been turned on near $0°$ cardinal. This is enhanced, turned higher, by any solar excesses, in their turn brought about by the placement of Mercury and Jupiter. Then Venus and Pluto are in turn enhanced by planetary aspects close to partile (exact in angle). Thus the heat generated at these times is not a constant, but functions in what may be termed a normal or average range, much in way the thermostat regulates the temperature of an oven. At other times heat may fall above or below the variable norm.

A further modification occurs with the slower planets Jupiter, Saturn, Uranus, Neptune and Pluto. At times, one or more of these remains in early cardinal for longer periods. The oven is not turned off. Note that two or more of these planets in early cardinal would also be in aspect, a secondary enhancement. It is easy, therefore to note the periods of increased vulcanism.

If we may infer the process of the gas belts, what might we infer regarding their size? Churchward, not a conventional man or an establishment scientist, was little interested in measurement and in his natural honesty made no effort to appease. But he clearly believed they were huge in a geological overview of them. He correlates them to a plowing of the earth, involved in the creation of mountains and the furrows of the oceans.

Unspoken by Churchward but obliquely noted by some tilt proponents, the breakup of Pangaea, obviously catastrophic, also might have catapulted the continents in the tilt, or pole shift and crumpled the mountains horizontally.

Cataclysm becomes an initiatory and recurring factor in both continental drift—today known formally as tectonic plate theory in an updated version—and horizontal mountain building, previously the domain of the gradualist whose mountains crumpled slowly. Vertical mountain building is considered the domain of the catastrophist. In general, western geologists are horizontalists while the former Soviet Union geologists often subscribe to vertical uplift and much energy is wasted on either/or positions. Common sense indicates both occur under their respective conditions.

Well here to recall the blind men and the elephant. In reading both esoteric and establishment geology one is struck by the overall failure to ``see'' beyond one's bit of the ``elephant.'' More correctly in terms of the analogy, one's view remains limited.

Another problem occurs at the process level. Geology has emphasized description, analysis and causality. But as process unfolds, that is, moves toward greater EM or even cataclysmic levels, cause and effect intermingle in an orchestration of magnificent synergism.

This is aptly illustrated with the Chandler Wobble. Ice, wind and quakes are the results of vulcanism increasing oscillation. On reaching the point of instability, when the earth is about to tilt, ice, wind and quakes would become contributing causes to the tilt.

This blending of cause and effect is also rampant in EM as vulcanism and quakes. Both effect, increase, or release the other as the processes unfold. Vulcanism nevertheless remains as the initial cause of all major EM.

Churchward believed that the gas belt system was on a scale as to effect continent, ocean and mountain formation. We are not talking city sewerage system dimensions.

Starting with level land as a horizontal base line, land rose as adjacent land fell. The furrow of a plow illustrates this crudely. Somewhat less than the furrow, continents rose as mountains grew from adjacent magma in the "furrows." On the other hand, longer distance horizontal transportation of magma also occurred through the belt system.

Not to muddy the waters, gradualist upheaval or subsidence is not considered out of the question. Here we note specific cataclysmic events involving subsidence.

Continuing with the plow furrow image, the furrowed land that built the mountains was an undermining. At some point the original land now spanning our furrow collapsed. Our furrow is the ocean. Churchward believed the Great Belts were involved in the disposition of mountains ranges and oceans.

There are rolling hills and continental shelves. There are mountain ranges and deeps, some as deep or high as five miles.

Returning to Atlantis, we might say the subsidence involved was slightly more than the depth of the Dolphin Ridge regions, in particular if the beaches of Atlantis have been found, as some writers believe.

We can thus say, subsidence can be of any depth with outside limits approximately the depth of the trenches. The "recent" uprising of the Peruvian and Chilean coastline and the inner-land, dry beaches of Venezuela and Brazil, result from the periodic subsidence of islands or sections of Mu and Atlantis. The ocean rushed into a void left by the falling land which in turn filled the void of the gas chamber. These periodic subsidence events leave records on these inland beaches. The higher the beach, the older the event. Archaeological finds off Europe and the Bahamas involve land subsidence.

The expansion (exposure of the American Atlantic coast also corroborates lower water levels.

In terms of Atlantis, this represents a series of chambers more or less a mile in height. In terms of diameter of the earth of 8000 miles we are speaking of a fraction of one percent. By way of contrast, the vein in a man's forearm at approximately 3/16" overall diameter—somewhat less inside—would represent approximately 6 percent of the thickness of a forearm. At a flash the chamber does not seem so ridiculous in concept nor huge in size. The gas belts and gas chambers have always been considered out of context. Man's natural perspective of matters, distorted and self-centered, has noted their size in terms of his tunnels and the vaulted ceilings of cathedrals.

If the height of a large chamber were 2 to 6 miles what might the width of a belt be? Let us postulate that the ratio is 100's of miles to 1 at the mid-chamber diameter, and narrowing down to a couple of miles at most points of the belt.

In terms of an arch, the chamber becomes too wide, or the engineering is not distributed evenly. At the center of the vault, in the keystone area, the mass is the thinnest. On collapse this point falls through, but damage on the sides may vary. With the gas chamber representing the arch opening, a tunnel might in fact be indicative of more total linear destruction in terms of the "arch."

Because the penchant for examining matters piecemeal exists in all Western thought, a perusal of geological writing on subsidence, uplift and sea levels soon becomes confusing.

Sunken structures in the upper latitudes off Europe and near the tropical latitudes of the Bahamas are in fact subsidence. Returning to our inland beaches, these are records of the North to South destruction of Atlantis. With each major Atlantean subsidence the ocean levels fell, ultimately exposing Central America and extending the Atlantic coast of the United States. The sinking of Mu, as put forward by Churchward, might then have resulted in the highest inland beaches, for it would have occured prior to the Atlantis sinkings.

In visualizing the belts I sense that I may be underestimating size here and there. I have not dealt with these concepts before in terms of attempting to explain them to others.

Thus at some 600 miles +/- from the coast, to the general area of New Madrid, MO., as measured across Churchward's Appalachian Belt Line, we might note the partial collapse of a minor chamber some 600 miles wide.

If a major chamber is two to six miles high and some hundreds wide how wide is the belt? Perhaps only a fraction of a mile, for like a hose or gun barrel it must concentrate propellant force. Churchward drew the Belts as lines. The collapse of a chamber would result in the carving of a new chamber in the belt nearer the magma origin. The belt at this point would also have to periodically clear itself. This would probably be through branches which Churchward notes. More probably through the reabsorption of magma into the viscous levels below the Moho, or in volcanic eruption.

As a hypothesis the belts invite scientific reexamination. The belts provide a common mechanism for vulcanism, in particular allowing a means of motion and horizontal movement.

The astrological signature of vulcanism is common to all locations and appears more or less cyclically, whereas the quake signature varies from location to location and quakes appear more or less random in timing. A volcanic eruption is a momentary event in the overall cyclic process of vulcanism. Thus it maintains the overall signature of vulcanism when noted in the chart.

It is well known that quakes and volcanoes often seem to show a direction of movement when noted over a period of time. Belt dynamics, including chamber collapses etc., offer an insight into the matter. This is important in location forecasting. I've noted that the next "New Madrid" may be New York.

The belts offer at once a system of safety vents, releasing magma and gases at rifts and lower latitudes, as well as the mechanism of catastrophic EM through overactivity or blockage. Finally, in a worst possible scenario, they allow for the build up of magma in the higher latitudes with its effect on the Chandler Wobble; this being a sensible hypothesis for the first cause of the Chandler Wobble increase—build up of magma in the higher latitudes.

If astrology indicates a general cyclical pattern for vulcanism covering the entire earth, there might well be a geological equivalent covering the earth.

Belts also explain the massive amounts of magma extruded, say in a Kiluea. Simply stated, an active volcano exists at a point where gas and magma rise vertically in a minor branch system. The earth is renewed and venting is accomplished. Whether or not the vertical system begins from a belt or a chamber is unknown. I suspect both, with a system originating from a chamber and involving a secondary chamber able to achieve rapid build-up of magma when the belt further on is blocked. This fits the *"nuee ardiente"* types of eruption and the occasional super events such as Krakatoa. However, should the event be slower in growing, or on going, as in Kiluea, one might suspect the vertical system arises from the belt. Thus the magma chamber right below a major volcano may or may not be a secondary chamber. I would argue for an upper secondary chamber being needed closer to the earth's surface for a major event. With a flow volcano like Kiluea, the primary (deep chamber), with only a vertical branch, is enough to explain the ongoing flow.

Belts in no way contradict the upwelling of heat vectors or magma from the inner earth. They merely offer a horizontal component to the system at what would be a natural juncture, the bottom of the crust. Such a system functioning smoothly aids in the equitable distribution of heat and magma in gradualistic or cyclical process. A breakdown in the system would in turn precipitate cataclysm. Average EM is normal wear out or release. Thus, present day volcanoes and even 7+ R events viewed in this context are natural whether viewed from the point of view of process or breakdown.

5

Catastrophism: An Overview

For much of the 20th century geologists have bravely defended gradualism, the 19th century victor over catastrophism, as a mechanism for geologic change.

Late in the 20th century an integrated catastrophism has been accepted. Periodically sudden and catastrophic events and periods interrupt the monotony of gradualism, both being natural processes of the living earth. This shows that thought can escape the scientific prison of either/or.

What follows is a compressed version of catastrophism, the illustration of dynamics. Some principles are drawn from, what for lack of a better term, I'll call Esoteric Geology, which perhaps now, in the over-specialized age of non-communicating specialists, deserves an objective review.

Most importantly, the living principle, the moving principle, is heat—more precisely vulcanism, which covers the production and motion of heat from the inner core of the earth to the eruption of a volcano or the slipping of stone masses in a quake. Along the plates water reenters the earth's mantle to supply the steam, primary fuel of EM on the crustal levels of the earth, and the belts more or less at Moho level.

6

Catastrophism: The Key To Major EM

Mind-set is a suble but tenacious force. Most people are locked in by their mindset. Often unaware of this, they remain unwitting prisoners. Mindsets abound and do not necessarily reflect the intelligence or circumstances of those involved.

The history of geology is to some extent based on two counter themes, its search for order and timing, and its problems in dealing with aberrations and randomness. There are several terms for each of these themes, but I'll use gradualism and catastrophism. The geological establishment is still heavily influenced by the mind-set of gradualism, though it is beginning to recognize catastrophism—providing it sits in those chairs with doilies on them and promises not to leave tracks in the parlor. They're still upset by the puddles left by Wegener, even if they did manage to banish him unto death to the Artic, then resurrect him in the revamped tectonic plate theory.

Geologists, as well as most of present-day people, are the victims of either/or thinking and over-specialization. Science breaks things down into ever smaller parts and it doesn't work to make connections since analysis wins out over synthesis.

The gradualist had a problem when it came to major EM, how to graft it onto the overall picture as he chose to see it. Thus EM, unto this day, is seen, studied and otherwise worked upon, in terms of being a component of the gradualist theory. Never mind that it never seems to fit, that just means the job will last longer.

It's a bit like trying to understand the gun fight at the OK Corral in terms of Christian theology. The idea of mindset is amazing. When nothing works, you just continue mumbling "It's scientific" or "It's not scientific," as the circumstances dictate. "It's not scientific" is the mantra of modern-day pseudo-religion.

I haven't digressed as far as you might think. For example: you buy a car and plan to keep it. Over the ensuing years it has minor breakdowns but you get where you're going. One day it *breaks down completely* and you take it to the dump to be buried, or carried to the smelter for transformation into new steel. The underlined are Plutonic transformation or renewal. Breakdown equals major EM. You never knew when the breakdown would occur when you bought the car, three, five, twelve years ago. You guessed maybe six or seven years.

Over specialization, another peculiar modern-day mindset, also influenced the study of EM. It separated vulcanism and earthquakes. While on an academic level vulcanism is acknowledged as having some relationship to quakes, the overall process is ignored as the end results, volcanoes and major quakes, are studied separately.

Vulcanism is the essence of all EM. That it is understudied is proven by the general absence of thought on the propellant force necessary to drive those rivers of magma up or sideways. Magma only runs downstream after leaving the volcano. And those piles of rock in the major quake rock can only fall into a cavity. It cannot fall up or sideways, it must be pushed.

What I am getting at, simply, is that major EM is not part of the process, but an end to it in terms of a major interruption. It is the period at the end of the sentence. It is the result of inevitable but acyclical breakdown in the system. Major EM means its time for serious repairs or a new car. Extending that analogy, a period of catastrophism would indicate a change in the means of transportation.

The separate study of volcanoes and earthquakes has led to ignoring vulcanism, the initial and propellant force of all EM. Imagine a large system of multi-layered pipes running in all directions including up and down, with steam driving a semi-solid through them. The days operations always result in steam venting at the joints where pipes wear. The whole system vibrates when venting occurs, here a lot, there a little, over there not at all, as the pressure is turned up periodically by solar activity.

Now imagine a major blockage. Several pipes blow apart, major volcanoes. Here and there pipes fall and twist with some of the falling pipes levering others upward, major quakes. Across the way is an old pipe system, all fallen and twisted. Not even the old pipe tenders remember when it happened. They don't think about it too much as they worry about today's slips and blow-outs.

You see? Analogy is more feared than scorned. It facilitates communication and thinking, secretly held as undesirable by those in power. Analogy shows that major EM is the result of blockage, blow-out or breakdown in the vulcanism distribution system, the essence of the living earth and the propellant force of all EM.

7

Chandler Wobble

Every field has an overworked area of safe mystery and inconclusivity. In literature it's *Hamlet*. In anthropology it's the Bering Strait (wet and dry). Doctors write of common colds, and geologists of the Chandler Wobble.

Major EM represents a breakdown, an acyclical punctuation in an ongoing cyclical process, the circulation of heat and magma in the living earth. This circulatory system is analogous to that of animals or trees, the life force in balance with its own rhythms of change.

Another chapter notes an area of extreme vulcanism in the North Atlantic—and a shunting system, with blockages moved toward the North in the Appalachian Belt. Let's say a blockage exists somewhere near Richmond and to the east of Iceland some 1,000 miles inside the former Soviet Union. This FSU position is entirely hypothetical at this writing, but Richmond may well be terribly real.

I recently reread *Pole Shift* by John White (A.R.E. Press, Virginia Beach 1980). It is a complete anthology of the pole shift theory. Anyone interested in learning about the ultimate geological event, the tipping of the earth on its axis, might begin here. Mr. White presents pro and con with objectivity and lucidity often in the words of the proponents.

Polar shift or tilt theory, as it is known today states that the earth, considered as a spinning top, falls on its side, creating a general mess. Shortly after, it will spin again on this new axis. Some say it has never happened. Some say it has happened many times. Some say it may occur again. Let us admit the possibility and move backward, prior to it. In the geology of tilt, believers and forecasters differ in opinion concerning the amount of tilt in degrees, on whether it occurs rapidly or slowly and on whether the entire earth tilts or if just the lithosphere (crust) slips. There is also a question of the final tipping mechanism. Scientist seem to keep coming back to the ice caps of the Poles—growing and out of balance—perhaps because, like mountains, they're there.

The first time I heard about the Chandler Wobble, I intuitively assessed the matter. I truly believe the answer to the Wobble is the ultimate in simplicity.

There is a great deal of vulcanism centered more or less in the tropics and in the nature of a spinning object, the equatorial zone would be the most stable. North Atlantic magma is probably shunted southward, and its steam vented in this direction as well.

The Chandler Wobble is perfectly understood by cooks and housewives. Walk to your refrigerator and take out some eggs. Leave some raw. Quick poach a few. Boil some hard. Mix them up, put them on the table and spin them. You can sort them out. PRESTO, the Chandler Wobble. I'm sorry if I shot down some grants. The earth is some what poached and some what hard boiled.

The Chandler Wobble on increase indicates the increase of magma (hard to poached to raw) far enough north or south to effect rotational stability. The earth's mid-section would be somewhat less susceptible. The Chandler Wobble on decrease indicates the decrease of magma far enough north or south through shunting to lower latitudes or through its hardening. The Chandler Wobble is at once caused by vulcanism, and indicates an increase or decrease in vulcanism.

In the cyclical process of vulcanism, increase and decrease of the Chandler Wobble would appear to be natural. It seems simple enough to correlate this since records exists for vulcanism and wobble. But can the matter get out of hand? Vulcanism should also confirm itself in the ephemeris by early cardinal emphasis.

What follows is a North Sea scenario. The main quakes of the early 20th century, due to the Uranus-Neptune opposition and the new ones as a result of the 1992 Uranus-Neptune conjunction, have weakened its northern magma shunting systems. Ceilings in the belt chambers have been burned through, too high. The belt sides have expanded beyond the point of support for the land above, that is the arch has lost a leg, weakened at legs or thinned too much at the keystone, in terms of supported mass, so cave-ins and blockage occur. The fires of the earth turn up, perhaps just in a natural phase, let us say extreme, in the sense of a bad winter, a little colder. More than usual magma is produced. Unable to move towards the equator, it builds up. It's beginning to look like an auto manufacturers parking lot in a recession, but while cars may sit there, magma won't. Following a path of least resistance, it begins to carve a new belt, but the belt does not move south. The North Sea has suffered repeated quakes and paths of least resistance move toward Greenland 70°+/-N in the West and toward Novaya Zemla 75°+/-N in the East. After some time, whether measured in human or geological moments 80° of longitude in high northern latitudes are awash in magma, as the new belt fills up. It has not yet cut an exit or volcano.

Scientists note the increase in Chandler Wobble. They do not connect it to the major increase of magma production and storage in the higher latitudes.

Has tilt occurred? I do not know. There is a lot to the argument that it has occurred. If it has, all legends reports, studies, prophecies, etc. generally agree that it is an acyclical occurrence.

There is an implicit argument for it in vulcanism, for vulcanism itself is ultimately a process of life and renewal for the planet earth. This would be the new cycle as both outer and inner earth begins anew, old lands and oceans, as well as inner belt systems, being rested.

Returning to Novaya Zemlya, gas and magma are backed up under it. The Wobble increases, along with great quakes, which probably accentuate it momentarily until the earth's stability, itself already almost lost, reaches some point-of-no-return to balance.

The tilt occurs shortly after Novaya Zemlya blows apart. Its remnants are now at 12° south latitude and its nuclear poisons flow back and forth in the equatorial currents.

Hanford, Washington also moved about 87° to the south and is more or less at 45° south. It was a full tilt. Washington State did not sink but all the shaking made a lot of spill at the Hanford nuclear dumps. Nuclear leakage levels pose no known threat to human health.

Spin those eggs. Keep an eye on upper latitude vulcanism.

Finally the question of wind, polar ice and earthquakes causing or effecting the tilt deserves note. Vulcanism integrates them. Great vulcanism will cause great heat expansion and both deep and shallow quakes of great size would be expected.

Vulcanism reaching the surface will create winds in terms of massive heat fronts colliding with the cold polar climates. The Blizzard of 1993, along the eastern United States, would be a moderate example of a heat front in this instance.

The question of super quakes is itself debated. Some of the psychics see possible 10 to 12 Richter events, while some scientists maintain that the 8+ to 9+ Richter events are in fact the outer limits since the greater energy cannot be stored.

Let us say, in the presence of greatly increased vulcanism, the number of great quakes of 7.8R to 8.5R increases. Should polar shifts prove a reality, I believe that vulcanism will prove to be the true destabilizer. As vulcanism increases, wobble would increase. At this point, the wobble itself might in turn effect the overall process, wind, polar ice, and earthquakes. Now at the point of imbalance, they in fact may be critical secondary causes of a tilt.

It is not a matter of one cause or one right party, again somewhere in White's book, the fable of the blind men describing the elephant is mentioned. Western man should look more closely at his fables. This is not only a fable about perception, but about communication; the failure to communicate and the problems of dealing with partial truths. A partial truth, alone or rejected, is tragic for it is a piece of the whole. When the puzzle is completed it is no longer a puzzle.

The purpose of this text is the integration of geology and astrology to forecast EM. Working backward from the ultimate castrophe, there are insights and truths to be learned which can be brought to the garden-sized problem of forecasting major EM in regard to population centers or nuclear sites. Both increase in size and number as EM's increase, perhaps in a normal 200+/- year cycle involving the outer planets Uranus, Neptune, and Pluto.

In dealing with the Chandler Wobble, it helps to examine it on three levels. The first is the innate wobble of something spinning. Why assume that it should spin perfectly and that there is not some wobble inherent to the spinning itself. Here the matter is observational. Since vulcanism is integral and constant in the life of the earth, it is also a natural part of the Chandler Wobble.

An increase in Chandler Wobble must have a cause. I have proposed vulcanism as a primary cause—noting the different properties of solids and liquids when spun using the well known example of eggs.

As increase to a point of imbalance increases other ``causes,'' wind, polar ice, quakes may become secondary causes—the straws that broke the camel's back. But note, an increase in the vulcanism alone would bring imbalance and collapse at some point.

In examining vulcanism related to Chandler Wobble, geology would be remiss in not considering the possibility of horizontal conduit system for ``gas,'' propellant and magma, here the destabilizer.

Returning to the gas belts of Churchward, which make more and more sense to me, and putting aside for the moment consideration of size, let's examine a couple of plumbing problems in a horizontal system. Let us consider a slightly different scenario.

It is a period of magma increase in the natural cycle, this period somewhat enhanced by some recent strong planetary patterns. Equatorial EM increases, but a major increase in northern activity occurs near Iceland. An old beltline is unable to handle the magma, carrying it on a southward leg, and a new beltline is being cut at 65° North running east and west, Magma is remaining in the less stable upper latitudes instead of flowing to the more stable equatorial latitude. In a blink, we are talking human time, some 35° of northern longitude are awash in an inner magma river. The fires of the earth continue both to fuel it and push it forward. With a new belt system of least resistance, the magma does not try to move southward.

Fortunately there have been enough release quakes down near the equator to stave off major quakes near several population centers, including temperate latitude California. Off the coast of the Yucatan, on both the Atlantic and Pacific sides, relatively innocuous 6.5R events cause collapses in the Great Central Gas Belt. Ring of Fire magma heads north west, tapping into an old belt, and soon arrives at the latitude of Portland. Safely under the continental plate, only minor quakes are felt in the U.S. Northwest. St. Helens vents, but this is rightly noted as a release event.

The Great Central Gas Belt is involved in stabilizing the earth. Some even suspect it is behind the equatorial bulge. Few consider its work as mainly planetary stability by shunting excess magma and gas into the Ring of Fire where it can spread itself thin in a wealth of minor volcanic systems, which are in fact the earth's safety valves.

On the Atlantic side the Great Central Gas Belt collapses some several hundred miles WNW of the Caribbean island chain. The Italian volcanoes have been venting and few know how much magma they've been shunting west. The back up here is immediate, and midway between the Azores and the Strait of Gibraltar. The Italian magma finds a weak point. It too cuts into an old belt and races North into, of all places, the English Channel and under the Irish Sea. Directly under Glasgow, Scotland the magma meets resistance. Its hot gases cut into an old chamber ceiling. The disaster of Atlantis is about to be revisited but that lies some years ahead - in human terms.

Geologists from all over the world are noting the Chandler Wobble increase. There is now a new wobble-within-the-wobble that causes mystification. They don't know that this is the result of the Tropical blockage in the Great Central Gas Belt.

The triple buildup of destabilizing magma now begins to cause 8R quakes and the eruption of dormant volcanoes throughout the world. While regional geological organizations attempt to examine their own EM sites, a few intuitively sense that synergistic energies are at work and wonder where it will end.

An incredible bulge forms under the sea between Iceland and Namsos, Norway directly north of the Faero Islands. Temporarily it subsides but quake activity is noted North of Jan Mayen Island, and echo sounders note a huge bulge under the Irish Sea.

A Russian geologist, who acquired a taste for forbidden literature, under the boredom of the old Communist regime, remembers the words of a crank named Emil Sepic (Sepic, Emil, *The Imminent Shift of the Earth's Axis*, privately published, 1960, p. 175):

> "There will be many oscillations before the shift happens. A new equator will begin to bulge outwards. The old bulge (equatorial) will begin to be pressed inwards and gradually disappear. This will cause cracking of the earth's surface, violent earthquakes, unheard of bad weather and many new volcanoes will come into action."

At this point the ice caps move, waters rise and the race is decimated.

8

Why Geology and Astrology Should Cooperate

Archaeologists know that old cities, cultures and economic empires were destroyed, buried beneath the rubble of major quakes. A growing number of the public also know this for documentaries of buried and destroyed cities are common on educational television.

Because of logistics, roads, ports, rivers, all necessary to trade, cities were rebuilt on the rubble of their destroyed predecessors. The economic damage in time was overcome. Just as often the circumstances of a rebuilt city changed.

In the earliest of times, man left his cave at the first rumbling of a quake or fled the area of an imminent volcano. Life was simple then. Plenty of land, few people, no buildings to speak of, and an economy as we think of it was not yet in existence. Both of these conditions existed right up to the 20th century. And then the formula changed. Major cities were built, or grew on or around, quake and volcano locations. Today, an 8R quake, perfectly centered to do maximum damage in Tokyo, New York City, Mexico City, would not only cause large loss of life and building destruction, but probable destruction of the economy of a country. The three cities cited are on known fault zones or sensitive locations.

Beyond the super damage to life and economy that would come as a result of a major quake in certain populous areas, the 20th century brought new and deadly problems. chemical dumps and factories, nuclear pollution (so called storage sites) and nuclear power plants. And these exist in major quake prone sites. Anyone who says a nuclear power plant can sustain a direct hit in a quake, like Alaska's Good Friday (March 27, 1964) 8R+ is certifiable, deluded, or a liar, depending on one's point of view.

The geological establishment needs to reflect, not just on the mechanics of forecasting EM, but on the purpose of their work which is adequate early warning. Since all indications are that EM forecasting will never be fail-safe, it falls to the geological establishment to warn of the inherent dangers of nuclear and chemical pollution, to the water table at the very least.

The New Madrid quake (there were several) took place December 16, 1811, and into early 1812. It is now overdue since the previous quake possibly took place in 1683. It was noted by Jesuit missionaries in Quebec. The secondary sources I've seen gave no date or time.

As the 1990s unfold, a horror show of nuclear pollution is narrated to the world by television, particularly the tragic pollution of the former Soviet Union. Nuclear pollution alone, especially its possible spread through EM, should by itself have all forecasting parties begging for a chance to corporate with each other.

Beyond the super economic damage of a direct hit to New York City or Tokyo, is the mega damage of a nuclear Dead Zone created by a 7R direct hit on a myriad of nuclear dumps and power plants.

Earthquake engineering is designed for 6R. There is simply no way to engineer for an 8R event. It is physically impossible and economically unfeasible. It certainly was not done on existing structures and dumps.

9

Evacuation

Evacuation means the safe removal or retreat of people from a disaster in the making or in progress. With or without practice, it has successes and failures on the small scale.

There has never been a successful large-scale evacuation where everyone escaped. Conversely some usually do escape from the worst of tragedies.

Evacuation is a modern concept dealing with saving larger populations present in metropolitan locations. As projected by governments, evacuation is nothing more that a soporific, however well intentioned. At worst it is a deadly farce. The government is afraid of giving a false quake warning because of damage to the tax base. The government will not give early warning for the same reason.

Logistical failure, e.g., blocked roads and communication failure, are not fully admitted and the human element is even less considered, panic. Earthquake drills, as in California, probably offer the best and most realistic chance for human life.

Simply, in the event of a direct hit by an 8R quake in a major city with skyscrapers, many will die. However terrible this may be, the lasting damage would involve chemical or nuclear pollution. This is what must be addressed by those in power.

Evacuation in the United States comes under the agency of FEMA (The Federal Emergency Management Administration). This is a bureaucracy whose primary function is to protect the Federal Government in event of nuclear attack. Most of its budget goes in that direction. It was exposed in a series of articles in Pent House magazine in the late 1970s and on CNN in March 1993 regarding these nuclear and high government propensities. It is inefficient and dilatory in dealing with major disasters. Ask victims of Hurricane Hugo and Andrew. It will be interesting to see how it handled the widespread disaster of the Blizzard of 1993. If it were to warn you of a quake, you wouldn't get out of town, because FEMA would have you filling out paperwork.

Information on damage and evacuation are dealt with in some detail by Jeffrey Goodman in *We Are the Earthquake Generation*. Somehow I sense that details only obscure the ultimate facts as outlined in these chapters. Loss of life may vary, but it will be present. Economic damages will be great. The truly lasting danger comes from pollution sources innate to our modern technology, polluted water table, nuclear pollution, etc.

10

The True Tragedy of Future Em

In 1972, I vacationed in Washington DC. It was my first experience, since repeated, at the Smithsonian Institute. I entered the main hall and saw a rope suspended from the ceiling. The rope coiled along the floor in a full revolution before stretching upward. At the point the rope left the floor, a cardboard sign noted the beginning of the Industrial Revolution in the early 19th century. From that point the rope shot to the ceiling. This was a population graph illustrating the maxim, "A picture is worth a thousand words."

In ancient times, at the premonitory rumble of a quake, men left their caves and camped in the open. At the venting of a volcano they left their fields or homes at a rapid walk.

There were victims. Some events came without warning or were too big to escape. But man became over confident, careless. The stone house, so enduring, was a death trap in a major quake.

In the first third of the 20th century great villains appeared, Hitler, Stalin and Hirohito. America's President Truman called in the clowns, Einstein, Oppenheimer, Fermi, and they let the nuclear genie out of the bottle. That genie has polluted the earth and the minds of man ever since. The nuclear genie is a trickster and his repertoire is simple. He makes a promise that captures attention and does not talk about his poison, all of which is still around.

We don't like to think of ourselves as a species that is subject to the laws of nature. That is unfortunate and one of the seeds of present tragedy. We don't acknowledge our animal nature, learn little from our human nature, and only sporadically use our divine or higher nature.

Other than each human death being a tragedy in itself and to loved ones, even a one or two billion loss of life through major EM would be merely a blip in the human population graph. We would replace the loss in about 40 years and living conditions would possibly improve in the early interim. Cynical? No. Factual? Yes. Europe has reproduced her loss many times over since 1945 and now has her own population problems.

If EM deaths are seen in terms of percentage, however great they might be, they are as nothing either in terms of the species or a nation.

What then is the tragedy? Simply this: sooner or later a nuclear installation or installations will be hit. We're talking multiple Chernobyls and everyone pretends that the Emperor has his clothes on.

On March 25, 1953, a 5.7R quake hit Oregon by surprise. We're getting near to Hanford, Washington. The nuclear genie has changed the game.

We're no longer discussing some simple culling of the species or minor herd reduction, but serious species damage, including genetic mutation. We're talking about poisoning the earth, whose choice flat areas are used for both farms and battlefields.

We are running out of time, because putting aside all millennium EM specials, any increase in EM, whenever it comes, will hit new and larger population centers than existed in the early 20th Century.

We're talking about normal 7.5R events with epicenters near nuclear facilities.

The true heyday of modern seismic events was the first decade of the 20th century when virtually every so-called quake area was tagged by a large one. This was the true era of earthquakes. 1976, often cited, is merely the time that a sudden uptick took place relative to a quiet period in mid-century. We still are not producing the first class events of the early century.

The EM events of early this century related to the planetary placement Uranus opposition (180°) Neptune.(Events listed in the Appendix section)

On February 2, 1993, Uranus made a conjunction with Neptune and in the spring the nodes of the Moon reached mid Gemini/Sagittarius, an indicator of full energy. (See Chapter 13)

Astrologically, the conjunction is traditionally twice as strong as the opposition. We're in for some serious shaking, but the potential for true tragedy is in nuclear accidents. This is why it is time for some very realistic cooperation between all parties, some serious changes of attitudes on all sides.

This text offers a workable system needing refinement. Under the best of circumstances there will be misses as well as hits. It's the hits that will count. At present geology offers no warning. Astrologers alone can do little better because of the geographic factor; that is, insufficient imput on location, history, and wrong approaches to the forecast.

We must learn to cooperate.

Section II

Earthquakes and Vulcanism

The Astrological Overview

11

Planetary Overview

In major EM events, whatever the planetary signs, whatever aspect complexes are present, the chart is well integrated with both aspects and concentrations of aspects. It is a high energy chart.

There are proven methods for reading charts, most of which define human activity. One of the problems in astrological forecasting of EM has been the attempt to view EM in terms of certain areas of astrology, usually as natal or mundane event. Both of these also involve horary principles.

Each of these areas involves people. Two problems arise concurrently. Not all the rules of human astrology work on EM. Secondly, little is done in forming and delineating an *EM astrology*. Astrologers in the main just continued trying to make human astrology work.

Taking the eruption of Mount St. Helens as a dynamic starting point for this work, the real functions of the planets in EM slowly evolved, and somewhere over the last 13 years the entire picture came into focus.

In the following chapters each planet is delineated by itself and its position in planetary groups is again noted. Here I wish to note the groups of planets themselves. Group is not a fancy word and I'd like a better one, but it will do.

- Each group requires interaction within itself.
- If midpoints are used it should be between or among the planets of a group.

In EM activity whether quake or volcanic eruption, group planets interact for a particular dynamic. Within a group certain planets will make the outside linkups to other groups.

The Sun, Mercury and Jupiter are the cycle builders, the switch as it were, sometimes on, sometimes not so on. An aspect relationship exists with each other when they are on. In the text they are also called the *initiating triad*, or *primary triad*.

Venus, Mars and Jupiter are energizers. At the time of a major quake they have usually separated from most of their slower counterparts and perhaps somewhat from each other, but again an aspect relationship exists each with the other. In the text they are sometimes called the *energy triad* or more often noted as *Venus-Mars-Jupiter*.

Jupiter, Saturn, Uranus, Neptune, and Pluto, the slower planets, also relate to energizing (in fact all ten planets energize). This is their general function, except for the Moon which carries the energies of other planets, a difference that is not important in the overall understanding of this text.

But Jupiter, Saturn, Uranus, Neptune and Pluto have a more specialized function in EM. As they move from sign to sign and make their aspects to each other, geographic locations are isolated. Certain locations seem to require aspects between certain of these five planets and certain signs. An imaginary example, Uranus to Neptune: at least one cardinal with Jupiter past Saturn, one of them in an earth sign. Pluto is usually not aspected by one of these four at the time of an event in location X.

The timing complex of an EM event, which is actually a release or blockage in terms of an overall vulcanistic process, is more complex than generally supposed. It is not just the Moon or Mars or Uranus.

The timing planets are Moon, Mercury, Mars, Uranus, and at times, Saturn. The specific nature of their timing mechanism is noted in their individual chapters.

Much oversimplified, the Moon opens a 2.5 day location signature, making an area susceptible to a quake. The Moon collects a final jolt of energy if Mercury is in a suitable position in terms of the Sun and Jupiter, and in the degree of another planet, and if Mars and Uranus have generated enough release energy. Saturn blocks, as it were, thus creating resistance. The planetary dynamic of Saturn and Uranus is tension. The planetary dynamic of Mars and Saturn is friction.

Reread the above. Note that a planet from one group as a member of another is capable of integrating the group energies. This allows the development of EM through an ongoing living dynamic process.

Lastly, Venus with Pluto seems to have a special effect as an indicator and energizer of solar events, especially when planets, including the Sun, are in very early cardinal degrees.

Jupiter is very important, functioning in three of four groups and relating to the timing process through Mercury, Mars, and Uranus. Jupiter appears to have a special integrating function, being a member of three or four groups, influencing the time through Mercury, Mars, and Uranus and indirectly reaching the Moon and Saturn as timers.

Again the process flow of energy is; solar event, increased vulcanism, eruption and quake. This is noted elsewhere in detail and is inferred by the degrees of cardinal signs at the time of events.

A similar dynamic appears to involve the Moon's Nodes (see Chapter 13) culminating in more release (EM events) at the time of early mutable and fixed positions.

Thus the EM chart is ten planets and the Moon's Nodes performing many functions over a cyclic process which involves at least eleven intersecting cycles (Sun through Pluto and Moon's Nodes) along with acyclic phases, timing, aspects and aspect complexes.

At the time of an EM event, actually an instance of surface catastrophism in a gradualistic ongoing process, these planets are highly energized, well integrated in terms of the planet group energies having access to other groups. The process must be well integrated in terms of aspect and aspect complexes to show high energy, and suitably dispersed by sign, aspect, and aspect complex to bring about an event, at a given time, in a given location. General separation and lunar enhancement are also present, especially in a major quake.

12

On the Sun

Since the Sun heads our planetary system and since throughout astrology it has a special place as the most important planet, I'll simply state that this continues in regard to EM.

The Sun is the powerhouse and channels its energies to the earth, modifying and specializing these energies through the planets. These energies reach the earth most usually through the Moon, which Frances Sakoian, one of the greatest astrologers of the 20th century, has called a "step down transformer."

The precise dynamics of the Sun in relationship to EM may not be known exactly, nor is it necessary to know or describe them precisely at this time. It is not necessary for Em forecasting.

During the last several centuries data on Sun spots, solar flares, and solar storms have been quietly and patiently collected by astronomers. Such solar energies are interactive with the other planets in our solar system, particularly those at angles involving multiples of $15°$ and $30°$ that is when, what astrologers term an aspect, is in effect.

Vedic astrology, also known as Hindu or Indian, is clear on one point, planets effect one another. Thus the angles of Jupiter, Mercury, Venus and Pluto may have much to do with the cycle of these solar events. But in turn, the activated Sun enhances the effects of these planets.

Along with the other planets, the Sun performs several functions. Each function is ultimately necessary to bring about a major EM event or to continue the ongoing course of EM and vulcanism as geological constants or processes. The Sun in very early cardinal degrees relates to solar events and the heating up of the core of the earth. This is the inner core and power plant as represented in legend by a god, Pluto, and in astrology by a planet with the same name Pluto.

The Sun in early cardinal degrees through the first $10°$ ($9°59'$), as with other planets in this placement, relates to general vulcansim as heat gas and magma move upward through the outer core and mantle where they break through the earth's crust or lithosphere. If the geology here is very simple, its because ultimately the process is simple; a heat driven process moving through several stages on the way to the end result of EM, quakes and surface volcanic eruptions.

The inner core is represented by Pluto, the outer molten core by Neptune, the fiery semi-molten contents of the inner mantle by Uranus and the solid outer mantle and lithosphere by Saturn which bounds it as a shell does an egg.

The Sun interacts with these slow planets infusing them with energies. As these slow planets interact with, or aspect, each other there are shifts in vulcanistic energy production, the isolation of geographic energy production and the isolation of geographic locations.

The heat and magma *wax* and *wane*, increasing or decreasing the potential for surface EM in particular locations. When sufficient energy has been stored in these locations, the other planets, also not idle during this process, will form some pattern suitable for the release of energy in this location.

The Sun thus interacts with the so-called slow planets to stoke the earth's furnace. This is the living earth of continental drift, ocean currents, atmospheric winds and the creation and fertilization of lands through surface EM of quake and volcano.

The Sun directs its energy in several ways through some intermediate planetary agents. Jupiter defines the solar cycles and supplies energy. Mercury directs it earthward by timing. Venus carries the energy to each planet where it is stored, including the Sun itself. Venus also helps initiate the solar phases with Pluto. When all is in order, Mercury will time the EM and through Mars or another planet will pull the ``EM Trigger,'' when the Moon has enhanced the location signature.

The Sun, Jupiter and Mercury form the main energy producing complex in terms of EM phases and cycles. Venus distributes this energy to the other slower planets including the Sun. Venus-related solar disturbance energizes the EM of our planet Earth.

The Sun with Jupiter and Mercury control the basic ebb and flow of solar energy, the inner vulcanism of the earth and EM or surface manifestations of earthquake and volcanic eruption. It goes without saying, continental drift and the life of the planet are part of this dynamic.

Like the Moon, the Sun changes aspect complexes by its motion through the signs. At one sign a month, it too creates focuses of energy through the planets it most strongly contacts. Remember that the overall pattern of the planets at any given time may be said to relate to specific locations.

At the time of major EM the Sun must be in some relationship to Mercury and Jupiter. It may be other than the so called classic aspects of astrology and often the relationship of Mercury and Jupiter are inharmonious.

Noting here that Jupiter is a major energizer, changing a sign each year, and that Mercury is the final timer, we may say that Sun-Mercury-Jupiter are the ``on switch'' triad of EM planets, the primary triad.

In summary the Sun functions in EM:

- Through its relationship with the Moon in lunations. Eclipses and ingresses are extensions of this principle. The purpose is geographic localization along longitude.
- Through the primary EM triad Sun-Mercury-Jupiter.
- As a chart integrator supplying energy to all other planets.
- Enhancing or creating aspect complexes and modality over a one month period.

13

On the Moon

Of all the planets, astrologers give the Moon an exalted position in EM forecasting. The Moon stars in the lunation chart, usually the New Moon, as well as eclipse and ingress charts. In the event chart the Moon is the timer. I'll examine both of these roles before revealing my hypothesis on its true but unnoticed major role. I will also point out some problems, perhaps best called misunderstandings, that have arisen within the lunation and event charts, such that they have become ingrained error.

Astrological tradition holds the Moon to be of utmost importance in EM. While this is true, what is less known is that it is perhaps the most misunderstood planet in EM. The Moon in EM charts is usually noted in retrospect. This causes an oversight, a slip of the mind, namely that any tight, hard aspect noted as a timer was only the middle aspect of three, one occurring about a week earlier, one to occur about a week later.

"This week" in terms of major quake prediction is "loose." If I were to state a large quake in X location two years hence would occur on day X, plus or minus seven days would be noted as close. True, but we would be talking about 180° of zodiacal longitude in lunar motion. Today, "three days before/after" is a common statement in an EM forecast. I've used it myself. We are talking 2+ signs or 80° of zodiacal longitude. Three days, centered on the middle day is also more than one sign and 40° of zodiacal longitude.

Frances Sakoian calls the Moon a step-down transformer. Completely passive, she transmits the character of the sign she is in, along with the energies of those planets already aspected while in that sign, with the more immediate energy of those planets she presently aspects. The behavior of these planetary energies is further defined by the specific aspect angle. In fact, she is a storehouse of energy, but in a sense she is not the final trigger as commonly believed. Her work as a timer is primarily related to sign, not aspect.

This is to say that lunar aspects have their weaknesses in forecasting EM. Factors other than aspect are needed to narrow the time frame when using the Moon. It is not lunar aspect that determines EM potential.

More confusion has arisen out of the ancient use of the Lunation, also used with some success by modern astrologers. It is not lunar aspects that determine EM potential. It is the Sun conjunct Moon relationship to the angles, and other angular emphasis within the lunation chart, that lay down a probable track of longitude which is noted through the Midheaven and Nadir.

A lunation chart seen as tight, stressed or in someway extreme, increases the likelihood of an EM, yes, and anything else too, from hurricane to heartbreak. But which terribly stressed lunation is ``the one'' to bring about major EM? The eclipse lunation became special and rightfully so. Included in this reasoning are lunar eclipses, actually enhanced full Moons. Ingresses function much as eclipses forming, like them, a long-lasting backdrop of time and providing corroboration of a lunation. Again angularity is of prime importance with either the lights and/or planets on the meridian axis (IV/X). The more of this, and closer to the Midheaven or Nadir, the better. An attempt at geographic isolation or pinpointing was going on. A strip of longitude was established. But within these charts it is transits to the planets near the angles, not transits to the angles that are noted.

In a small world, using the seven planets Sun through Saturn, astrologers forecast local events. Success would depend not on aspects, because these reappear with regularity, but on chart patterns and aspect complexes which appear in a less regular fashion. This was looked for in the event chart, here was the location isolator. In this similar reoccurrence of chart pattern and aspect complexes, planetary aspects, sign similarities and differences would come into play.

This is how the Moon truly functions in EM. As the moon moves through the signs, it changes major planetary patterns and aspect complexes every 2.5 days. The Moon enhances aspect complex patterns, modality, and net polarity. It creates patterns, modalities and polarity, And then shifting kaladiscopically, changes them every two and a half days.

Let us examine where we stand regarding future event X in an imaginary location. Note in passing that the lunation, eclipse and ingress maps are used similarly. Any one of them may be used alone, any two of them or all three of them. Perhaps the best and most common usage is linking a lunation to a prior eclipse. Lunation planets transit to eclipse points. Let us say there is good interaction with Sun, Mars, Uranus and Pluto. Both charts have strong angular emphasis at the location including some Nadir and Midheaven emphasis. For our example we will use the Aries Ingress, said to last for a year. It occurred two months after the eclipse and it interacts well with both the eclipse and lunation planets and angularities (location). The lunation follows the eclipse by five months and the ingress by three months, prime EM time.

We find a pattern similar to a previous quake in the location. Nine days into the lunation, planets have changed signs, moving into the water element. A long standing cardinal T-square involving slow planets continues. Transiting Sun in Cancer makes it stronger this month. Transiting Moon moves into the empty water sign Scorpio, eight days into the lunation. We now have Sun in Cancer, Moon in Scorpio and Mars in Pisces. The Moon has aided the Sun, which has strengthened the T-square. The Moon has completed a Grand Trine Water circuit, which when with another strong complex, in this instance the cardinal T-square, forms the overall signature for a strong quake. In fact this might be said to be the universal signature (Grand Trine Water with additional complexes).

But this is not all the Moon has done. A planet is in early Taurus in an early degree related to EM. Fixity is enhanced and the degree is energized by transit. Thus the Moon in Scorpio has enhanced the modality involved—fixity. Two hours after the Moon forms a trine to Mars, the 6R quake goes off, causing little damage in the uninhabited land beneath the sea. Three other events, two moderate quakes and a volcano venting occur in apparently random areas in the next 36 hours.

To recapitulate, using the Moon, one cannot forecast by lunar aspect as the timer. Secondly, the lunation chart is in fact a geographic indicator involving a band of longitude and according to the lunation chart a varying degree of time. An eclipse is an enhanced lunation.

How can the Moon be used in forecasting EM? Simple, What matters is the sign. As the fast moving Moon moves through the signs at two and half days per sign, it changes and intensifies the aspect complex pattern of the chart, each change empharizing other locations. I call this Lunar Enhancement"; it is the prime function of the Moon in EM.

Thus with planets in two water signs the entrance of the Moon into the third water sign would create a Grand Trine Water and possibly create a T-square somewhere else. Grand Trine Water is one of the indicators of a major quake that can occur just about anywhere. I personally believe it is the nearest universal indicator of great quakes we have. But then other subtleties within the chart would narrow the location and the lunation would narrow the matter further, as would eclipses.

Simply, lunations involving eclipses lay down the same type of track, that is strips of longitude, but the imprint lasts longer, a year with a solar eclipse (conjunction) and months with a lunar eclipse (opposition).

While rules have been laid down which relate to the duration time of effects, to the duration time of obscurity or shadowing in the eclipse, and relate the area of effect by the visibility of its path, it would be just as logical to say the path of a solar eclipse lasts until another solar eclipse occurs in the next sign of the Moon's Nodes. This would also explain the ``months'' duration of a lunar eclipse as well.

A given eclipse path may be stimulated by a subsequent lunation too. It is important to indicate that a layering of geographical indicators is occurring with the eclipse and lunation, or one without the other with subsequent aspects that corroborate that path (location signature). These are geographic indicators or isolators, and the Moon is especially important as it is what changes these aspect patterns every two and half days.

Thus, from the eclipse and/or lunation, there must be transits to it, and these must form an aspect pattern that the transiting Moon will relate to a geographic area, on some point of the longitudinal strip, sensitized by the lunation/eclipse/ingress. Such a pattern may be somewhere other than this sensitized longitudinal strip. I do not believe every earthquake is eclipse or lunation keyed. The most glaring argument for EM, independent of a given eclipse or lunation, is the fact that a series of EM events often appear closely connected in time but widely scattered by location (see Appendix I). Usually this involves one major and several minor events. Is the major event always eclipse keyed? I have not at present done this research.

In summary, the Moon moving through signs indicates the EM location of the moment. The overall aspect pattern would fit previous quakes in these areas. Suitable time must elapse between major quakes in a given location to store seismic energy. A very strong, perfectly fitting aspect pattern, might create a premature release of stored seismic energy which drains the stored energy in a minor event.

An aspect pattern may seem correct but in itself may not have enough astrological energy (separation) to trigger an event.

Either of the above may store energy for the future, this is why many events fail to occur. In fact additional energy storage is not noticeable generally, or usually considered. Geology at present does not measure stored energy (see Chapter 24).

It is the Moon that finally completes these aspect patterns. An argument for this also may be inferred from the large amount of aftershocks that immediately (same sign) follow a major quake.

The Moon does in fact also trigger or time an event. Usually it involves recent contacts with Mars, Saturn or Uranus, but these are not of primary use in forecasting, nor is the Moon the final trigger. The location would have been isolated by the Moon forming a definitive aspect complex and the general time frame, two and a half days, narrowed.

Mercury, Mars and Uranus, sometimes Saturn or Pluto would have to be considered to see if the two-and-a-half-day pattern will trigger off. Only then may the Moon be factored in.

Little value is attached to the Moon as a final timer, day and hour. Its relationship to Mars, Saturn and Uranus etc. varies too much, involving orbs of approach or separation. In some locations Jupiter and Pluto would appear to replace Mars, Saturn and Uranus. Like the imfamous Uranus conjunct Midheaven/Nadir or whatever, it is only seen after the fact.

An analogy will go a long way to resolving the problem. If one were to attempt to forecast an assassination he would have charts relating to the potential victim and previous assassinations, but he would not have the chart of the unknown assassin. Precise lunar timing for EM, like the assassin out there, is always unknown.

The Moon's Nodes

The Moon's Nodes are changing points 180° apart along the ecliptic, and astrologically sensitive. In terms of EM they relate to eclipses, for eclipses take place near the nodes each year. The eclipse chart, an emphasized lunation, is used to determine geographic location for future EM. This is the path of the eclipse noted as a band of longitude.

During years of noting earthquakes, I tried to integrate the Moon's Nodes into the EM event chart with no success. Unlike some astrologers examining quakes, I also draw up the moderate ones I happen onto as well as minor events from a few locations. Finally, I drew the Moon's Nodes in my EM charts but largely ignored them for my signature work.

The nodal key came unexpectedly when I saw a table of intensity on quakes, page 51 in Ann E. Parker's *Earth Quake Prediction* (first book). The majority of intense quakes take place with the Moon's Nodes in fixed signs, Taurus/Scorpio and Leo/Aquarius; most of the balance occur with the Moon's Nodes in mutable signs, Gemini/Sagittarius and Virgo/Pisces; and few occur with the Moon's Nodes in cardinal signs. Actually none occurred in the time frame of her table.

Finally, the Moon's Nodes move retrograde about three minutes a day average. The key word is retrograde. From a cardinal sign, the Moon's Nodes move into a mutable sign and fianlly from the mutable signs into the fixed signs.

Assuming as I must that vulcanism is directly or indirectly present in these intense quakes with fixed Moon's Nodes, I offer the following hypothesis: vulcanism begins to build up in the cardinal and mutable phases and peaks during some point of the fixed phase. Strong energy may be existent by mid-mutable positions.

Using the principle of separation and my balloon analogy, it is probably that the final phase of the fixed Moon's Nodes carries declining vulcanism, this carrying into the cardinal Moon's Nodes, where at some point the process begins again.

Conversely, all phases of the fixed Moon's Nodes would have maximum energy build up signified—filled balloons—what happens to them?

Thus another key to the phases, tides or cycles of vulcanism is available which may be integrated in some way with the transit of planets through the cardinal signs. Solar events and some volcanic EM, first nine degrees cardinal, volcanoes erupt, second decanate and third decanate, quakes.

A full nodal return involves some 18 years. Thus one phase of the heating—cardinal, mutable, fixed—invovles some four and a half years. This may be meshed with cardinal vulcanism.

14

The Other Planets

On Mercury

In one of his books, Joseph Goodavage said he suspected Mercury was more important in EM than his understanding of it at the time. I kept that in mind and acknowledge his intuition as I soon noticed that Mercury was usually in the degree of another planet at the time of a quake or volcano.

The Ascendant, Midheaven and Moon were not used since they cannot be used for conventional EM forecasting. I was not paying much attention to the Moon's Nodes for EM most of the time and do not look for Mercury in the degree of the Nodes. I've still to deal with the nodes outside of the eclipse chart, though hypothesizing an energy buildup from 29° cardinal through mid-mutable, then a release in fixed signs.

Mercury is often in the degree of one or more of the other planets, Sun, Venus, Mars, Jupiter, Saturn, Uranus, Neptune and Pluto at the time of a major event.

Mercury was in the degree of Neptune in both the 1906 and 1991 San Francisco quakes.

Noting the eight planets used above, only eight degree numbers out of 30 are possible. That would mean Mercury is in the degree of one of them only every three events.

However in major events, Mercury not in the degree of another planet is the exception, not the rule. If not in degree, it is often found to be in one of the following situations.

- In the degree of the Moon, this known from timed events, but again unknowable for forecasts.
- In some 15° type aspect—15°, 45°, 75°, 105°, 135°, 165° (in particular 165°).
- One degree approaching or separating from a slow planet degree.
- By midpoint with the Sun or Jupiter, the midpoint degree is the same as one of the other eight planets.
- As midpoint of a stellium.

This generally applies to both volcanoes and earthquakes, and to both major and lesser events. In specific locations Mercury may tend to occupy the degree of a particular planet.

The slower planets have danced and Jupiter has repeatedly transited them, Jupiter is the bridge planet. Ingresses, eclipses and lunations have provided energies to a given location, or at least astrologically indicated it. Sun-Mercury-Jupiter have stoked the furnaces. Venus-Mars-Jupiter have energized those planets the've contacted. The Moon moves through changing patterns, as does the Sun. An event is ripe and Mercury hits a certain degree. The hammer is cocked, Mercury is the timer. The passing Moon, having created a pattern of aspect complexes and enhanced mode and polarity, will brush near or past a certain planet, signaling Mercury to pull the trigger. They are secondary trigger planets. The Moon, often transits last, by conjunction or other aspect, Mars or Uranus. Sometimes it is Jupiter, Pluto or Saturn. With volcanoes it appears to be Saturn in most instances.

Note that whatever the speed, Mercury can function within that two-and-a-half-day Moon sign phase. Mercury is the timer, it's that simple. Whatever Sun and Jupiter have done, Mercury now regulates time.

Thus a chart may appear to resemble the chart of past events. An astrologer looks and all appears to be in place, but no event.

Perhaps Mercury is not in place in reference to the Sun and Jupiter, or is not in degree. Not so, Mercury is in place and degree.

Perhaps there has not been enough cumulative separation of major aspects by the planets in general, especially Venus and even more especially Venus-Mars-Jupiter as the energy triad.

Lots of separation, but Venus, Mars and Jupiter should aspect one another in some fashion. Their three energies must get through at once, forming a cosmic sledge hammer blow.

Venus-Mars-Jupiter are in aspect. Still no event. Perhaps the Moon is not in the right sign. The Moon is in the right sign, but no event.

The locations involved in this signature lack sufficiently stored energy, either from several small releases over a period of time, or through a past major event that requires more time for re-energizing the location. That location, for the moment, is dormant.

Remember that geological moments are not the same as ours; 50, 100, 500, 1,000 years are all equally geological moments.

On Venus

Venus probably maintains separation power for the length of time it takes her to go 15 degrees from a major aspect. Thus Venus is often at a 15° type aspect, or in the early degrees of a sign, which means that it has separated from all slower planets.

As Venus hits a 15° type aspect, eg. 15°, 75°, 105° or 165°, that planet's energy is restimulated and energy buildup for the EM in question is increased. Or this may be an energy peak point.

Venus and Mars are often in very early Aries or Cancer at the time of major volcanic eruption (Mt. St. Helens 1980 Venus/Cancer, Mt. Pelee 1902 Venus/Aries, Krakatoa 1883 Mars/Cancer).

Venus conjunct or just past Pluto, or Venus in very early cardinal, especially Aries and Cancer, relates to strong events—solar storms and volcanoes.

The occurrence of solar and volcanic events show overlapping much of the time. Observation by date and event clearly show the very early Sun and earth cardinal degrees. These early cardinal degrees and overlapping infer that the Sun's energies reach Earth quickly, as known from Nelson's radio static observations for RCA.

As well as contacting all solar planets (the primary triad Sun-Mercury-Jupiter) through Jupiter, in an on going process of bringing energy to the future event, Venus also has several other functions:

- In solar storms, which are said to be root or forerunning events, by a contact with Pluto, or by placement in very early cardinal.
- The formation of aspects within an event chart. It should be determined if Venus forms an aspect with a particular planet in regards to a geological area or location chart. This applies to both quakes and volcanoes
- The Venus-Mars-Jupiter complex with mutual integration and aspects, as well as other aspects, and separation involved.
- While Venus often has separated from all major aspects involving all or most of the slower planets, she often forms several minor 15° type aspects at the timing of the event. These are new infusions of energy, enough to bring about a ripe event now that she is in contact with Mars and Jupiter.

On Mars

Mars performs several functions in EM charts.

- As part of the major Venus-Mars-Jupiter energizing complex where separation is important. Separation may be thought of as storing of energy.
- Forming aspects with slower planets, in particular Uranus, for Moon, Mercury, Mars, and Uranus are part of a tumbler mechanism timing process.
- Mars may form an aspect with a particular planet in a given area. Particular aspects by sign, angle and planet may be a part of the Venus-Mars-Jupiter complex's functions, also involved in isolating locations.
- Mars has usually just contacted and separated from, slower planets in many quakes.
- The formation of highly significant midpoint sequences, Mars/Uranus, Mars/Jupiter, and Mars to Jupiter/Uranus among others. Of note, midpoint positions are often exact (partile) or approaching at the time of EM.
- Mars with Mercury and Saturn is a volcano complex (see On Saturn).
- Ancient astrologers noted the closeness and color of Mars. I have not dealt with this, and leave it to others.

On Jupiter

Jupiter has a key position in two complexes, Sun-Mercury-Jupiter and Venus-Mars-Jupiter. It is also part of the slow planet dance.

In the first, I believe that the relative positions of Jupiter and the Sun with Mercury, set up the waxing and waning energy patterns that act upon the geological areas. More importantly this complex turns on vulcanism, both on the Sun and Earth. In this they are aided by Venus which is important in jump-starting these solar disturbances and vulcanism, which in turn energize earth's vulcanism, which energizes earthquakes. What is often overlooked, there could be no earthquakes without heat. Or to be more precise, earthquakes would be limited to downward vertical motion or collapse.

Jupiter also forms part of the energy complex Venus-Mars-Jupiter, previously treated. As in Venus and Mars, separation is important, here from the slower planets Saturn through Pluto.

But Jupiter also has a more subtle influence. Just as Jupiter is the planet separating the faster and the slower planets, it also influences time within the major quake ``cycle'' that is, the overall time periods involving recurring volcanic or seismic activity in a given area. It does this by aspect with one or more slow planets. The subtlety of this can only be apparent when a whole series of events in one location are charted.

In forming this type of aspect, let us say, hypothetically, Jupiter 90 plus Saturn, 60/120 Neptune, a year past Pluto conjunction, the actual time frame for the event is keyed. A location is isolated and energized.

Jupiter, as the largest planet is a prime factor in producing the year's EM energy which may be stored, dissipated in release events or brought forth in certain areas as major EM. This energizing is a result of all the mutual contacts involving 15° or 30° sequences made by slow planets to each other, as well as faster planets to Jupiter.

Jupiter increases all energies and symbolizes expansion, eg. the bulge in a volcano. Jupiter's relatively fast motion, of a sign per year, is at present an indeterminate factor at moving locations in and out of imminent EM. I feel certain that the collected quake histories of locations, including minor, intermediate and failed events, will prove this.

On Saturn

Saturn is part of the slow-planet complex forming a part of the slow-planet location signature and overall energizing system.

Saturn symbolizes boundaries. It resists the swelling action of Jupiter. Ultimately pressure is created, friction heat results and Uranus will act upon this bringing release. This creates a flow (Neptune), or a slip. Neptune releasing, and transforming the stored energy, Pluto.

In volcanoes the passage of the Moon over Saturn by conjunction or other aspect may indicate the final energizing of a given location, especially in volcano charts. Mars may be involved since often, in both volcanic and seismic events, near simultaneous Mars-Saturn transits may result. Obviously at this time, Mars and Saturn are related by aspect.

Mercury-Mars-Saturn is a volcanic complex. They are interrelated at the time of first activity and of eruption.

It is probable that the ancient astrologers could relate Saturn to their location EM events. As the slowest planet of their time, at 29 plus years per cycle, it would have a place in the historical records or tradition.

On Uranus

Uranus, like all the planets, performs multiple roles in an EM event. First and foremost as the architect of sudden, dramatic and unforeseen change. He is the moment of slip in an earthquake, or the *nueé ardiente* in a volcano, the eruption and the release of the flow in a lava flow, itself Neptunian.

As a slow planet, it has a role as a long-term energizer. Again, by its relationship to the other slow planets, energy distribution to a given location is created and indicated. As it is energized by the Venus-Mars-Jupiter complex, when all is in place, it will be one of the trigger planets.

In major events it may be the planet contacted by Mercury or the planet in the degree of Mercury.

All EM events that occur without warning, and the reawakening of long dormant volcanoes, are ruled by Uranus. Such charts will show a strong Uranus.

On Neptune

As with all the planets, the slowest also perform many functions in EM. Modern astrological tradition, modern because of its discovery since that of Uranus in 1781, places the ``slow'' planets Uranus, Neptune, Pluto, beyond the control of man, as indicators and timers of great change in the social structure and influencing generational attitudes and progress.

In EM, Neptune may be said to represent the flow of the matter. This would include the magma, especially its flow upward through the earth's layers, its internal heating system stimulated and ruled by Pluto. Neptune also rules the spreading and diffusion of the new magma flow system, its containment within a channel of stone, and its immediate system of closed circuitry leading to the point of EM, ruled by Saturn, which by Saturnian restraint creates resistance, pressure, friction, etc., all non-conducive to flow.

Neptune also rules the sea water, for it is from sea water that pressurized steam is created that is so much a part of magma flow, but perhaps not related often enough to quake activity. Neptune also rules the steam produced, which is a Mars matter when produced by direct heat (Mars and Neptune) and Mars-Saturn when produced by friction (Mars, Saturn, Neptune). Magma pushed through the magma conduits is a Mars, Saturn, Neptune process.

So Neptune is a significator representing materials and process. In terms of energizing, like any planet slower than another, it will supply energy to the faster planets as they aspect it, and have its own energy focused through the faster planet. Eventually this collected energy will be enough that when it breaks forth, a major EM event is created. Along the way minor events, quake tremors, swarms or volcanic leaks and ventings could occur. A medium event may drain the energy and be a primary cause for the failure of a forecast, on one hand, and the randomness of events in a location on the other.

This collected energy shows in the EM chart at the time of a major event by strong aspect complexes or concentrations. Lastly, there is usually much separation at the time of EM. Faster planets have reached and passed exact aspect to a slower planet. For the purpose of EM, this separation may be considered as a measurement of the most recently stored energy. This becomes a consideration in the timing of the EM forecast.

Noting this between Uranus and Pluto is appropriate, for these slow planets, which store or focus the energy of the faster planets, are keys to major EM. Ancient forecasting, using only Sun through Saturn, was doing the same thing, picking up on patterns. In the smaller world of the ancients, events forecast were local ones, the signature of the location in which the astrologer operated.

Neptune, as well as Uranus and Pluto, remain in a sign a long time: Uranus approximately seven years, Neptune 14 plus and Pluto with its extremely elliptical orbit, from 12 to 30 years. In a given sign they imprint locations for present or future major EM. Neptune by sign, will emphasize certain locations as a significator (magma, steam, diffusion, flow), storing energy there. Such locations may then be further emphasized by certain slow planet combinations, for example Jupiter or Saturn in certain signs.

Finally I believe that there is an aspect theme involving the slow planets for any given location. Working with Neptune in one location, an aspect between Saturn and Neptune might appear consistently at, or near, the time of EM. This might be accompanied two out of three times by Jupiter or Pluto contacts. In our imaginary location, Uranus may make aspects only with the fast planets at the time of EM. These energies can be easily assessed through Michelsen's *Tables of Planetary Phenomena* (see Outer Planet Aspect Intensity). I believe that small and medium EM, for effective research, should be carefully observed in relationship to a given location.

On Pluto

Pluto is the most recently discovered planet of our solar system and the farthest from our Sun. Small and cold, nevertheless it seems to represent the extremes of transformative energy. In astrology it represents both the survival and death process in terms of the life cycle. Conversely it rules reproduction. Similarly in EM, I believe that it represents cycles within the Earth and the Sun that both begin and end EM sequences.

As a significator, Pluto represents the core of the earth, the life processes of a living Earth, and through its self-generating heat it keeps the Earth's vulcanism in motion, fertilizing the Earth, creating wind, ocean currents etc. Pluto, as core of the Earth, melts magma starting an upward convective flow of heat (Pluto) and magma (Neptune). The surface of the planet Earth is represented by its opposite sign Taurus ruled by Venus and co-ruled by Earth itself. Taurus rules the mouth in astrology, here the mouth of the volcano or the location of the quake.

Since it is the slowest of our planets, but known to leave generational imprint on humans, it appears to have a strong effect on the major EM of a given location. I key it to the location's super events. Given the brief, known history of the New World, and much of the Third World, it is hard to chronicle a location's events but the inference is clear. It would seem the study of Chinese, Japanese and Italian records would bear fruit.

Pluto is the Earth's nuclear furnace and her life force. In some way it transforms the energy of the Sun radically, giving life itself or the most violent of events.

How can I relate Pluto to the Sun? A strongly aspected Pluto often appears at major solar events, flares and storms. It is accompanied by an aspect to it from Venus, its counterpart as defined by the Taurus/Scorpio axis. That there is a cyclical level in this, is corroborated by early cardinal placement of a planet, 1 to 3 degrees in many of these solar event charts.

In terms of EM charts, the sign of Pluto is the most important in defining locations. Since we know that many locations have major events occurring in the slightly less than 250 years of Pluto's motion through the zodiac, check element and mode. Check aspects to it by slow planets, Jupiter through Neptune and whatever other aspects these slow planets form between themselves.

Lastly, note fast planet aspects to Pluto approaching, exact and separating. Mercury in Pluto's degree may indicate significant EM both generally and as a location.

Ann E. Parker, whose excellent work on earthquakes has emphasized eclipses and solar astrology, notes Pluto is, of all the planets, most frequently on an angle at the time of a quake, corroborating indirectly a solar connection.

I would note again that any planet on an angle is useless for forecasting as each planet passes through the four angles of the chart every day. Such an observation is astrologically interesting, but in terms of forecasting only means that in retrospect the train was on time. As repeatedly noted, this has been the greatest of astrological dead ends in EM forecasting. Playing around with planets on angles is quicksand at the end of a path that must have more bones than the LaBrea tar pits.

Conversely, a matter generally missed but more easily studied now, would be the placement of Pluto on an angle, especially the MidHeaven or Nadir (noon or midnight position), of a solar eclipse chart, as there it might function as an extreme eclipse. In such geographical locations as the eclipse path crosses, a new EM cycle may be beginning or a major event about to take place (ending). It could signify major energy build-up in an ongoing process for such a location.

In passing, the rulership (home) of Pluto is the sign Scorpio. That sign is square to Leo, ruled by the Sun, trine to Cancer, ruled by the Moon and opposed to Taurus, co-ruled by Earth. Since a solar eclipse involves Sun, Moon and Earth a strong Pluto, particularly near an angle, may have predictive significance for EM on the eclipse path (geographic locations).

One of the truly amazing things about astrology is the preciseness of its symbology when it is viewed and understood in semantic terms as a symbolic language. Pluto is seminal, birth and death, the beginning and the end, the species, continuity. Pluto in geology is the causal inner core of the earth and the force greater than nuclear bombs in EM events.

Pluto probably defines the beginning and end of location cycles. With the other slow planets, by both sign and aspect, it isolates geographic locations and participates in energy build-ups.

Pluto probably intensifies the results (EM in a given location) of an eclipse, if placed strongly in the eclipse chart. Pluto is significant in solar EM, known generally as solar flares, solar storms and sun spots, stimulating the heating of earth's, vulcanism, in turn creating quake activity.

All quake activity ultimately has its origin in vulcanism, ruled by Pluto, both at Earth's core and the volcano's crater, as well as the Solar vulcanism underlying its events.

15

Planetary Groups in EM

Sun-Mercury-Jupiter are the primary triad or energy triad, while Venus-Mars-Jupiter are the secondary energizers.

Sun, Mars, Uranus, Neptune integrate with major long-term timers and energizers. The slow planets create both energy and geographic isolation. This combination will often figure in a major complex.

Moon, Mercury, Mars and Uranus are the timing complex. Saturn figures in volcanoes.

Jupiter, Saturn, Uranus, Neptune, Pluto—as a group their aspects energize, give long-term timing and geographically isolate through their varying aspect combinations and the signs they occupy.

Mercury is the three-day timer, often through touching off Mars, Jupiter, Uranus, Neptune, but any planet will do. In the absence of a planet in the degree of Mercury, check the Sun-Mercury-Jupiter midpoints. The three-day timer in a forecast is one day before or after a point chosen by Mercury in degree.

At the event, with built-up energy in place, the slower planets wait to be contacted by the Moon and Mercury. If Mercury is in degree, and the Moon contacts Saturn, in some cases Uranus by degree,(some 30 degree aspect) and separates moving on to Mars, the time may be ripe.

16

A List of Simultaneous Events

The following is a list randomly made:

- One week covers three Moon signs. The EM's were noted on a one week basis Sunday 0 GMT thru Saturday, then repeated.
- Six days, the event plus or minus three days, would cover two plus signs for the Moon. That is three location signatures. More importantly six days allows a variety of Mercury transits. Near stations it might move a couple degrees in a week; more than two degrees a day at its most rapid rate of motion.
- The change of the Moon's sign means a change in the location signature. Thus EM events, in widely separated locations *if the Moon sign is the same*, may be said to respond to the same planetary signatures. However, the actual energy build up is not necessarily the same. Geologically speaking, a great event may occur here, a minor event there.
- These same signature locations should be checked for previous eclipse emphasis, especially the path of the eclipse.
- Lunations, eclipses and ingresses should be noted for amount of slow planet emphasis, or a stellium near the MidHeaven/Nadir Axis (Noon/Midnight) of the chart.

The purpose is to establish those locations likely to respond to the same location signature, for each location under the eclipse path is not equally likely to have a quake, an obvious but often overlooked point.

17

Drawing the EM Event Chart

All events are drawn with an equal house, 0° Aries Ascendant. This is known as the zodiacal or flat Aries chart. Place the ten planets in the chart using degrees only. Place the Moon's Nodes on the outside. If the angles from a timed event are known, these too go on the outside.

The mode of the Moon's Nodes may well key the likelihood of major events by both area and intensity: cardinal, weak; mutable, moderate; fixed, strong. Since the Moon's Nodes move by retrograde motion, note that this sequence indicates energy build-up. A partile point, by analogy, or an inferred energy buildup of major proportions, would occur at 15° mutable. Strong EM occurs under separating fixed Nodes

Of course the nodes function as part of the eclipse chart being the path of the eclipse. The eclipse chart MC serves to further localize events. Transits to the eclipse chart, in a subsequent, suitable location signature dispersion chart, would give an approximate time of a potential event.

The common, necessary, and more or less precise quake indicators are then assessed, whether in terms of forming a location signature from past events, or forecasting a future event (location signature known).

In summary, the plantetary angles are irrelevant. The Moon's functions, most important by sign, have no reliability in timing an event in terms of approaching, exact or separating aspects. Lunar exactness in EM is always random and always in retrospect.

Just as the human brain is the greatest computer, so the eye is the greatest scanner. I believe I'll be vindicated when I say that visual scanning of the ephemeris, and Aries zodiacal charts, will prove more efficient and productive than the computer. Since building an actual location signature is in effect a layering process, the eye can do it faster.

The most helpful tool in analyzing quakes is this simple, uniform chart. Visual habit aids acuity and what I have explained here is in fact done in a minute or two.

18

Signs and Aspect Complexes

In the chapter on properties of the Moon (Chapter 13), I examined a hypothetical chart to illustrate what I call the principle of lunar enhancement. That is the main function of the Moon in EM, the others are collector of planetary energy and a part in the triggering process. Oversimplified, lunar enhancement is primarily geographic isolation and peaking the energy, this last is the true trigger nature of the Moon.

In the chapter on the Moon the importance of the signs of the zodiac was mentioned. Signs are of an immutable character and a planet, which is the active dynamic in astrology, passing through a sign takes on the character of the sign, or is influenced by the sign. Mars in Scorpio might lead to calculated revenge taken cold, while Mars in Aries would indicate a violent outburst, using a human example.

The signs in EM astrology relate to geographic location and this is layered into the rest of the signature. For example, a Japanese quake usually has a planet in Virgo, California often one in Pisces and a West Indian quake usually has a planet in Cancer. Bet your money, you'll come out ahead. When such a key location sign lacks a planet, thus failing to complete a geographic signature, the Moon may leap into the breach, one of the functions of lunar enhancement.

The signs also have two other qualities: element (fire, earth, air, water) and mode (cardinal, fixed, mutable). Element denotes a type of energy. Mode denotes a manner of energy use. With four elements and three modes, each mode has one sign of each element for the 12 signs.

The signs, through character, type and manner, influence the energy of a planet there. Similarly a planet (or planets), if not the ruler of the sign, will have an additional effect on the sign where it is, and on its own sign. Scorpio is ruled by both Mars and Pluto, but to continue with that Mars example, Pluto and those ruled by Pluto in whatever sign it falls, will be the cause of recipient of the ``cold revenge'' of Mars in Scorpio.

For the purpose of EM signs, elements and modes, the latter two being properties of signs, subtly alter the energy of planets passing through them. In the matter of EM, the mere presence of a planet in key signs appears to complete that part of the signature.

Signs have two other functions as opposed to properties. They are the foundations of aspects, aspect complexes and polarities. These three culminate in the powerful aspect complexes, of which four are key.

The Grand Cross—four or more planets square (90°) each other in two polarities and four elements.

The T-square (90°)—three or more planets forming an opposition (180°) with one or more of the planets square those of the opposition. The planets in the opposition are of the same mode and polarity, the planet square to them, the same mode but different polarity.[No two adjacent signs are of the same polarity. Same location signature have predominance of one or the other fire/air (positive) or earth/water (negative). Some polarity signs and their aspects 60, 120, 180 give flow to the energy. Different polarity signs and their aspects give alternating flow (either/or), creating resistance, the square for example. In the T-square, the square planet is the trigger. The energy strength concentrated by midpoint and the release-point use of energy is also there. The grand cross would have more release points (four), and is in fact stronger, but its energy is more diffuse than the concentrated energy of the T-square.

The Grand Trine (120°)—three or more planets in trine to each other from the three signs of the same element (fire, earth, air or water). They have also the same polarity at all points. This is an aspect of flowing energy, self contained. A planet square or opposed one of the trine's three points lets energy in or out. The planet in opposition creates the classic kite formation. This may be a factor in EM ripeness or release.

The Stellium—three or more planets in one sign is concentrated, self contained, integrated energy. The planets themselves, with the sign involved, would thus function more or less effectively and more or less powerfully. It can compensate for a lack of planets in the other signs of the same mode.

For example, a super strong stellium might involve three planets of the same element, exalted planets, and the Moon. Example: Sun, Mars, Jupiter, Pluto, Moon in Aries. This is not complete but these four complexes are the strongest.

Other complexes relate primarily to a general dispersion of planetary pattern.

- Planets in consecutive signs—alternating energy.
- Planets in every other sign—flowing energy.
- Planets in two or more sign on each side of the chart—seesaw, equal flow plus alternating energy.

In major EM two or more major complexes may be present. Aspect complexes are immediate keys to location, chart integration, and much energy. Note the separation and position of triggers, energy patterns and the relationship of planetary groups like Sun-Mercury-Jupiter; Venus-Mars-Jupiter; Moon-Mars-Uranus; and in a volcano, Moon-Saturn and Mercury-Mars-Saturn. Note slow planets, Jupiter through Pluto, aspects, and Mercury by degree, especially to planets Mars through Pluto. Note the respective aspects of Venus, Mars and Jupiter to slower planets and separation among themselves and the slower planets. Note Venus to Pluto. These indicate new events and solar events.

In summary let's touch on planetary energy in the various forms necessary to activate major EM. The aspect combination by sign and mode, element and polarity, as well as planetary dispersion and lunar enhancement, isolate location.

Strongly configured Uranus may indicate events without warning, or in so-called inactive areas. Both of these factors were present in the Cairo 1992, quake. Many planets, or a planet in early cardinal degrees, may relate directly to strong vulcanism as cause. Note chart location signature and check actual geological activity.

19

What the Ancients Can Teach Us

Allowing for historical exaggeration and apocrypha, some ancient astrologers still made successful EM and weather forecasts. Putting aside their known use of fixed stars and Arabic parts, the modern day astrologer must ask himself how they could do it with just seven planets, ending with Saturn. My own attempts at reconstructing their circumstances encouraged me.

These were not global times. A couple of hundred miles was a major journey except for a chosen few on military or mercantile expeditions. These routes were known and usually no one wandered too far from them.

Astronomical measurements were hard to come by and planetary positions weren't projected too far into the future, although the methodology existed for their future positions. Lunations, eclipses and ingresses were the most commonly used charts and we can infer that astrologers coaxed a lot out of them. The Saros Cycle of eclipses was known, and there probably existed a special body of knowledge on Mars. The positions of the fast bodies (Sun, Moon, Mercury and Venus) were well known.

We know there were traditions of astrology in various places and eras and that knowledge was passed from generation to generation. We know that astrology in practice was localized and may infer from this that most EM studies and forecasts related to local events. They certainly weren't tracking the Ring of Fire.

They used ingress, lunation and eclipse charts, and seven planets. Within the 30 year period of the Saturn cycle there were two and a half Jupiter cycles and about 12 Mars cycles. These were the three heavies that comprised the ancient's tool box.

I can visualize the lines or pictographs on tablets, parchment or papyrus: "When suitable time has passed since the last earthquake, four or five generations and an eclipse appears in sign . . . with the Nadir afflicted a quake will come when all planets are in watery signs and Mars or Jupiter are in. . . ."

- Some time must elapse since the last event.
- An important chart, or a series of charts, lunations, eclipses, ingresses gave a warning.
- This probably required a transit.
- It also required a suitable planetary dispersement pattern by sign or aspect to accompany that transit.

Perhaps because I'm not mathematically inclined and notice the failings of science, I was free to form this vision. A solid argument could be that too much computer generated information, undigested in the isolation of scientific specializations and elitism, has obscured EM issues on every level.

The living earth in its geological cycles rearranges its skin bit by bit, exactly as an eagle loses one wing feather at a time; small, but utterly necessary to life, the feather and quake.

This study began with the eruption of Mount Saint Helens. Somewhere, I obtained a list of quakes and wrote the planets into a Grant Lewi decanate wheel (each sign divided in three parts, 10 degrees, 36 parts). I noticed that the quakes of Greece and Italy did not resemble the quakes of South America.

Patterns visible to the naked eye, glyphs spread over 12 signs, I picked up pencil, paper and book, and turned on the greatest computer of them all, the human mind.

Only seven planets. I quickly picked out Sun, Mercury and Jupiter. It was years and hundreds of charts before I picked up on Venus, Mars and Jupiter. The Moon and Saturn were left. The little chronactor and the great chronactor.

British astrologers of the 19th century and earlier wrote on the eclipses. They noted their properties by sign, element and mode. This leaves the Moon's Nodes, in the same sign in most cases, and I believe the sign of the Moon's Nodes indicates likelihood for a given area.

Ann E. Parker's work is heading in this direction, though I don't believe she specifically states it this way. It would seem from her lists, that fixed sign Nodes indicate the greatest likelihood of quake, cardinal the least. Note that in the backward motion of the nodes, fixed signs follow cardinal, with the cardinal Nodes representing gathering force. The mutable nodes are in fact intermediate in quake action. Fixed nodes indicate strong energizing and EM.

Remember the eclipse chart always refers to locations. Since there are more or less the same number of 6+R events in a year, both location and severity must be assessed. Tradition notes the power of fixed signs in quakes, especially Taurus/Scorpio. After drawing many charts this does not make much sense, unless the reference is to the nodes. I believe this to be true, that the ancient warnings about Taurus/Scorpio referred to the nodes in this position and thus eclipses in Taurus/Scorpio. They returned to Taurus/Scorpio February 1, 1994 with the Moon's North Node at 29° Scorpio.Early Taurus/Scorpio are quake degrees as well, but are not in every event

20

Why I Do Not Use Ascendant Charts in EM

Ascendant charts represent in some ways the human being; this is true also in the mundane chart (geopolitical or mass event). The only exceptions are the lunation, eclipse and ingress charts where the angles represent a place; all planets pass over all angles every day. In EM it doesn't matter which planet is where. It doesn't matter what time of the day it goes off. In EM charts houses do not apply as in the lunation chart, nor do angles. Signs do. Houses relate to human activity, angles to place.

Angles are useless for forecasting because:

- In order to forecast a given planet in a given angle or angles, you'd do better betting on greyhounds.
- The position of planets conjunct angles, including such examples as Uranus or Pluto to the Midheaven, or the Moon made a perfect conjunction to planet X, are all after the fact in the EM event chart.
- Showing a planet conjunct an angle has nothing to do with forecasting future EM, for it occurs every day.
- A two hour framework of time has nothing to offer the human being in an EM area. Even the slow witted would tell you they'd like to leave a little sooner.

The earth is wired with instruments that can only record ongoing events. At the same time, the EM is divided into quake and volcanoe specialties. Quakes have been over-defined in terms of California and volcanoes over-defined in terms of Hawaii.

Much of the above comes across as assertion, but I believe some light can be shed on the inadvertent misunderstanding which has led to the "Uranus-on-an-angle-morass."

Lunation and eclipse charts, as well as solar ingresses, are used in both weather and EM predictions. By observation, astrologers know the angles are sensitive, especially when outer planets are present near them. This is an empirical fact.

The lunation, etc. is a natal chart representing potential for a period of time. It is the transit of a planet to natal planets in angles that is emphasized, not angles themselves, which indicate the location. Such a chart notably would be said to have an active fourth house for example, the weather house in mundane charts.

To clarify, I will illustrate with Uranus conjunct the IC, the harbinger of all manner of blowing and shaking. This is a very strong Uranus, as strong as you can imagine, and in fact your forecasts are exactly right.

The planet transits to Uranus indicate the time. The angles have nothing to do with the event. They indicate the location of your forecasts. As forecasts were made, we did not say at midnight, but gave a day, or two, or three.

The hurricanes and quakes came. We charted them. These event charts are not used to forecast future EM or weather events, though we know in retrospect that outer planets often seem to appear near the angles at the EM event. This is not that strange considering the daily rotation of the earth, but sometimes we forget that this has no forecast value, even as we turn to the next lunation for EM and weather events.

We must go on to the next lunation, etc. and start over. Again, these event charts are not used to forecast future EM or weather.

21

Why I Don't Use Locality Charts

Most locality charts, such as the state of Hawaii or Alaska, are in fact human events. In terms of EM, it is akin to reading a neighbor's chart to find out what you are doing. Even that is not a good analogy for event charts and EM are not read in the same way.

To my knowledge no astrologer currently knows how to progress an EM chart or work transits and solar arcs to it (for the non-astrologer, the principle techniques of forecasting). This does not mean that it can't be done. One would begin with several long sequences of quakes in exactly the same locations.

The often long periods, a century or more between major events in a given location, and the historical lack of data for such events, remains the problem. For example, the New Madrid Fault System, had a major event in 1683 as well as the documented quake of December 11, 1811, with several more in 1812. Virtually nothing is known of New York City which has a fault system more or less under 14th St. As noted elsewhere, one begins with the EM of Italy, China and Japan, to my knowledge the only places with accurate records of more than 400 years.

The records of the New World cover more or less 400 years. Of principal interest are the South and Central American events. Unfortunately all EM records were noted and preserved in a haphazard fashion. Few minor or failed events were noted. Late in 1993, I secured a copy of the *Catalog of Significant Earthquakes*. It is a remarkable work and samples for given locations are better recorded than I thought. I truly believe precise location charting is the correct route to follow. Several promising examples are featured in the text and appendices.

22

Midpoints in EM

Midpoints are becoming more popular in all areas of astrology. There are 78 midpoints using just 10 planets, Ascendant, Midheaven and North Node. When a third planet is integrated, the combinations rise to 924. What the astute user of midpoints does is to note the obvious ones, or ask what the appropriate one would be for the chart and matter at hand. He or she might choose to use just one, and gain much insight.

Since only a few are needed for EM, they can be hand-calculated. The zodiacal minutes are not necessary. The EM system is one of simplicity, and if you don't need the midpoint don't use it. Most astrologers know how to calculate midpoints. Geologists and laymen can learn in 30 seconds. A midpoint is the mid-distance between two planets in question. Add the longitude of the two planets.

Aries 0°	0-29	Libra 0°	80-209
Taurus 0°	30-59	Scorpio 0°	210-239
Gemini 0°	60-89	Sagittarius 0°	240-269
Cancer 0°	90-119	Capricorn 0°	270-299
Leo 0°	120-149	Aquarius 0°	300-329
Virgo 0°	150-179	Pisces 0°	330-359

Divide by two. If the midpoint moves to the far side of the chart, subtract 180° and this will return it to the near middle of the two planets concerned. In close opposition (180°), I sometimes use both sides of the chart.

Example: Sun, 0° Aries, Jupiter 0° Cancer, midpoint 15° Taurus. If a planet is at 15° Taurus, there is a blending of the three planetary energies, giving observed results. Skilled users can derive matters of timing, content, and the significance of the midpoint. Assuming all planets here are of the same time or chart, a transiting (future) planet at 15° Taurus, or other positions aspecting it, would be the key to timing. It would also refine content according to the nature of the planets involved.

How are they used in EM? As noted in Chapter 37, the actual events of EM contain a greater degree of separation in terms of the overall chart than is usual. Or, put another way, the astrologer should read separation in EM charts.

Research showed me two things. First, while the aspects were separating, often exact midpoints were formed to a third planet in the EM group, or a third planet representing the third partner in an aspect complex, e.g. Grand Trine or T-square. (Note the void-of-course Moon at 28° Aries in Cairo 1992)

Saturn 311° (11° Aquarius and Mars 105°—15° Cancer—form their midpoint to the Moon at 28° Aries. As noted, I saw relevance in this for the Moon and Mars are triggers and Saturn has a trigger function with the Moon in volcano charts, or those involving vulcanism.

This leads to the second use of midpoints in EM. Note what is missing in the chart, or what would enhance it in terms of the EM planetary groups. These groups in general define the practical use of midpoints in EM. The purpose is to come up with a missing signature component.

Sun-Mercury-Jupiter	Initiators
Venus-Mars-Jupiter	Energizers
Sun-Mars-Uranus-Neptune	Integrators
Jupiter through Pluto	Slow planet aspects
Moon-Mercury-Mars-Uranus	Triggers
Saturn	Volcano trigger
Mercury-Mars-Saturn	Volcano complex

Mid-Gemini/Sagittarius often appear. These are earthquake duads. Use only midpoints of the planets in each group.

Example: In Cairo 1992, Mercury was not in degree (trigger) and its position to the Sun and Jupiter seemed weak. Note that the Mercury/Jupiter midpoint (initiators) resolved both matters.

Example: The signature of location X requires a Jupiter-Pluto aspect and a Saturn-Pluto aspect as well. As we forecast, in the face of known new geological activity, these three planets appear to float about, lost. Try the midpoints Jupiter/Pluto=Saturn, Saturn/Pluto=Jupiter, Jupiter/Saturn=Pluto. Visually eliminate or choose one. You have your Jupiter-Pluto, Saturn-Pluto connection in no more than two moves.

As noted, EM usually has much separation in planetary aspects. Often enough, a common midpoint degree may be found within a complex. This may be usable as a timer and deserves serious study.

Example: 16° Pisces, 18° Cancer 20° Scorpio yields 18 in our imaginary GTW (grand water trine).

Example: Jupiter 5° Aries, Mars 25° Aries, Jupiter/Mars=15° Aries (90°) Sun 10° Cancer, Venus 20° Cancer, Sun/Venus=15° Cancer.

Finally, a certain midpoint might correspond to an eclipse degree. This should probably be confined to timers such as Mars/Uranus=Eclipse Sun.

This represents the better part of significant EM midpoint work. There is no magic bullet, but often a missing component to the signature appears almost magically. Midpoint theory maintains it was not missing. In summation, use midpoints when necessary and with purpose.

To the astrologer who would like to become acquainted with midpoints for other astrology, I recommend *The Combination of Stellar Influences* by Reinhold Ebertin. Each two-planet combination is defined by principle, psychological correspondence +/-, biological correspondences, sociological correspondence and probable manifestation, Ebertin's terms.

23

The Rolling Signature

As the planets orbit, new patterns are formed. While the overall 10 planets are always in different positions relative to each other, their overall dispersion patterns are duplicated. Thus there is a repetition of:

- Sign—yielding element and mode
- Aspects—angle between two planets
- Aspect complexes—linked aspects
- Dispersion—over 90° zodiacal longitude, scattered, 90° link up emphasis, 120° link up emphasis, half the chart or bowl, etc. It is this dispersion that gives a location signature, as well as the high energy necessary for an EM event.

Location signatures, as they recur, may be subtly different, or only subtly the same. Something missing here, but enhanced there.

The other conclusion is, a planet in a sign or complex is the important thing, rather than a planet itself, as this simply cannot always occur. This is not to say that planets, particularly the faster Sun through Mars, don't often reappear in the same signs in recurring events for a location, but they will not always reappear in the same signs.

Next, certain areas may respond to a secondary signature. This may be the grand water trine type, which I believe is the nearest to a universal quake signature, or simply a very differently dispersed chart. In South American events one suddenly comes across the wedge chart (90°) of zodiacal longitude. Full knowledge of an area's events might well indicate:

- A primary signature.
- A secondary signature.
- Susceptibility to the universal signatures grand trine water, or Cancer/Capricorn axis.

I suspect that over a long period of time, long meaning a century plus, or a geological blink, there may be some overall change in the primary location signature. I call this in particular, and the matters noted here in general, the rolling signature.

24

Stored Energy

Stored energy is a descriptive term for energy built up between major events in a given location. It is pressure, resistance, friction, heat, rebound, etc.

In terms of astrological forecasting it may be inferred that energy is somewhat generally stored in locations, and more specifically in the locations sensitive to the planetary pattern of the moment.

It may be inferred that energy storage covers passages (transits) of 30° in the zodiac, 15° approaching, exact aspect (partile) and 15° separating. This explains the large number of more or less exact 15° type aspects in EM charts.

Theoretically the classic aspect, say 90° would be partile, midway between 75° and 105°, both 15 degree type aspects. What occurs at this time?

The power of the classic aspects, 0° 60° 90° 120° 180°, each divisible by 30° except the conjunction, is indisputable. We know that most astrological rules and guidelines function in EM as elsewhere.

What occurs at the partile classic aspect, in the time prior to the EM, as the location signature comes together? Common sense says that a major burst of planetary energy at this time results in a major build up of stored energy.

Think about those balloons again—an extra strong burst of air, why the balloon is half full.

The 30° energy storage transit also makes sense in terms of Jupiter, one of the solar initiators (with Mercury and Sun), since it moves through a sign in one year, and periodically, by sign and aspect to the slower planets, strongly energizing a given area.

The concept of stored energy is itself inferred from the indisputable fact of planetary separation in EM charts. The EM event occurs after the partile classic aspect, but the very nature of the partile classic aspect is indicative of great energy.

25

Outer Planet Aspect Intensity

In assessing the overall potential for EM at a given time, we have arrived at two methods for assessing the increase of vulcanism: planetary motion through the cardinal signs and the Moon's Nodes by modality - cardinal, few major quakes; mutable, some; fixed, the majority of intense earthquakes. This is all in terms of the sequence equation, Solar event = Vulcanism = Quake.

How else might an increase in EM vulcanism with its subsequent eruptions and quakes be noted? I offer another hypothesis. A key assessment factor lies hidden within the outer planets. How can we measure their intensity?

Periodically, astrologers quantify the value of a planet's energy. The basic principle is simple. A numerical scale is created for the question at hand. I wish to quantify outer planet aspects for a given year. With the publication of Neil Michelsen's *Tables of Planetary Phenomena*, this is easy.

Based on conventional astrological principles that relate to the power of aspects, and the principle that the slower the planet, the more powerful its energy, I developed an integrated numerical value system for the planetary phenomena; Jupiter, Saturn, Uranus, Neptune, Pluto, 0°, 45°, 90°, 120°, 135°, 180° Aspects 1700-2050.

1	2	3	4	5
45°/135°	120°	90°	180°	0°
1	2	3	4	5
Jupiter	Saturn	Uranus	Neptune	Pluto

Thus the strongest possible assessment would be a conjunction (5) of Neptune (4) Pluto (5) for a total of 14. The weakest would be a semisquare 45° (1) of Jupiter (1) to Saturn (2) for 4. The Uranus-Neptune conjunction of 1993 had a value of conjunction 5 Neptune 4, Uranus 3 for a total of 12.

We know that some years produce more EM than others. Here are the aspect values for 1900 through 1910, when the world was buffeted by strong quakes in all quake areas, perhaps under the early Uranus opposition Pluto 1901 followed by Uranus opposition Neptune 1906.

Year	Value	Year	Value
1900	39	1906	78
1901	51	1907	81
1902	62	1908	93
1903	79	1909	77
1904	72	1910	68
1905	48		

1992 had a value of 30 but 1993 with the Uranus Neptune conjunction, etc. had a value of 98.

Just how would I integrate this into EM forecasting? Remembering eclipses and location signatures as shown in EM charts, some places are building, some getting ready for release.

In February 1994, the Nodes moved into Scorpio/Taurus. With maximum buildup aspects for 1993, I would forecast strong EM for 1994.

Here, concepts of energy buildup, the Moon's Nodes as intensity indicators, and outer planet aspects, merge into a cohesive whole. Regarding 1994, in most instances, EMs would use a large infusion of energy build-up received in 1993.

This hypothesis can be examined and refined by matching a catalogue of 6R quakes against the year's outer planet aspect intensity. I suspect the principle of buildup and separation may mean many EM show in the following year, or years, after a large aspect intensity count.

A strong year by aspect intensity, with cardinal Moon's Nodes, might produce little in the way of overall EM. A strong year by aspect intensity, with mutable Moon's Nodes, might produce moderate results. But I believe its built up energy will carry into the following year's EM when the Moon's Nodes go into fixed signs, e.g. 1994, with a value of 64.

That year, if strong by aspect intensity itself, will further increase EM potential with the Moon's Nodes fixed, especially if preceded by a strong outer aspect intensity year, or years.

26

Planetary Patterns Forming the Signature

For lack of a better term, interlocking planetary conditions are involved in setting off major EM. This complex interlocking, involving groups of planets, with each planet involved in several groups and in necessary patterns, reduces the number of major quake patterns. Thus a pattern applies to several locations—events occurring at the same time in different locations. Similarly, enough conditions, both geological and astrological, may be present to set off a minor event at the time of a major event. Geologically speaking this would cause a release of energy and the location is back to square one, delaying a major EM. Again consider the apparent random occurrence of major events in a given location.

An astrological result to the above is the occurrence and reoccurrence of patterns in the dispersal of the ten planets through the signs. This signifies stronger than usual activity, activity in several areas, or designates a major event or a particular location. These patterns in fact, narrow time and location. They include:

- Grand Trine combinations, especially the GT Water which has figured in many major quakes.
- The Grand Cross combinations
- Predominately trines
- Predominately squares
- Predominately negative planets (earth and water)
- Predominately positive planets (air and fire)
- Predominately of Mode (cardinal, fixed, mutable)
- Combination of the above
- Stellium—three or more planets in one sign
- Mixed squares and trines including Grand Trine and Grand Cross. Strong Taurus/Scorpio axis
- Strong Cancer/Capricorn axis
- Fixed square combinations
- Extreme Wedges or Splays (three or four signs—eight or more signs)

These are not all of the major patterns, but an ample illustration. In fact, these can combine in three- or four-way combinations, but it is important to be able to note groupings and patterns in the ephemeris or chart, and relate them to times and locations.

27

The Use of Aspects in EM Forecasting

These are the classic aspects:

- 0° Conjunction
- 60° Sextile
- 90° Square
- 120° Trine
- 180° Opposition
- Parallel/Contraparallel (planets parallel on the ecliptic)

These have been in use since antiquity, when the difficulties of calculation made time of the essence. In the 20th century, astrological establishments reinforced these six aspects somewhat dogmatically, perhaps to bring back some discipline to a field overgrown with weeds.

During antiquity and the present, the 45° angle or semisquare, and the 135° angle or sesquisquare, have always been in use, or more exactly, available to those who cared to use them. They are divisions of the 90° and 180° aspects, thus frictional or dynamic. The 360° lunar cycle is also divided into semisquares (45 degrees) for phases of the Moon.

Note that all the classic aspects are divisible by 15 and/or 30. What happened to the others? Stated in utter simplicity, they've been lost in the shuffle. Do they have value in EM? Most certainly. Any and all aspects that will give corroboration in timing or locating an EM have value. This system of forecasting is based on the matching of signature as seen in the line of the ephemeris. No calculation is needed.

To complete our aspects, the quincunx or 150° aspect was revived. It is a 6/8 aspect that is unpleasant in natal astrology, involving sickness and work (sixth house) and death and crisis (eighth house). While some spiritual astrologers might not have liked its more sordid qualities, there is another twist to it: the issue at hand is not resolved, the energy balance constantly shifting from one planet to another.

The semisextile, sometimes called half a sextile. It is 12/1 when unfortunate and 1/2 when fortunate, and Vedic astrology deems it negative. Astrologer Carol Griffin, sees it as a sign of bickering, basing this on the behavior of married couples with consecutive Sun signs. Note that both 30° and 150° have planets in different polarities, modes and elements.

These aspects are present in the signature of some locations. British quakes seem to have a 150° opening between the leading and trailing planets.

On October 12, 1992 at 3:09:57 a.m. EET, an earthquake measuring 5.9R struck Cairo, Egypt, 30N03, 31E13 (F.E. Cairo Earthquake, *Today's Astrologer*, January 22, 1993).

Farouk Elhiddiny wrote, "Both charts (preceding Full Moon and event) show a remarkably large number of inconjuncts and semisextiles, which are the hardest aspects in the Egyptian system." He then states, "Conspicuous by its absence is the trine." Perhaps these aspects relate to the Egyptian signature. I will show elsewhere that the grand trine water is perhaps the nearest we will come to the ``universal'' signature of a major EM.

Weather astrologers have long noted and used 15° aspects in their forecasting. These are 15°, 75° and 165°.

Years ago I noticed the 75° aspect and defined it in terms of excess. Note also the resurgence of solar energy, often negative in the old, as progressed Sun hits 75° from the radix Sun. The point being, I believe it is a solar aspect. I believe 15 degrees is also a solar aspect. It is the approximate distance the Sun moves from New to Full Moon.

Thus, 165° is a lunar aspect from the New Moon Sun at the time of the Full Moon and compliments the 15° aspect. EM charts are full of them and these are often close or exact.

Comments on the so-called lesser aspects should stimulate interest in them for they need to be noticed.

My system of EM is nothing more than the search for a planetary signature that can be located in time and space as read from the line of the ephemeris:

- No astrological theory.
- No math or calculation.
- No minutes of degrees.
- The elimination of angles and the Moon as primary timer.
- The use of the Moon to create or enhance a location signature, defining quake locations for two and a half day intervals and the probable time for major EM; thus the same two and a half days.
- The defining of stored energy.
- Noticing the trigger planets, more than one.

There are three other aspects in use along with their multiples: the septile, 51+°; the quintile, 72°; and the nonagon, 40°. In natal (personal) astrology these are most often used in karmic or spiritual terms. Respectively, in utter briefness, they deal with fate, gifted or innate skills, and hindrances or blockages. Given that I've stated any aspect is useful in creating an EM signature for a location, I'll just note that these are covered by the concept of approaching or separating aspects—45°, 75°, 45°.

28

Simultaneous Events

Anyone who becomes interested in EM soon notices the phenomenon of simultaneous events. Noteworthy quakes and volcanic eruptions often appear in widely separated places on the same day, or many events occur over several days.

A period of seven days involves the Moon's passage through three signs of the zodiac. This creates three separate signatures in terms of lunar enhancement (see Chapter 40).

Events occurring with the Moon in the same sign (two and a half days) obviously respond to the same location signature. My observation of charted quakes shows that widely separated areas respond to a given overall signature and that conversely, some quite close locations respond to a different signature. The latter is true of California (see Chapter 62).

Given that eclipses, lunations and ingresses would indicate location strips (longitude), and that a period of one year and three months might involve several eclipses, five ingresses, 15 New Moons and 15 Full Moons, it is safe to assume that several of these simultaneous events were indeed localized by longitude.

Here is where the tedious detail work begins. It would be necessary to track areas by past events, and even more importantly those times of good location signature that pass with no event. This is relatively simple, especially with computer generated charts. A given location would also need 30 charts a year, specifically to see if the Midheaven (longitude band) has been sensitized.

Were all events in a lunar enhancement period sensitized by Midheaven location (longitude) indicators or eclipse paths? I'm a betting man, and everytime I've found something ``sure'' in this research, I move on to an exception. I'm quite sure the exception operates here as well.

I believe there will be examples of major EM events that cannot be shown by location sensitizing. Exceptions are ever present in EM; they are an ongoing reality to any forecasting system. EM is not scientific in the sense of a chemical reaction. Failed events or surprise events do not invalidate the forecast system. They must be accepted into the system as jokers, or wild cards.

Proceeding with the assumption just outlined, two conclusions are immediately apparent:

- The location signature by itself may be enough to trigger an event, given sufficent and previously stored energy.
- There may be a connecting geological factor.

Both of these must be considered geologically. An indicator of sufficient stored energy would be an overdue period of time for the location's EM. At this writing, Mount Pele in Martinique is overdue. Its last major eruption was in 1902. This is known by several major eruptions dating from the 17th century, when for all practical purposes, Caribbean EM was first noted.

The Caribbean began the 17th century with the subsidence quake of Port Royale, Jamaica. The subsidence was approxmately 15 feet. Premonitory events would also be an indicator.

The second consideration is what James Churchward calls the gas belts (see Chapter 4). Here and there I've noted that EM study is overspecialized—quake, volcano and ocean currents. These are all resultant events and little thought is given to the causal and connecting factor, vulcanism.

In 1931, Colonel James Churchward published the first two books of a four part series on MU, an earlier Pacific counterpart to the lost continent of Atlantis.

Naturally, any lost continent literature accepts cataclysmic geology and this is true here. The concept of the gas belt has old Tibetan origins according to Churchward. These gas belts are huge systems that conduct magma and super heated gases, mainly steam, in a worldwide system of tunnels or belts.

Many simultaneous EMs appear connected, in so far as they are on the same belt system as described by Churchward.

I believe these belts are located along the Moho Line where the crust meets the semi-molten outer mantle, but where the mantle still maintains much structural (rock-like) integrity. They are not studied much, and indeed may not be well acknowledged by the geological establishment. It is easy to infer the existence of these belts. Krakatoa's, five mile high eruptions and the lava rivers of a modern Kiluea, HI or an ancient Western Shield in the northwest United States, did not come from cracks in rocks or energy mains the size of city water or sewer aqueducts. Furthermore, the magma eruptions of a Kiluea or the Western Shield indicate a sustained source of propellant energy which infers a delivery system. This differs from trapped or built up energy of a boiler type explosion, receiving energy on the spot. (See Appendix I.)

29

An Astro-Geological Overview

The general requisites of an EM chart have been delineated in individual chapters and here and there combined and illustrated by example. Common factors are planetary groupings and energizing factors such as planetary integration and lunar enhancement, separation etc.

What follows is an attempt at geographic isolation, to narrow down probable locations in order to forecast future events. The astrology of this is best understood by noting some geological perspectives.

The number of seismic events registered every year is 50,000 plus. Ninety-eight percent of these are unnoticed, or barely noticed, and may be considered by analogy as the stretching and creaking of the earth. The final 2 percent, starting at 3+R, are easily felt and noted.

Of that 1,000, about 100 are 6R or more. Of these about 10 are 7R or more. An 8R event occurs once or twice annually, sometimes not at all. Years separate the occurrence of high 8R events.

Naturally it is those 100 quakes that catch the interest of the geologist or astrologer, for these are the quakes that can cause severe damage and loss of life.

Of these 100 quakes most occur in the sea, in particular around the Ring of Fire in the Pacific, and plate junctures elsewhere. A small and varying remainder hit land masses. Statistically, the majority of these will hit unpopulated areas, but this will change as more areas grow populous.

A very small remainder hit populated areas. Depending on the ground conditions, that is the extremes of hard rock that pass the vibrations, or the filled earth of a Mexico City that attracts and holds the vibrations and, depending on the epicenter, damage varies considerably.

Human loss of life usually occurs through burial under rubble. Of particular danger are areas with generally unreinforced masonry construction, areas directly on or beneath mountains, and night time quakes when people are caught asleep. These three conditions exacerbate the loss of life.

Occasionally a secondary factor is even more dangerous, for example fire in Honshu 1923, and tsunamis off the Pacific Coast of South America.

In the developed world, new threats from earthquakes appear. They are the rush-hour quake, San Francisco 1991, and the direct hit to a nuclear facility or power plant. Thankfully I have no example of the second. Unfortunately it is an inexorable eventuality and for the first time man will lose habitat from a quake through secondary damage.

So, we are interested in a half dozen major events a year which have the potential for grievous damage to life and property.

The trick is to isolate these from, an ongoing, worldwide process, at the same time as the entire question of process is ignored, in varying degrees, by both the geologists and the astrologers. From this perspective the apparent failure of both parties in forecasting is not surprising.

The geologist is bereft of timing factors and has inadvertently forsaken process in separating the study of quakes and vulcanism.

The astrologer is bereft of geographic referents, usually working without current seismic data (ongoing activity) or without the history of an area, a series of events.

Furthermore, astrologers have, in the main, persisted in viewing EM from the perspective of natal astrology, both in rules and concept. EM charts have some rules of their own and might be more likened to death charts. Put differently, major EM is the fruit, not the blossom.

Both astrology and geology have de-emphasized minor events, but I believe these are extremely important in the timing of future major EM events.

Before a location can experience significant EM there must be a build up of energy over a period of time, both of these in accordance with the geological nature and history of the area.

Energy build up, as correlated by the planets, is at once intermittent, cyclical, acyclical and seasonal, from a solar perspective. At the time of EM, the basic rules of the EM chart are in effect and usually there are differences indicating the locations.

The key word is usually. Both astrologers and geologists must learn to accept the wild card factor, in astrology, the Uranian event, as part of the paradigm of forecasting.

The wild card may be an actual or perceived forecasting failure or neither. It is always a surprise.

It is a rule of forecasting that anything goes if it works. That is, a forecasting indicator's only requisite for admission is that it be part of successful forecasts.

The location signature and the incipient event signature, chart differences and trigger factors, must come together in an otherwise developed chart; the planetary patterns in effect and the basic EM requisites in place.

Before moving to the location signatures themselves, let's note again that widely separated areas respond to similar location signatures, that adjacent locations may respond to different location signatures, and that location signatures are perfected by lunar enhancement, and change to other location signatures as the Moon changes signs every 2 1/2 days.

Among the basic location indicators are planetary dispersion patterns, the ``shape'' of the chart as it were, the nature, sign, element, mode and polarity of aspect complexes, and the preponderance or absence of the same outside of the complexes.

A planet in a sign, or a specific planet in a sign, may be relevant. Certain degrees, aspects, and slow planet conditions may recur. Planetary separation must be present.

All these and more have been dealt with in the text to this point, but the question of how to show these signatures created many problems. Should I draw all the charts? How ``predictive'' should the presentation be? I settled, simply, on noting the contents of the randomly collected charts for a given area. With random probability they should give a true general signature.

Almost on a whim, I decided to include sections on Churchward's gas belts, since vulcanology has sidestepped the issue of a propellant in magma. It can only be steam with other gases as by-product of the heat processes involved in volcanology. The process heats stone as magma rises, and a rift converts ocean water to super-heated steam.

We have seen cutaway pictures of volcanoes with a neat tube of vertically rising magma. Of course we are not supposed to ask what happens to the magma at the bottom of the picture, rather where it comes from.

Unfortunately, I don't believe many geologists ask either. I see a purely vertical concept of magma rising as nothing more that a *deua ex machina* concept. The Ring of Fire is a horizontal system. The word rift has horizontal connotations, just as the word volcano has vertical connotations.

Putting aside geological conclusions, the concept of the gas belts may be checked through past, present and hopefully future EM events occurring simultaneously in widely separated locations.

On August 20, 1993, simultaneous quakes occurred: a 6R+ Pacific seaquake which I haven't heard of again, and 5R+ events in California and the Dominican Republic.

Mercury in Libra was in the degree of Neptune and Uranus. Cardinal Mercury square Neptune by degree is a signature component of California quakes as noted elsewhere.

Note the strong Libra with lunar enhancement. Moon, Mars, Jupiter square to Venus in Cancer just separated from opposition to Uranus and Neptune in Capricorn, a six planet, cardinal T-square on the Cancer/Capricorn axis, an indicator of quakes in many locations.

The gas belts, at least as a hypothesis, might reunite the studies of volcanology and seismic events since vulcanism is clearly the driving force behind most seismic activity. The ephemeris clearly shows that it precedes seismic activity with vulcanism's early cardinal degree emphasis.

30

Cairo 1992

Delineation of a Quake: Past, Present and Future

This method may be used to delineate any quake, using only the ephemeris. I have chosen the Cairo 1992 Quake as an example of extemporaneous delineation.

- Major aspect pattern is a grand cross cardinal: loose, six planets, including Sun and Moon (strong).
- Stellium in Scorpio: Mercury, Venus, Pluto, with Venus exactly conjunct Pluto (partile.)
- Other aspect patterns: quincunxes, fixed square, strong water trine involving a planet of the grand cross and the Virgo stellium, doubly strong as the integrating aspect between two major complexes.
- Sign emphasis Virgo 3
- Polarity emphasis 6+ 4-, even
- Mode emphasis, cardinal 6
- Element emphasis water 4

This would form a basic signature chart, patterns of planetary dispersion, aspect and complexes with sign properties, etc. that one could look for and compare, past and future, for the this particular location. Now we examine the planets themselves.

Separation: Moon void-of-course has passed all planets. Venus has separated from all slower planets and makes an exact conjunction to Pluto. Mars has separated from Saturn and is one degree past Uranus and one degree from Neptune. It makes an exact 75°, and powerful, aspect to Jupiter. The link up creates a double trigger emphasis with Mars and Uranus. Here we note separated cardinal Moon in Aries.

Sun separates from Jupiter, Mars, Saturn, Uranus, Neptune; Mercury from Sun; Jupiter has separated from all slower planets, entering a new sign, the powerful cardinal mode. (I have begun to note the separation of Jupiter and Saturn by sign. I feel there is validity as they bridge the truly fast and truly slow planets.) Saturn separates from Uranus and Neptune in Capricorn.

Planetary groups: Sun-Mercury-Jupiter, the initiators, must be related. Sun and Jupiter are in the same sign and separating from 15° with Mercury separating from semisextile, 30° to Jupiter. More intense, Mercury/Jupiter at 19° Libra and Sun at 19° Libra fulfills the Mercury degree. Venus-Mars-Jupiter, the energizers, in a strong quake must be related. Venus trine Mars and Mars 75° to Jupiter.

Slow planets: Uranus conjunct Neptune strongest, then Saturn square Pluto by sign. Note strength of Saturn and Pluto by mutual antiscia. Note strength of Pluto in own sign. Note strength of Saturn through Sun/Jupiter trine. Note strength of Jupiter, strong by conjunction, cardinal, midpoint with planetary partner Mercury to other planetary partner, Sun. Note the aspect of 75° from much aspected Mars to Jupiter, slightly separating.

The Sun, despite being in detriment, is made strong by being the midpoint of its partners Mercury and Jupiter, by aspects to Mars, Jupiter, Saturn, Uranus, Neptune, made more powerful here by separation from all five of them. The Moon has aspected the Sun and separated, but remained to create a cardinal grand cross having separated from all planets.

Moving to the Moon, it enhances the cardinal by creating the super-strong cardinal grand cross. Note that three of the planets, Sun, Mars, Moon, are themselves cardinal in nature. It creates the missing element of fire and adds to the balance of the polarity, making it almost even (6-4+ with Moon).

It enhances aspect complexity, forming a separating quincunx (inconjunct, 150°) from Venus and Pluto and separating opposition (180°) from Jupiter, Sun and Sun/Jupiter for the entire two and a half days, since on entering Aries, it immediately opposed Jupiter.

Astrologically we must now examine the triggering mechanism. This involves four planets, Uranus, Mars, Mercury, Moon. Other planets function passively in relation to them.

Uranus strong by approaching conjunction. All four of these planets often time exactly in other areas of astrology. Uranus is as exact as they come. We accept the approaching two degree orb to Neptune. Uranus is powerful through its recent square to Sun, and Uranus conjunct Neptune is 105° partile to Jupiter (an aspect of 15 degrees). Uranus is part of the strongest aspect complex, enhanced by the Moon by sign, mode, aspect and separation.

Uranus also forms an exact one degree separating opposition to Mars, another trigger planet. A Mars-Uranus connection is powerful in all EM as well as very strong in weather since it is a combination of two trigger planets. It is close to Uranus, 1 degree separation, but has already separated elsewhere.

Mercury is the timer par excellence. Mercury denotes the likelihood that a major event will occur at the time, by the following functions. It must relate to its partners, Sun and Jupiter, though not always by classic aspect. It should connect to Jupiter in a dissonant or negative manner. It should be in the same degree as a slower planet. This occurs the most often and is the secret of Mercury. A 1° orb from the degree of a slower planet approaching or separating may be allowed.

Should both of these not be present, as happens in this chart, I then examine the Sun, Mercury, Jupiter midpoints. Note the exact hit of Mercury/Jupiter to Sun here, fulfilling both degree and dissonance. Mercury functions as a trigger with perfection. So far 3 of 4 triggers have functioned to perfection. In the reality of EM charts, sometimes Mercury is not in degree.

Finally the Moon has a long tradition as a trigger in EM, but I don't believe many astrologers have analyzed this function carefully.

By degree, the Moon will have separated from an aspect to Mars and/or Uranus. In this quake the Moon has separated from a square to Mars, formed about two hours after its aspect to Uranus. Note that it forms approaching 15° type aspects to both Mars and Uranus (75° Mars, 105° Uranus). The Moon too, has performed its function well.

Saturn is a trigger planet in vulcanic matters, particularly eruptions, but also vulcanism. I noted the Moon last passed over it by conjunction, indicating the possibility of vulcanism. I also noted that the Moon is close to midpoint Mars/Saturn and decided to calculate it. Degrees alone suffice.

Saturn	312
Mars	+105
	417

Divide by 2 = 208+ or 28° Libra; then move to the closest side Mars/Saturn= 28° Aries, the Moon 28°Aries.

Geologically this would lead me to consider the possibility of vulcanism. I look for Moon/Mars, Moon/Saturn and Mercury-Mars-Saturn as part of a location signature.

Similarly, I would look for Sun aspects to all or most slow planets, again as part of a location signature. The separation of the Sun would relate to timing in terms of these Sun, slow planet aspects.

Major quakes are relatively rare in Egypt. While 5.9R is barely a major quake, it sneaks into that category by virtue of a direct hit 20 milessouthwest of Cairo. Geological formations and human building faults, and the site of a major city allowed it to become a peculiarly significant EM despite its relatively small "size".

I would refer to earlier quakes and compare their signature to this one. Then I would examine the immediately preceding solar eclipse considering this the most important. Hopefully I might find a signature and project it into the future. Or, is it independent of eclipse paths. I noted some clues about past and future quakes:

Coming without warning, it was clearly a Uranian quake, corroborated by the very strong Uranus in the Cairo 1992 chart. There may be vulcanism involved, so I would assess Cairo quakes in terms of the nearest active spots for vulcanism. Perhaps in this case, the rift running through Africa, African volcanoes, Italian volcanoes, and whatever quakes took place nearest Cairo, to establish if it is a shared signature or not. Vulcanism here is denoted by Jupiter in early cardinal and the Moon last over Saturn. Planets in the first decante cardinal relate to volcanoes in appropriate locations.

It is a new cycle. The chart is extremely strong and hopefully sufficient release has occurred to leave the populous city of Cairo safe for a while. Newness of the cycle is seen through 0° cardinal and Venus conjunct Pluto. Both are common in solar events, which I maintain function in the following sequence:

- Solar event
- Increase in vulcanism, volcanoes
- Quakes

The possibility, that instead of a release event indicating the quieting of the EM cycle it is a premonitory event, must be assessed in terms of past events and their charts. Geologically, the possibility of a preemptory event should be assessed through the nearest adjacent, or new vulcanism.

Personally, I believe it was a release event. That is based on the fact that a strong chart, perhaps fulfilling most of the necessary location signature, was subjected to extreme triggering. Note the perfection of all four trigger planets and the extreme beginning aspects of a perfect Venus, Pluto conjunct in Scorpio, and a strong Mercury/Jupiter = Sun in the initiative energy and forming a powerful conjunction, cardinal, this at 75° to Mars, all cardinal.

31

Geological Timing for EM: A Method

Ultimately, there is some level of arbitrariness in measurement. One must start somewhere in establishing the standard of measure. This applies to the cyclical time of EM. Geology has no means to measure EM time for it is bereft of time measurements. Historically it has a spotty collection of past event data. These events would appear to occur haphazardly, without a standard of timing or correlation, which in fact geology does not have. Their seismographs record a series of isolated present moments. The planetary positions as given in the ephemeris serve to time both the flow and uneven cycles of EM, as well as correlate them to probable areas by planetary dispersion and to indicate the probable time of an actual event.

The Sun's ingress into the cardinal signs is indicative of the new season and beginning. The timing sequence of EM related to the cardinal signs is indicated below. Early cardinal, 0° to 4°, solar disturbances in general, often with Venus, Pluto aspects. We are in fact dealing with solar vulcanism, strong energy charts with many aspects. Many basic EM chart rules would apply to solar disturbances, but in fact we are looking for points in time, correlating planets in early cardinal with solar disturbances. Such periods of solar disturbances in early cardinal times stimulate the earth's vulcanism which occurs, both heating and eruptions, during the time that planets are in the first decanate or 10° of cardinal signs. Major earthquakes occur with more of these cardinal degree planets now in degrees higher than 10° cardinal.

- Solar disturbances = very early cardinal
- Earth vulcanism in general = 0-9° cardinal
- Quake activity in general and large events = 10°+ cardinal

Despite overlap and exceptions, this observation is indisputable. This involves weighing the total of the cardinal degrees added together, 0° through 29°, in batches of event types. In practical terms, a strong solar event occurring with planets in early cardinal will probably indicate a surge in vulcanism almost immediately and lasting as long as there are planets in 0° to 9° cardinal. Quake activity follows as these cardinal planets move past 10° cardinal. What are some of the conclusions that may be drawn from this?

- Quakes showing early cardinal usually relate to the more vulcanistic locations.
- Quakes not usually showing early cardinal may be said to be less directly influenced by vulcanism, or to require a longer period of buildup.

- Solar disturbances of all kinds, in particular if major and occurring at times of planets in very early cardinal, are an early warning sign.
- Vulcanism is behind all quakes. It creates continental drift, and rock slip is a minor co-manifestation of continental drift. Using the San Andreas Fault, the energy build-up results from resistance to off-shore plate tectonics, fueled as always by vulcanism. No vulcanism, no continental drift.
- The cardinal position of planets when related to their planetary separation, approaching and separating aspects involving a minor volcano or quake, should show whether this event indicates near-future buildup or release.
- The premonitory event, an indication of whether it is a minor release event, indicating a present decline in the energy build-up, the waning of a phase or short term cycle as it were, is also revealed by the cardinality and separation present in the chart.
- Events with earlier cardinal positions of planets, moderate separation of planets, with fair signature formation of planets, may well be premonitory, especially when noted in terms of history of the locations events.
- Moderate events, with earlier cardinal positions of planets, moderate separation of planets but with exceptionally strong planetary aspects, signature formation or aspect complex strength, may signal the occurrence of a premature event. Build-up is decreased and a large event is postponed. Conceivably so much energy might be released that the location must again begin its energy build-up.

A major event occurs. Cardinality is relatively late in terms of its being a volcano or a quake. Separation is major. The event is accompanied by what is known as aftershocks. These usually immediately follow an event, probably while the lunar enhancement is still present. This is more or less total release of energy and a new cycle will begin.

At some time after a major event, weeks, months, years, but well short of the usual time frame between major events in terms of years, a moderate event occurs under strong planetary patterns and with strong separation is present. This is probably a final gasp. The energy build-up is totally broken down. In terms of vulcanism a period of dormancy would have begun.

At times two major events, large enough to be rated as separate major events (Tbilisi, Georgia FSU, October 24, 1992, April 29, 1991 and December 7, 1988), occur within a very short period of time. This can only be the results of increased vulcanism reaching that area and heating it up again.

Contiguous known areas of vulcanism, in all directions, should be noted. There is reason to believe that both magma and superheated gas may travel long distances horizontally in large volumes. This matter has not been sufficiently studied, due in large part to the widening separation and overspecialization in the fields of ocean currents (NOAA), vulcanism and quake activity. The fact that geology in most countries is government funded and/or controlled, has not been conducive to communication among its different branches or related studies, such as water current studies by NOAA.

Lastly, the event signature of volcanoes appears to be more general or universal. All areas of vulcanism should be quickly noted before emphasizing known hot sports.

Conversely the signature for a quake may be highly specialized. I noted several in California alone.

Note: El Nino is vulcanism pure and simple. Recently the U.S. Navy, using the latest equipment, discovered thousands of previously unknown volcanoes while mapping unknown areas of the Pacific (reported by CNN in February 1993).

These would be mini-volcanoes or vents covering a gigantic hot spot in the Pacific and vent it. It is probably related to El Nino. The increased heated water in a vulcanistic waxing phase would have to show sidewise drift as it moves to the surface. These so called volcanoes are probably large fumaroles.

32

EM Degrees

Astrologers have long noted recurring zodiac degrees in specific types of charts. Now the computer has saved the astrologer calculating time and made possible large collections of charts.

During the 1980s this all led to a reassessment of degrees in terms of the matter at hand. I call them the tarot of the zodiac. Rosie Cosentino has baseball degrees, I've listed violent degrees, Eleonora Kimmel lectures on anatomical degrees, and Ann E. Parker emphasizes geodetic degrees in her quake forecasting system.

The concept of a single degree definition (more importantly, eliminating contradiction) as indicated through various collections of degrees is no longer generally accepted. Degree observation however, is booming in all fields of astrology. Recurring degrees can now be quickly isolated. I believe most degree isolation begins with the duad, or two and a half degree increment, counted from zero degrees of a sign.

Thus, 0° to 2°30′ Aries is ruled by Aries-Mars. 15° to 17°30′ Aries is ruled by Libra-Venus. 27°30′ to 29°59′ Aries is ruled by Pisces-Jupiter-Neptune, the twelfth sign to Aries. 0° to 2°30′ Taurus is ruled by Taurus-Venus, etc. This duad system is the classic and most commonly used of both Western and Vedic astrology.

Duads of 2°30′ seem to have a general significance in the four signs of a mode. In EM we might note 15+ mutable. The next stage is the division of the duad into 12 signs and rulers for segments of 12 and a half minutes. The Vedics have done this for centuries.

Then comes the labor of analyzing them both in terms of planetary position and the ruling planets and their positions. If all this sounds like a lot of work, it is. One method of screening out superfluous work is to know exactly what you're looking for. It is not necessary to catch every degree or to know its actual significance. Their occurrence in sufficient number should be the prime factor considered, for this is how they indicate a time, place or both.

The foundation of Ann E. Parker's system is degrees. She holds that the Geodetic Ascendant, Midheaven and Vertex are significant indicators of location when an eclipse of the Sun or Moon has one of those degrees.

On May 21, 1960, a quake of perhaps 8.9R hit Chile at 6:00 p.m. Conception coordinates are 36S50 and 73W03. Previous eclipses were: solar, 6° Aries, February 27, 1960; solar, 17° Aries, April 8, 1959; lunar, 22°

Virgo, March 13, 1960. Parker also used heliocentric positions and the future eclipse at 2° Pisces on August 16, 1961.

The Geodetic Ascendant was at 17 Aries, Mars at 7° Aries, Venus at 21° Taurus, and North Node at 22° Virgo, well illustrating her system. The position of Mars just happened to be a classic indicator, conjunct the degree of a solar eclipse. Geodetic degrees indicate both time and place and I refer you to Ann E. Parker's works for further study.

Moving away from the geodetic degrees, planets in eclipse degrees are indicators in time. Other general earthquake degrees are early Taurus and Scorpio, especially the first duad, and late Leo, especially the last duad. Taurus and Leo are also antiscia (solstice points) in this instance.

Mid-Gemini/Sagittarius, especially 16° to 17° Gemini, appear frequently. None of these are constants and often the Gemini/Sagittarius degrees are by midpoints. Other degrees are the recurrence of a degree in location charts, the very early cardinal solar degrees, and the first decanate cardinal for vulcanism.

In summation:

- Eclipse degrees the same as geodetic angles or Vertex and future transits to these degrees.
- The transit appearance of one or more planets, especially Mars, in eclipse degrees, that is the position of either the Sun or Moon. This includes the square and opposition (mode).
- Several duads which seem to have inherent quake properties.

Much degree work in EM remains to be done.

33

Significance of Minor EM

location is the key. The present day tabulation of major events alone, or rather their subsequent emphasis by both the geological and astrological establishments, is another dead end.

Planetary patterns indicate build up of EM energy in a given location. Small and medium EM in the location will often show a strong chart, but there was not enough built-up energy. Conversely, the chart may seem weak. This may indicate a lot of stored energy, but the planetary timing and energy were not such as to really set it off. Either way, small or medium EM indicates the release of energy.

Only through the accumulated charts for a given location, as well as planetary separation in the present or near future charts, can one guess whether this is a premonitory event, a precursor of a major EM, or a delaying event, releasing such energy that major EM is postponed—again, until sufficiently stored energy encounters a suitable planetary pattern for the location, and this pattern is sufficiently strong in planetary separation, planetary grouping, lunar enhancement, etc. Then we may search for the triggers.

Certain locations, notably California, have some major EM when Mercury is in the degree of Neptune.

I believe local signatures reveal themselves in the charts of these minor events. Events having the same coordinates—truly the same place—seem to have specific signatures. Elsewhere I noted by example the promise of this: Tblisi, Tokyo and Bakersfield, California.

34

EM Weather

Laymen, astrologers, and geologists are familiar with what is commonly termed earthquake weather, so I will forego examples.

When a major quake occurs, planetary energies run strong. Everyday events continue but hurricane and heartbreak enter. Major weather patterns, near or far, may in the main be considered independent occurrences. But at the time of a major quake, there may well be some local weather caused by geomagnetic disturbances. This is an area needing much observation and recording.

The scope of this book is forecasting. In the modern day, with crowded cities and overburdened road systems, quake weather, whether simultaneous or caused, would be too close in time to the event for safety or predictive value.

Volcano weather, through heat, relates to wind and rain. It is a generally accepted phenomenon and appears to have no forecast value. Seismic observations and the perception of quake swarms are used. This volcano weather is in fact caused by the event, though this would again be in context with astrological lunation, weather maps or the general energy potential, as well as the season of the year, rainy season or not.

Because of variation, closeness in time to the event, and overall lack of knowledge on an EM caused, or simultaneous occurrence, EM weather is not important in forecasting.

Careful recording may in time give some accompanying weather signature of value if keyed to season and location.

35

Forecasting the EM Event: The Difficult Made Succinct

The major EM event is forecast by picking a time of maximum planetary energy, accompanied by substantial planetary separation. Mercury should be in the degree of another planet, usually a slower one (not the Moon). Hopefully, eclipses and lunations have shown the longitude, narrowing the search.

Suitable signs giving elements and modes, suitable aspects and aspect complexes accompanied by the right Moon (lunar enhancement) give probable locations.

Lunar enhancement in the presence of the above indicates a probable event time during two and a half days, the Moon's passage through one sign, as well as the probable locations.

Carefully assess the group planet relationships to each other (Chapters 13 and 14).

The shifting planetary patterns are readily seen by drawing the weekly chart. I use the 0° Aries chart, Sunday 0° GMT and the planets' degrees (minutes are absolutely unnecessary).

The background material, both astrological (past events, recent eclipses) and geological (registered activity) is dealt with in individual chapters.

Encapsulated, the overall method would run thus:

- Examination of time and strength of strongest recent or near future sun spot activity.
- The noting of significant seismic increases and declines as well as any new seismic activity at that time.
- Examination of vulcanism charts and correlating volcanic activity to the above two activities.
- Relating the increase/decline of EM or EM energy to the tightening transits, compared to an earlier event in the same location pattern (aspects, aspect complexes and dispersion or type).
- Assessing time and location from the above.
- Noting other probable locations (the multiple event).
- Using secondary indicators from both astrology and geology.

36

Final Timing: The Hour

Seismic activity in an area, and knowledge of the recurring location signature, form the long term forecast projection. A record of the location events, including weak quakes and ``failed'' events, may give an indication of severity. The intensity of the upcoming location chart may also give clues.

Assuming that it is an event with warning, premonitory minor quakes or swarms etc., the two and a half day period may be assessed by lunar enhancement.

The placement and degree of Mercury is probably most indicative of the event, and could indicate the day as well of the three days in question. But don't bet the farm. Mercury may be a degree earlier than other planet degrees, or a degree later. Sometimes it must be found by Sun-Mercury-Jupiter mutual midpoints.

Finally we come to the hour. The Moon does not time accurately for the hour in EM—a fact. Recent or upcoming aspects to Mars and Uranus must be read in the two and a half day lunar enhancement period. Pick any 30 to 100 quakes and confirm this for yourself.

My distaste for Uranus on the angles or some other planet there, Mars or Pluto is noted elsewhere. Approximately 15° on each side of the angle would cover eight hours of a day and sometimes Uranus and less famous brethren are not near an angle at event time.

Uranus on the angles happens every day everywhere and thus has no predictive value at all in the upcoming event chart. This is not the same as transiting Uranus to the Midheaven of a past chart, in particular one involving human activity. As stated elsewhere in the text, Uranus near the angles in a lunation, etc. is indicative of weather and EM potential, when transited by another planet, a matter which may involve several days. Astrology is a symbolic language so be aware of its semantics.

But, can I tell the hour of event? Possibly. The answer lies neither in astrology nor geology. Over the years, in observing minor West Indian quakes, I've noticed that a sequence of quakes often went off near the same time of day. Importantly, that will change. I wouldn't use last year's time periods for example.

Let us say California, City X, with warning, 2+ to 3.5R events have occurred for six to seven weeks from 3:00 to 5:00 p.m. There is an increase in low-level seismic readings at this time too.

Center the recorded times. Expand them to six hours. Go with 1:00 to 7:00 p.m. Not exact, but you are betting the favorite.

Working the hour is unsure and potentially dangerous. Ironically this most dangerous move will be useful to nuclear power facilities and gas line companies unwilling to shut down early. Remember the hour is a horse race, so you should be just as prepared the rest of the day.

The most useful idea I can come up with regarding the hour is extra warnings if this indicator showed the quake would occur at rush hour, etc.

37

Approaching and Separating Aspects

Establishment thinking, regardless of the establishment, crystallizes. Saturn rules both establishment and crystallization. Reverting to form, establishments are creatures of habit who think as little as possible. Along with blind paths and overspecialization with its jargon, and the inability to communicate outside their own fields, ever-present in the establishment is ingrained habit.

One of astrology's ingrained habits is to stop, come up short, when the approaching aspect becomes partile. This is when the faster moving planet, approaching the slower one, comes to the degree that exactly defines the aspect in question, it is partile. (Mars 8° Pisces conjunct Jupiter 8° Pisces Mars 8° Virgo 180 Jupiter 8° Pisces are partile examples showing the exact aspect.)

Astrologer Robert Hand likens an approaching aspect to an approaching plane. Power and relevance are important in seeing it early on. Sensing an approaching aspect, its effects and energies is much the same. In most cases an aspect is most powerful as it approaches exactness (partile). There has been an increasing building effect, which now climaxes and the energy begins to dissipate quickly. We may find ourselves with results or reactive activity, but the activity is no longer initiatory or dynamic.

This is all true most of the time, but not for everything. EM, and probably certain illnesses and cycles, act under separating aspects. This may well be because their essential nature is one of results.

What's the point? Ingrained habit. The astrologer comes to the partile aspect and stops. He doesn't look further. This has gone on for hundreds of years without being thought about. Separating aspects are probably the least examined matter in all astrology.

Regarding astrology in general, paying some note to separating aspects will integrate a chart, stop it from being just points of *partility*, if such a word exists, and give it some living sense of sequence.

In terms of forecasting, it has thrown astrologers off for centuries. One seeks partility in forecasts. It does not come to pass at all, or it happens much later. The mistake is repeated ad infinitum.

I truly believe there are inherent limitations to EM forecasting with astrology, but that is not what I'm discussing now.

In fact, not only has our astrologer failed to consider separation, but he hasn't even imagined 15° type aspects. Separation and 15° aspects are frequent in most EM charts. To digress but complete the picture, his concepts of the EM trigger are hazy, usually involving fragmentary concepts of the Moon, Mars and Uranus.

Since 15° type aspects also appear in weather charts, we may infer that they could refer to the build-up of energy. Perhaps the 15° type aspect is itself the indicator of great separation from the smaller major aspects. In some way the energy still builds or is conserved; e.g. Jupiter 15° Mars 29°—separation from the conjunction.

There are often many separating planets in terms of major aspects. Furthermore, each planet should be examined in terms of its separation. The Moon void-of-course has separated from all planets. This applies to other fast planets as well.

I do not count retrograde separation. There is enough separation in the direct planets. Should I? Maybe, but I am also seeking simplicity. To overcomplicate a forecasting system is to invite certain failure.

Having examined separation in general, and the problems of many astrologers with it, just what is its link to the EM chart? Once again the clue comes from the weather charts. The build-up of energy. Furthermore, there is something solar and lunar about these 15° type aspects, if only from inference.

I began this study around 1980, and soon after came to the concept of balloons which I related to the actual geological build-up of energy, and only much later to planetary separation.

Fill similar balloons equally and tie (partile). Certain balloons in fact are weaker than others. They explode and break at different times for different reasons. They lose air at uneven rates and become empty or half empty. We do not exactly know when they will break or empty.

Time passes and we decide to refill our balloons. Some burst or cannot be filled. Some with leaks will not accept build-up. There are some, almost empty, that look like new, but these are likely to burst, with a bit more air than before, since the rubber is weaker.

The balloons are filled automatically. One had more than half its air left and it got a full amount of air. Some hours later it pops, especially loud. Call it 6 Richter, one of the 80+ EMs of the Earth's 50,000+ measured annual tremors. Call it eruption, as opposed to venting in regard to volcanoes. Call it hurricane force 5.

In some way the almost exact 15° aspects relate to the larger classic aspects. I would say that the storage of energy is ongoing, with perhaps a large infusion at the time of an exact major aspect. The breaking point often occurs when one of these 15° aspects is reached.

What happens is not of the most importance. What is the most important in EM is the simple correlation. Causality, the lack of it, synchronicity, are all irrelevant to the forecasting process.

Section III

Location Signatures

38

The Location Signature

The location signature was my earliest observation. Others followed in fits and starts over the years since Mount Saint Helen's erupted.

One of the earlier astrology books I happened upon was Grant Lewi's, *Astrology for the Millions*. Before I learned how to calculate a chart, I was inserting planets into his zodiacal Ascendant (0° Aries) wheels divided into 36 segments of 10 degrees or decanates. While this was not advanced astrology, the same Ascendent for all charts created visual awareness. Draw up 30 of these charts and the eye begins to respond to patterns. This is considerably harder to do with fully calculated charts since the overall dispersion is rotated 30° every couple hours.

It was fairly simple. Drawing up the charts on some famous quakes, I noticed the quakes of southern Europe and Asia Minor in general, varied in pattern from those of South America. At the same time, when drawing up volcano charts, I picked up on planets in the first decanate cardinal.

Anyone following EM at all is familiar with what I'll term simultaneous events, quakes and/or volcanoes coming in clumps in several distant locations (Chapter 28). These refer to the same signature. They would not be the only ones, as other locations for the signature would lack ripeness or the stimulation of a recent eclipse, etc. This makes sense, after all there are more locations than basic planetary dispersion patterns.

Then I secured a listing of California quakes. Much to my surprise California has several signatures of its own which are noted in the chapter on California Signatures.

Midway through this, I became aware that the Grand Trine Water (GTW) was especially significant. It showed up everywhere so to speak and graced some of the most important quakes of the 20th century. Grand Trine Water means a planet or planets in all three water signs, Cancer, Scorpio and Pisces.

Cancer is ruled by the Moon with her multifaceted functions in EM. Cancer also opposes Capricorn, one of the cardinal signs allowing energy to flow into and out of the Grand Trine Water, closed energy system.

Cardinal signs are very important in EM. They relate to volcanoes, whose charts usually have planets in the first decanates of cardinal. In quake-prone areas, adjacent to or involving volcanic areas, e.g., Japan, cardinal signs, usually involving planets slightly higher than 10° are frequent, as well as the frequency of early degrees.

The grand trine water may be called the universal signature, followed by a T-square involving the Cancer-Capricorn axis. Often enough the two have combined in serious EM.

Summarizing:

- The same signature applying to widely separate locations.
- Very different signatures for neighboring locations.
- What might be called a universal signature, GTW, present in major EM occurring just about anywhere.
- With Pluto in Scorpio from 1984 to 1996, one leg of the grand trine water is always in place at this time. With the Sun in Cancer or Pisces and the Moon in Cancer or Pisces there are not too many days in the year without grand trine water. In fact there are often periods of sustained grand trine water.
- One of the most prolonged recent periods involved the late 1992, early 1993, five month transit of Mars and its station in Cancer. Successively, Venus, Sun and Mercury kept a grand trine water in effect for most of the first four months of 1993. Transiting Mars opposed the Uranus-Neptune conjunction in Capricorn. Surprisingly, few noteworthy EMs occurred, and I'll answer that in terms of my work.
- The Moon's Nodes were still gathering energy in cardinal Capricorn.
- The 1992 slow planet energy quotient was a low 30 points, but 1993 had a high 98 points (See the chapter on Weighting the Slow Planets).

Using the principle of separation, 1993 slow planet energy may well become critical in 1994. This year itself has an above average slow planet energy quotient of 64, to be the immediate or integrating energy infusion, as well as the Moon's Nodes in the release axis, Scorpio-Taurus.

On July 8, 9 and 10, 1993, with the Sun in Cancer and the Moon in Pisces, an apparently strong configuration existed. Separation was good and Venus, Mars and Jupiter were alright. However the release potential of the Moon's Nodes is just beginning (11° Sagittarius) and Mercury was not in degree. Not much happened.

A critically important point that I want to reemphasize is the gathering of a quake history for a given location, including minor, moderate and failed events. On January 29, 1994, Saturn moved into Pisces for about two and a half years. With two legs of the grand trine water in position at any one time, the transits of the Moon through Cancer each month may become momentous EM events. Into early 1995 the Moon in Cancer will also oppose Uranus and Neptune in Capricorn.

In June 1994, Sun and Venus are in Cancer. In the second half of August and into early October, Mars is in Cancer.

Jupiter moved into Scorpio in late 1993 and Venus is in Scorpio in September 1994 along with Jupiter and Pluto. 1994 should be an interesting year, in particular the second half of August through September.

39

Methodology of EM Sample

The first quakes charted were those I came across first, usually major events. I began 13 years ago and continued throughout the writing of this book. I gamble, so I understand probability theory, and choose probability over statistics. Statistics have the potential for being flawed. In probability any error will eventually average out and restore the sample to equilibrium.

Probability has universal constants. If I roll double sixes three times in a row, the odds are 1 in 36^3. Nevertheless this is routinely done, and I am just one man of millions rolling dice.

Thus, any quake occurring at any time added to my sample at anytime, or under any conditions, should in some way support the hypothesis in question. This does not preclude variations. Variation may be inherent to a system. Two dice have 36 throws.

Some years into my research, I heard about *Catalogue of Significant Earthquakes 2000 BC to 1979*, US Department of Commerce. I decided to finish the work without it. Randomly collected quakes and volcanoes should be able to indicate a true direction of themselves, exactly as two dice cannot throw one or thirteen.

The sample came from works in geology and astrology. I secured several lists of quakes, historic, 6R+"86, California by location, and New Zealand.

In some instances a hypothesis was formulated before examining charts, in others, through the charts. Astrology and geology cross fertilized each other. Since EM is, semantically speaking, not prediction but forecasting, practical knowledge of geology was imperative, so it was studied.

My results are observational, empirical and used in synthesis. I am one astrologer who does not wish to see astrology joined to the Procrustean bed of science, for its definition has come to fit the needs of a proponent.

Having read geological texts for years, I see it too, as an observational field. It can't prove many of its hypotheses nor is it in agreement on all of them, e.g. mountain building. It does not have agreed on positions as a field, nor can it ``predict'' EM, though it would lead us to believe it can.

The geological establishment presents an orthodox view, for the moment. Though implied that this view is scientific, it is merely observation, with some corroboration, subject to change and schism.

Geology was begun by amateurs who were bored with the leisure time activities of their class and began looking at stones. Gradualism, catastrophism and continental drift are all the ideas of amateurs.

The size of the sample is about 1200 EM. Collected randomly, the exact number is without value. The hypotheses have arisen from the first dozen of the sample until the present. Corroboration is ongoing. This is a work in the making - there can be no clear end or perfect conclusion. The study of EM, like the events themselves, will not be pigeonholed.

40

Lunar Enhancement

I regard lunar enhancement as one of the breakthrough insights of this book, and like many insights it is simple. As the Moon changes signs every two and a half days, it defines new locations subject to EM. It thus provides the true forecast time, the Moon within a sign. As it changes signs, the aspect complex pattern is altered and a new location is subject to EM.

Enhancement consists of supplying a necessary element, mode polarity or aspect completion. Example: With planets in Pisces and Scorpio, the Moon moves into Cancer.

- Completing the GTW
- Augmenting water
- Augmenting cardinal
- Augmenting negative polarity
- In this instance supplying a strong jolt of energy being in her own sign.

The energies of lunar enhancement include completion, energizing and compensation. Enhancement is her prime function. Following her entrance into a sign, her contacts with the triggers occur. This is apart from the overall concept of lunar enhancement, which first and foremost isolates locations.

ically the same signature. All respond to the Grand
41

The Signature of Alaska, Aleutians, Katchamka Peninsula, Kuril Islands and the Bering Sea

These locations are discussed together because they are basically the same signature. All respond to the Grand Water Trine and the Grand Fire Trine. The basic signature in most cases is a combination of cardinal squares, mutable squares and fire trines. Fixity usually involves Leo and Scorpio; water trines usually involve Scorpio.

Churchward shows the Great Pacific Circuit Belt as passing through the Banda and Ceram Sea beneath Ceram and Holmakera (Indonesia) beneath the Philippine Islands, along Japan, up the Kuril Islands, by the Katchamka Peninsula, up the Aleutians and beneath them into Kodiak. The signatures of Japan and the Philippines will reveal their similarities. The entire area is subject to strong vulcanism with emphasis on Pinatubo-Philippines Islands, Unyen-Japan, and Redoubt-Alaska during the 1990s.

The quakes of these Northern Pacific locations are clearly related to vulcanism. This shows in the charts by the frequent appearance of planets in first decanate cardinal and the relationship of Mercury-Mars-Saturn, a planetary complex signifying vulcanism.

- Frequent presence of planets, up to three, in Virgo; presence of planets in Pisces or Virgo-Pisces. This is true also of Japan and the area noted as the Pacific Grand Circuit Belt should be studied as a whole.
- The entry of the Sun into a sign occupied by a planet other than Mercury or Venus, particularly if Mercury or Venus move in with the Sun.
- A grand cross mutable.
- Planets in Taurus if none are in Leo, considered with the rest of the signature.
- The presence of Sun, Mercury and Jupiter in Aries. This occurred in the Good Friday Quake, March 27, 1964 and in a moderate release quake 4.5R felt in Fairbanks.
- The chart at a glance fits the bowl (180°), locomotive (240°) or bucket type (180° with a planet as handle.
- Frequently when the planets are bunched (wedged), the Moon and/or Jupiter restores one of the above patterns; that is they occupy the rim of the bowl or the handle of the bucket. Similarly, Moon and Jupiter may frame the open space in the locomotive chart 240°.

- Venus-Mars-Jupiter triad strong but varied.
- Sun to Jupiter varies by aspect, sign, or separation.
- The polarity is more or less balanced 6-4, 5-5, 4-6 being most frequent.

Example: On July 9, 1986, a 5.7R quake, epicenter 40 miles southeast of Adok Island, Aleutians, occurred. This was a grand trine water with Cancer-Capricorn. The Sun was in Cancer, the least frequent of the water signs for this location.

It may be said that the universal signature can indicate a release type quake. A location whose energy is not fully built up is forced to release whatever energy it holds.

In this minor quake the Moon enhanced fire, moving into Leo with Mercury and Venus (three planets/sign), strong fire trines and fixed squares to Pluto in Scorpio and this with the universal grand trine water and Cancer-Capricorn.

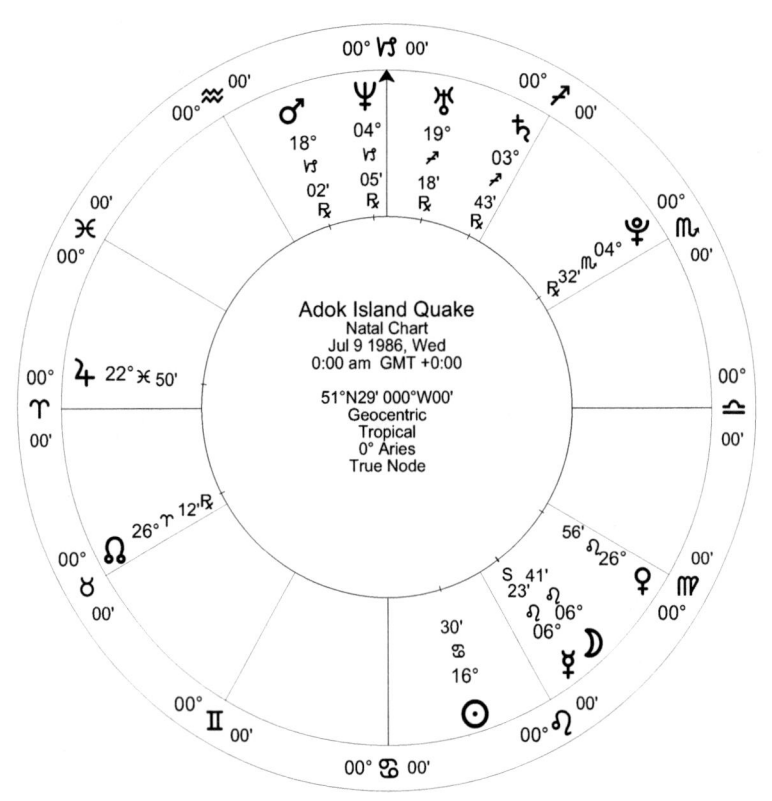

- Mars is usually, not always, clearly and widely separated from its last classic aspect to Uranus.
- Mercury is not always in degree, but if so it may be the degree of Neptune, Uranus or Mars.
- Rather than particular conjunctions, I would note the appearance of two or more planets each, in three different signs.
- Venus separation variable.
- The overall signature shows both emphasis and flexibility.
- During 1994 to 1996, the position of transiting Saturn in Pisces and the 1994 position of Jupiter in Scorpio should somewhat increase the quake potential for these locations. This especially when:
- Another mutable sign, e.g. Gemini or Sagittarius is occupied.
- Planets in Virgo.
- Planets in Aries or Libra.
- A planet in Cancer or a strong Cancer stellium completing the grand trine water circuit.
- A stellium in Leo.

Lunar enhancement is clear. It isn't the sign of the Moon that is important but its filling a needed slot in the signature complex. Frequently it is square, trine or opposition the Sun by sign, either approaching or separating. Again it would seem its enhancement is more important.

Alaska 1964 is also a perfect see-saw (oppositions) with Aries-Libra, Taurus-Scorpio and Virgo-Pisces.

As in many locations, a strong stellium may compensate for planets not in other signature signs. This is mainly in regard to square complexes and as usual involves location-emphasized signs, e.g. Aries, Leo, Virgo.

The Aleutians, with basically the same signature as the other locations included here, seem slightly more susceptible to planets in Cancer than the others; The same is true of Katchamka and the Kuril Islands. A strong Scorpio stellium and Sun, Neptune contacts appear at times in the Kuril Islands events.

Slow planet (Jupiter—Pluto) positions appear inconclusive, this by visual scanning approach. Separation and 15 degree type aspects are all present in varied contexts. The 15° type aspects may be closely approaching or closely separated.

Slow planet conjunctions and major aspects are by definition infrequent. A partile or exact conjunction or aspect does not appear to be significant in quakes for these locations.

Two slow planets in the same sign seems to come under the general series of loose conjunctions categories and is not of significance in itself. Major quakes appeared when all slow planets were in different signs as well, again, inconclusive.

Randomly Collected Sample

October 30, 1988	5.1R	60m NW Homer, Alaska
March 6, 1988	7+R	S. Coast 210m S of Cape Yakataga
November 30, 1987	7.4R	100m SW Yakutat, Alaska
November 16, 1987	6.9R	270m ESE Anchorage
April 18, 1987	4.5R	Felt in Fairbanks
March 21, 1987	6.2R+ 6R	Adak Island
July 9, 1986	5.7R	40m SE Adak Island
December 30, 1985	5.2R	Palmer, Alaska
November 4, 1985	5.1R	Anchorage
October 9, 1985	6.5R	Alaska
March 9, 1985	6.3R	110m NW of Fairbanks
February 14, 1985	5+R	Alaska
July 24, 1984	4.3R	Anchorage, premonitory release
July 30, 1972	7.6R	SE Alaska Mut. Grand Cross, Leo Stellium
May 2, 1971	R?	Adak
April 16, 1970	R?	Gulf of Alaska
May 14, 1969	R?	Amchitka
March 27, 1964	8+R	Anchorage (Good Friday)
July 10, 1958	7.9R	SE Alaska
April 7, 1958	7.3R	Central Alaska
March 9, 1957	8.3R	Aleutians
August 22, 1949	8.1R	S Alaska
October 9, 1900	R?	Alaska
September 10, 1989	8+R estimated	Near Yakutat Bay
May 2, 1987	R?	Aleutians
October 31, 1985	5.7R	25m NW Dutch Harbor Aleutians
September 12, 1969	R?	Aleutians
March 9, 1957	8.0R	Andrean off Islands
April 1, 1946	R?	N side of Aleutian Trench
November 10, 1938	8.7R	Bering Sea

March 7, 1929	8.6R	Aleutians
August 17, 1906	8.3R	Aleutians/Alaska
June 2, 1903	8.3R	Aleutians
November 1, 1985	6.4R	Katchamka Penn E
May 4, 1959	8.2R	Katchamka
November 4, 1952	8.4R	Katchamka
February 3, 1923	8.4R	Katchamka GTW
May 1, 1915	8.1R	Katchamka GTW
June 25, 1904	8.3R	Katchamka
June 24, 1973	7.5R	S Kuril Islands
June 17, 1973	"Strong Shock"	Kuneshin, Kuril Islands
February 25, 1973	8.5R	Kuril Islands GTA
August 11, 1969	R?	Kuril Islands GTW
June 10, 1965	7.2R	Kuril Islands GTW
October 13, 1963	8.2R	Kuril Islands
November 6, 1958	8.7R	Kuril Islands
September 7, 1918	8.3R	Kuril Islands

42

The Signature of Japan

The isolation of a location signature is as ongoing and sporadic process, but there is nothing complicated about it. Collect quakes, place notes on the charts and collate as the notes grow. The sporadic nature of this is good for giving fresh insight. I look at a location's charts many diferent times. The sporadic nature is not as good for rating the overall picture.

The first location signature I included in this book, one I rewrote from charts and notes, were the Alaskan and Aleutian Island signature. At some point in my research I had related the Aleutian to the Katchamka Peninsula that in turn had related to the Kuril Islands. I was somewhat surprised to find a common signature (basically common). I did note a bit more Cancer as I moved west and south into the Katchamka Peninsula and the Kuril Islands.

I started with Alaska because it started with A, but it now seems sensible to move on down the Great Pacific Circuit Gas Belt. The gas belts offer a hypothesis for the process of vulcanism, an explanation for Chandler Wobble, and a tenative location factor in the location signature. For example, the ``disappearance'' of Cancer planetary positions in several Grand Pacific Circuit Belts locals around 1970.

It makes sense that a distribution system for super heated gas and magma exists, and geology has not done much research on the propellant factor in vulcanism. Magma "floats" up and one sees pictures of mountains with red sections beneath them. Vertical magma, vertical mountains.

Moving south on the Great Pacific Circuit Gas Belt, my overall guess is that signature will follow the belts to a significant degree. I think a lot of widely separated locations will end up on the same belt having similar local signatures. I speak here of the simultaneous but unrelated events that puzzle geologists because one area does not appear as active as another. The astrologer, at the same time sees only that a location was under the eclipse path.

Japan is serious earthquake business. Even the most optimistic seismologists recognize that a major event could hit Tokyo at any time. This takes us to the North American division of the Great Pacific Circuit Gas Belt.

Five branches snake North, the westernmost in the Pacific, the easternmost, from about midpoint on the U.S.-Mexico border through Montana into Canada. There are a multiplicity of signatures in California which may in some way relate to the branches, as well as the particular faults.

In keeping with belt theory, where the principal activity occurs at ends, active areas or blockages, seismic activity in Utah, Colorado, Arizona and New Mexico is less than that of California, Nevada, Oregon and Washington to the west and Wyoming, Idaho and Montana to the north. Witness the venting system in Yellowstone National Park.

The Great Pacific Circuit Gas Belt moves up the west coast of South America and moves under Central America where it branches in a more or less parallel fashion. The Great Central Gas Belt crosses into the Caribbean/Atlantic through, (under) Central America.

Maximum internal heat flow, and minimum lithosphere pressure occurs in the same area which happen to be subduction zones and/or volcanic areas. Heat flow continues beneath the mid California area now technically dormant. This on the same order as the technically active Japanese area. All the deep quakes take place in cold, descending slabs. The heat sources of the lithosphere or crust of the Earth occur as:

- Rising from the mantle.
- Compression by subduction.
- Radioactive decay.
- Change of minerals to denser phases (the flow occurs here)
- Friction

The soft region of the mantle is made viscous, which is called asthenoshere. It is generally believed that the rise from the mantle and the change of minerals give the most. According to the same source, these also probably give the most heat. The point is that one doesn't hear much about the horizontal transferal of heat, which would have to be of the nature of steam gas under extreme pressure with or without magma according to the circumstances. Such a gas system would also act as propellant of magma, whether horizontally or vertically, utilizing the snorkel principle. In short, if the west coast of the United States is more or less tectonically dormant (low subduction) the gas and magma must come from somewhere else.

The Japanese Islands have three major quake areas. Hokkaido or the North Island, quakes here are referred to as Hokkaido. Central Japan includes Tokyo, Yokohama and Osaka. Honshu is the name of the main central island. The Bay of Honshu lies NE of Tokyo. The population of the central island Honshu runs to the west from Tokyo. Some serious quakes here are called Honshu others are termed ``Tokyo'' or ``felt in Tokyo.'' To the south and west the small island of Kyushu also receives a few quakes. Thus most quakes felt in populated Japan occur under the island of Honshu or in the surrounding sea. I'll note several examples of Hokkaido or the North Island first.

My sample is six quakes, five major, one minor, collected randomly. January 15, 1993, 7.5R and March 4, 1952, 8.6R are grand trine water. Mars is in water signs in both. The Cancer Capricorn axis, with a stellium in Capricorn, is present on

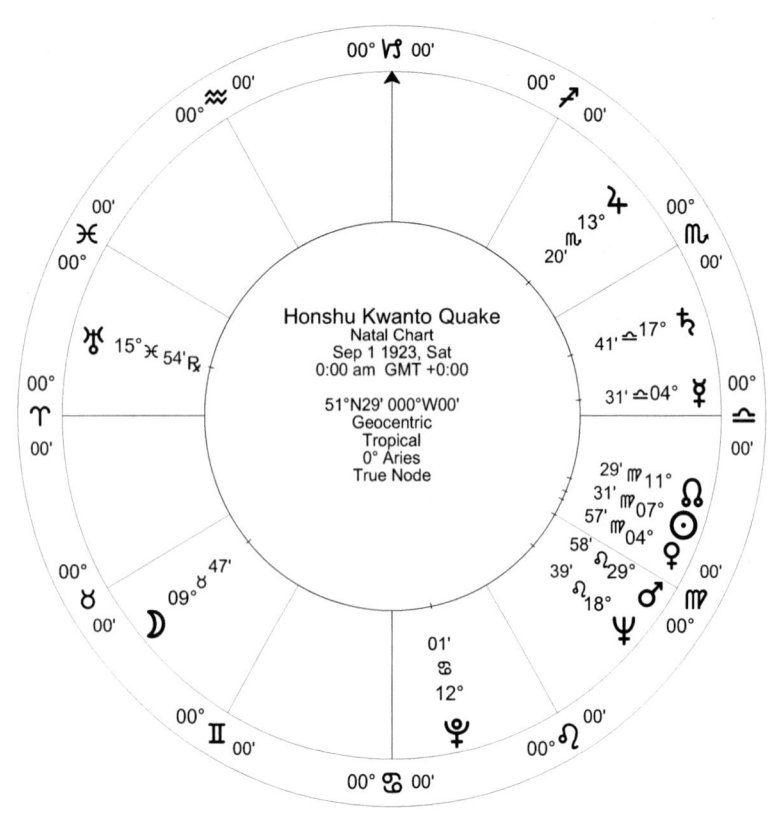

January 15, 1993. On March 14, 1952, a cardinal T-square is formed from Aries/Libra. Libra has two planets in both events Saturn, Neptune 1952, Moon, Jupiter 1993. 1952 has a grand trine air. A fixed square involving Scorpio is present, Leo 1952, Aquarius 1993. Planets in Pisces are present in five of six, including Saturn in Pisces on December 30, 1730.

Air Trines are present in all six. June 17, 1973, 7.7R, has a grand trine air. In this quake, Mars is in Pisces (water) and Mercury and Venus are in Cancer (more emphasized it seems as we move south).

Mars also appears in Aries, Libra and Aquarius. Moon once in each air sign (air trines important). Moon in the same sign as Jupiter twice and Uranus once. Mercury, often not in exact degree, but three out of six closest in degree to Neptune, once each Sun, Saturn and Uranus.

In five out of six, a planet or planets in first decanate cardinal, Moon relates to Saturn and separates usually, trines, opposition, recent conjunction or a sextile; the volcano triad, Mercury-Mars-Saturn connection present. While the overall signature may resemble other locations, the isolating factors would appear to be:

- Air trines
- Planets in Libra
- Planets in Pisces and Virgo

Polarity varies but is not extreme. Nodal axis mutable or cardinal, in particular North Node Pisces (2). Usually both cardinal and mutable squares or T-squares. Planetary conjunctions by sign appear to take place in cardinal, especially Libra, and least (none in my sample) in Aries. They take place in all four mutable signs, and Aquarius. The air trine is important in the Hokkaido event.

Regarding the slow planets, the relationship of Jupiter and Saturn is of interest.

Sample Quakes

January 15, 1993	7.5R	12½M from Kuchino Hok. Jupiter 14° Libra Saturn 17° Aquarius
September 22, 1988	5.1R	Hokkaido Jupiter 6° Gemini, Saturn 26° Sagittarius
March 4, 1952	8.6R	Hokkaido Jupiter 16° Aries Saturn 13° Libra
February 28, 1950	7.9R	Hokkaido Jupiter 20° Aquarius Saturn 16° Virgo with Sun 8° Pisces
June 17, 1973	7.9R	Hokkaido Jupiter 11° Aquarius Saturn 24° Gemini
December 30, 1730	Major	Hokkaido Jupiter 9° Virgo, Moon Virgo Saturn 16° Pisces

The recurring signs, aspects, omit separation, or lack of it, are self explanatory. Clearly there are various possibilities in keeping with the concept of the rolling signature (see Rolling Signature) but the possibilities are clearly narrowed down. This is the real world of geographic isolation.

Southern Japan or Honshu

Honshu is heavily populated. When lack of space for general human needs in Japan is spoken of, it is Honshu, in particular Tokyo, and its environs. Quakes here when mentioned in world news are usually noted as felt in Tokyo or miles from Tokyo, usually in the Japanese Trench.

As in other quakes of the Great Pacific Circuit Belt, volcanic regions are clearly recognizable with a planet usually in early cardinal, others in mid cardinal, with quakes following vulcanism.

The signature of Honshu is complex, that is to say it varies, especially at first glance. Cardinality, Mutability, Air, Water and Virgo/Pisces are important as in Hokkaido. But, regarding planets in the key signs Virgo, Libra, Pisces, all combinations or absences occur.

Secondly, a stellium may replace specific signature needs, Capricorn, all cardinality, Virgo or Pisces, all Mutability. Similarly an exalted planet may give the air requirements Mercury in Aquarius, Saturn in Libra.

Jupiter aspecting Pluto is important, especially in major events and especially when strong to the Sun, Sun-Jupiter as primary energizers of the initiative triad. In the quake 6.6R, February 20-90, in the sea 70 miles south of Tokyo, Sun 1° Pisces, Pluto 17° Scorpio, Jupiter 0° Cancer.

Given that there will be many quakes in Japan, we may then infer that there will be a greater variation in signature, especially in the details and in how the necessary signature components are met.

Both astrologers and geologists have one thing in mind when they think of the Japanese event - a major quake as a direct hit in modern Tokyo, a human ant hill and world trade and banking center.

On September 1, 1923 at 11:57 AM, Tokyo was hit squarely by an 8R+ event that killed 143,000 and left 500,000 homeless. Like San Francisco, 1906, fire did as much damage as the quake. Referred to as Kwanto, Honshu or Tokyo, it epitomizes the dreaded major city direct hit.

In terms of the Japanese signature, note the perfection.

The universal grand trine water was in place involving the planets, Uranus, Jupiter and Pluto. Jupiter and Pluto then made a midpoint with the Sun in Virgo. A kite was formed. A second kite was formed with Moon in Taurus. Moon enhanced with fixity, earth and aspect complex intensification (grand trine water to kite and yod to Saturn). Note Saturn in Libra (exaltation) in fact made the cardinal T-square quite strong.

Ann E. Parker notes that Jupiter at 13° Scorpio was conjunct the Geodetic Ascendant at 13° Scorpio.

Two opposing yods were formed, Pisces to Leo-Libra and Libra to Pisces Taurus.

A small stellium in Virgo, Venus-Mars-Sun is intense with energizers, Venus and Mars conjunct. Venus separates from Mars.

A strong midpoint complex links two triads, Sun-Mercury-Jupiter and Venus-Mars-Jupiter in early Libra. Here is that interlocking so commonn in truly great quakes.

It is the layout that is important. A major aspect complex duplication by all or most of the same sign planets, might be hundreds or thousands of years apart. Check the layout of 8.3R March 13, 1909, Honshu, and nNote the lunar enhancement, fixity, water, grand trine water. Finally, note Mino-Wari one of worst quakes in Japanese history 8R+ October 28, 1891. It rocked half of Japan and lasted 30 seconds, 7000 dead and twice as many injured (Ritchie, *Ring of Fire*, page 26.

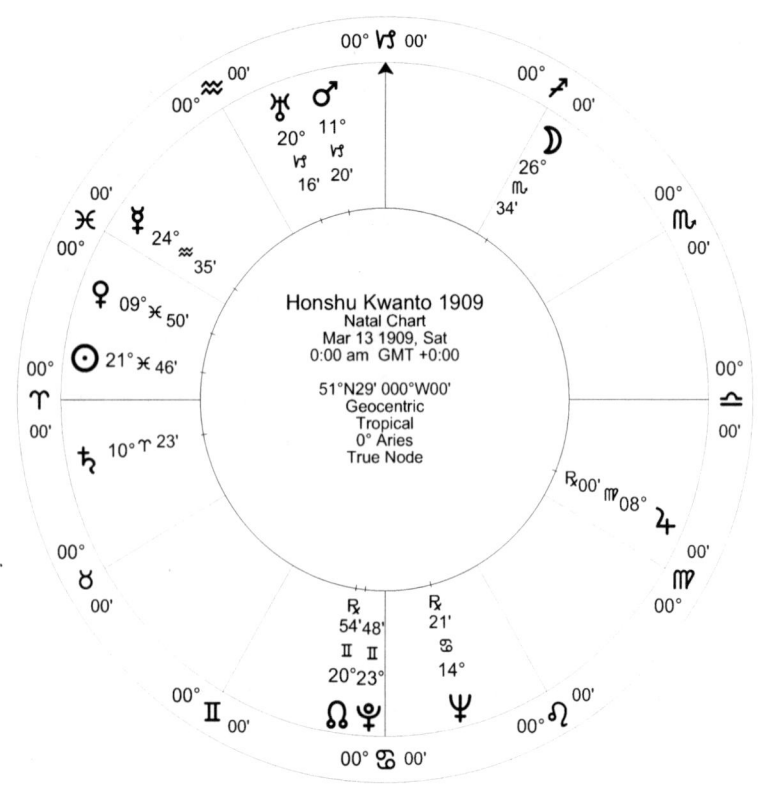

This quake is an example of the compensated signature. There is no grand trine water but Scorpio is stronger by stellium and Jupiter is ruler of Pisces. There is no cardinal complex, but Venus rules Libra and Libra is the most important cardinal sign in the Japanese signature. Neptune-Pluto conjunction in Gemini trine Venus in Libra means Air is intense.

The mutable T-square is awesome, involving at each of its points a planet ruler, a major slow planet conjunction, Mars and Saturn in the same sign, with lunar enhancement of earth and mutability.

Concluding, the great Japanese quake may well involve the universal grand trine water perhaps intensified to a kite. All the basic Japanese signature components will be made extremely strong. Note carefully the layout and composition of Mino-Wari as compared to Kwanto.

The 5R to 6R+ events show general characteristics of other locations on the Great Pacific Gas Belt, especially in the influence of vulcanism by early and mid-cardinal planetary positions.

Given the importance of a major Japanese event. I did a little extra planetary assessment and using the same randomly collected quakes to be listed, came to these conclusions.

- There is a decidedly mutable emphasis in both number of planets and the fast planets, Sun through Mars. Jupiter appears to be evenly distributed by mode with a slight preference for the signs Virgo and Capricorn. Saturn has fixed emphasis, and of this, probably most frequently in Scorpio. Uranus is most often mutable, and least often fixed, midway cardinal. I do not have sufficient 18th and 19th century quakes for full cycles of Neptune and Pluto. Indeed, Saturn and Uranus might need reevaluating, if a clumping factor is present.
- Moon is most often in Sagittarius.
- Mars is most often Gemini-Sagittarius.
- Mars is not present in this sample in either Cancer or Aquarius—this through September 18, 1984 when the tabulation was done. Best to simply say it is infrequent in those signs.
- Sun and Jupiter by sign are least in the same sign and most in trinal signs. Squares and oppositions follow with frequency. The second most frequent Sun-Jupiter position is the semi-sextile or adjacent signs. The Sun, separating from a conjunction, usually accounts for this. Again, all by sign not orb.
- Sun and Uranus by sign are least in the same sign, equally most in trine or square to each other by sign, and about equal in semi-sextile (solar separation) quincunx and opposition.
- Uranus is clearly a trigger planet. That there is a virtual lack of Sun sextile Uranus, may be taken as inferred proof of separation and the storage of energy. Sun has separated from conjunction. Nothing occurred in next sign; matters not ripe, no release. Energy has not yet begun to rebuild—the square, energy imput beginning at 75°.
- The Sun-Moon angle by sign is most frequently square or trine by sign, least often, new or full.
- Moon-Uranus aspects by sign are in-

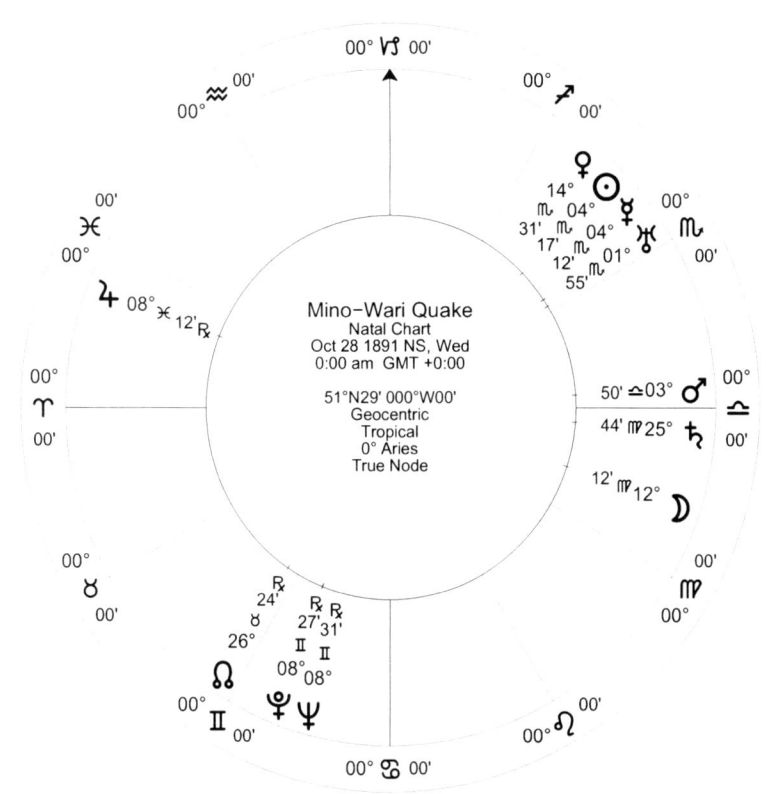

Mino-Wari Quake
Natal Chart
Oct 28 1891 NS, Wed
0:00 am GMT +0:00

51°N29' 000°W00'
Geocentric
Tropical
0° Aries
True Node

conclusive. Here again the classic truths of astrology reaffirm themselves. No planetary combination is more volatile than this. For the non-astrological reader, this is nitroglycerine on the paint shaking machine. All aspects are about equal with a small prefernce for the conjunction. Again by sign and again, clearly inconclusive.

Randomly Collected Sample

Date	Magnitude	Location
May 31, 1990	6R+	Off coast felt in Tokyo
February 20, 1990	6.6R	Epc in sea 70 m S of Tokyo
July 9, 1989	5.5R	Iza Peninsula (2 events)
June 30, 1989	Swarm Begins	Iza Peninsula
June 17, 1989	6.8R	310m S of Tokyo felt in Tokyo
April 27, 1989	6.4R	Off shore
September 26, 1988	5.9R	
September 13, 1988	5.5R	Near Toriskima 360 M S of Tokyo
August 12, 1988	5.3R	Felt in Tokyo 12,000 Tremors and up this month
December 17, 1987	6-6.4R	Honshu
October 4, 1987	5.9R	Off shore
January 9, 1987	6.9R	200 m N of Tokyo
October 13, 1986	R?	East coast
March 24, 1986	6.6R	Sea
October 4, 1985	6.2R	Strongest in Tokyo since Grand Trine Air July 27, 1929 with Moon in Gemini
March 28, 1985	6R	Sea
September 18, 1984	R?	Sea of Japan (simultaneous event in Turkey)
September 14, 1984	6.1R	Osaka
August 29, 1984	6.1R	Sea Quake
August 6, 1984	6.5R	Kyasha also Indonesia
March 6, 1984	7.9R	Sea of Japan
September 29, 1973	7.2R	Sea of Japan
December 4, 1972	R?	Japanese Trench
February 29, 1972	R?	Hachijo Jimo
January 14/25, 1972	Swarm	Izo-Osima
August 2, 1971	R?	Hidaka
May 16, 1968	7.9R	Tokachi
August 3, 1965	Swarm	100m NW Tokyo
June 16, 1964	7.5R	N11GATA
November 25, 1953	8.0R	Honshu
June 28, 1948	7.3R	Fukui
December 21, 1946	R?	Sea quake, all Japan, Honshu and neighboring major islands, tsunamis destroyed several thousand ships, 2000 drowned, 500,000 homeless
January 12, 1945	7.1R	Mikana

December 7, 1944	8.3R	Honshu
September 10, 1943	7.4R	Tottori
March 2, 1933	8.9R	Sanriku (Long Beach, CA quake 10 days later)
November 20, 1930	7.1R	Izu
July 27, 1929	R?	Tokyo; Moon, Pluto in Cancer-water enhancement
March 7, 1927	8.0R	Tango Peninsula, W Japan; 3,000 dead, 14,000 buildings down; almost as destructive as Kwanto
September 1, 1923	8R+	Kwanto, Honshu, Tokyo severely damaged, 143,000 killed
June 15, 1911	8.7R	Ryukyn Is.
April 12, 1910	8.3R	Ryukyn Is.
March 13, 1909	8.3R	Honshu
January 21, 1906	8.4R	Honshu
June 7, 1904	7.9R	Sea of Japan
March 22, 1900	R?	Japan
June 15, 1896	R? probably 8	Sanriku
October 12, 1894	"Strong"	Shonai
October 28, 1891	R? probably 8+	Mino-wari rocked half of Japan

The Tokyo Signature—A Note on Tokyo

In this sample, three quakes are noted as severely damaging Tokyo. As repeatedly noted, there are variations, rolling signatures, basic signatures, enhancements, compensations and details.

At first glance these Tokyo quakes show their differences but there is an important detail: planets in Virgo.

September 1, 1923	8.3R	Kwanto or Honshu GTW; Mars 0° Virgo, Venus 5° Virgo, Sun 7° Virgo
July 27, 1929	R?	Tokyo, Moon-Pluto in Cancer, lunar water enhancement; Neptune 0° Virgo, Mars 13° Virgo, Venus square Mars from 19°Gemini (separates and is strong, see Kwanto)
October 4, 1985	6.2R	Tokyo, Saturn-Pluto in Scorpio, Saturn separates; Mars 15° Virgo, Venus 15° Virgo, slightly separated

Synthesis for Tokyo

- Mars in Virgo
- 0° Virgo sensitive
- Two planets in Virgo
- Venus and Mars in Virgo
- Venus separates form Mars
- Mars in Virgo aspected strongly by separating Venus
- Venus conjunct Mars, close but separating
- 1923 Mercury 4° Libra, Venus 5° Virgo
- 1927 Mercury not in degree

- 1985 Mercury not in degree
- 1923 Jupiter separates trine Jupiter 13° Scorpio, Pluto 12° Cancer by 1°
- 1927 Jupiter separates semisquare Jupiter 9° Gemini Pluto 18° Cancer by 6°
- 1985 Jupiter separates square Jupiter 7° Aquarius Pluto 3° Scorpio by 4°
- 1923, 1927, 1985 Mars in earlier zodiac sign than Saturn.
- 1923 Mars Virgo 48 Saturn Libra, 12° separating sextile, 3° applying semisquare
- 1927 Mars Virgo 101 Saturn Sagittarius, 4° separating 105° aspect, 11° applying square
- 1985 Mars Virgo 70 Saturn Scorpio, 5° separating 75° aspect 10° applying sextile

Conclusion on Mars, in Virgo, in an earlier sign than Saturn, related more closely by 15° type aspect and this most likely separating.

43

The Signature of the Philippine Islands

Continuing south we come to the Philippine Islands, an archipelago whose land outline resembles that of hummocks left dry by receding water. The clear ring position of some archipelagos is not apparent at first glance. The midpoint between the northern and southern sections is scattered. This infers a change in the points of volcanic eruption, particularly below sea level.

The capital of the Philippine Islands is Luzon, the large northern island matched in size by its southern cousin, Mindanao. The capital Manila is in Luzon. Quakes are most noteworthy in Luzon and Mindanao because of population, concrete buildings and economics. They are often referred to as Luzon or Mindanao.

The sample consists of 20 quakes from 1863 to 1990, collected randomly. With some of these, the island is not clear. A general signature is noted:

- Predominately, but not always negative (earth and water planetary emphasis).
- Usually oppositions and squares, but not T-squares.
- Many easy oppositions (with sextile/trine between).
- Planets often in Taurus.
- Mars in Taurus.

The Luzon quake often has Taurus/Scorpio planets with others in Capricorn or Virgo (earth trines in an easy opposition). Luzon may or may not have planets on the Aries/Libra axis.

Manila is in the southern part of Luzon and appears, in the main, to share its signature with Mindanao, the large southern island.

Manila usually has Aries/Libra with square to Cancer or Capricorn. Often planets in Virgo. Note the Venus-Mars-Jupiter energy triad midpoints here in the major July 3, 1863, quake. There is an easy opposition to Aries/Libra or from Gemini or Leo.

In Manila the cardinal T-square has two planets from the initiation triad Sun-Mercury-Jupiter, or two from the triggers, Moon-Mercury-Mars-Saturn-Uranus. Manila Quakes—July 3, 1863, August 1, 1968 and April 25, 1972.

Mindanao, the large southern island, has more or less the same signature as Manila. Davao is the largest city in Mindanao and the quake may be known as Davao.

All Philippine Island quakes fall somewhere in between these two signatures with part of one or the other missing.

In a grand trine water quake, six planets, Lanao Philippines Islands April 1, 1955, 7.6R both location signatures are present with midpoints to Virgo.

July 16, 1990	7.7R	Luzon
November 17, 1988	5.1R	Philippine Islands
April 25, 1985	6.2R/6.0R	Luzon
November 19, 1984	7.2R	Philippine Islands
August 16, 1976	7.9R	Mindanao
December 13, 1972	R?	Mindanao
April 25, 1972	R?	Manila
April 7, 1970	7.7R	Luzon
March 30, 1970	R?	Mindanao
January 10, 1970	R?	Davao-Mindanao
January 30, 1969	R?	Mindanao
August 1, 1968	7.7R	Manila, Casagurian, Luzon
April 1, 1955	8.3R	Lanao, Philippine Islands
January 24, 1948	8.3R	Philippine Islands
May 25, 1943	8.1R	Philippine Islands
April 14, 1924	8.3R	Philippine Islands
August 21, 1902	"Major"	Philippine Islands
September 21, 1897	?large	Philippine Islands
July 3, 1863	7R+	Manila

Given the blending of signatures at present, current geological knowledge is necessary. Generally one might say Luzon north of Manila for the northern signature, Manila and south including all Mindanao for the southern signature.

During the 1990s onward, Uranus and Neptune in Capricorn and 1994 Saturn in Pisces, should sensitize any Virgo planets. Uranus and Neptune also are permanent triggers (Capricorn) to the Aries Libra axis on the Manila-south-Mindanao signature. At present (1990s onward), release of energy before 8R is more common.

The Great Pacific Circuit Belt branches south of New Zealand and one branch runs through New Zealand to New Caledonia, through the Solomon and Admiralty Islands, above eastern New Guinea and on to the Philippine Islands, where it passes north of them.

Some details of the Philippine Islands signature are listed below. Note the signature changes, which by their short spans (about 50 years), indicate changes in the rolling planetary signature as opposed to major geological change.

- Earth signature, grand trine earth, earth trines, Mars in earth, stellium (several planets) in Virgo. Always at least one earth planet which functions strongly (Mars, Saturn, Jupiter and Neptune).
- A definite relationship with Sun-Jupiter-Uranus, the first two initiatory, Jupiter also slow planet, Uranus slow planet and timer with aspects of 30° frequent.

- Rules regarding planetary separation appear not to apply to this Sun, Jupiter, Uranus complex.
- Mars more often in earth than water, one each in air, least in fire.
- Either first decanate cardinal or this recent development, early second decanate. This of course is indicative of, or relative to, vulcanism.
- Mercury often not in degree, but often functions as a near midpoint.
- Quakes after 1948 show five to seven planets negative in earth or water. Four negative now infrequent, but four negative common prior to 1948 (see Rolling Signature).
- Jupiter mostly in earth, then water, three times in Aquarius air, once in Libra air, seldom fire. Basically Jupiter, also an energizer, has the same sign preferences as Mars.
- Sun most frequently fixed or cardinal, Leo-Aries. Taurus/Scorpio frequent. Seldom in Virgo, not in Pisces or Cancer, when Sun may be in adjacent Aries or Leo if planets are in Pisces and Cancer.
- Prior to 1970, Cancer appeared in the signature, but in the subsequent rolling signature it has been eliminated. The Capricorn emphasis from 1988 on, may relate to this or change the signature again. Note that pre-1970 quakes did not usually need or have Capricorn emphasis. This recurs in the New Zealand signature.
- Planetary dispersion is usually locomotive (120° space left open) or see-saw (a series of oppositions, 180°). No clear cut bowls in the sample (planets form semi-circle). Wedges (90° or less dispersion) have a singleton as handle (one planet opposite) often Saturn.
- Since 1972, the dispersion has been nearer the bowl (180°) with one sign more or less than the bowl common and Moon, Jupiter, Saturn as singletons.
- Squares or T-squares are usually cardinal, again vulcanism.

44

The Signature of the Celebes

Moving south of the Philippine Islands the Great Pacific Circuit Gas Belt passes midway between Celebes, the major island of the group by the same name and West Irian/New Guinea to the East.

Many quakes in this area are sea quakes which do relatively little damage, especially as noted by the Western press which usually designates the quake by the sea involved, Celebes, Molucca, Banda, Ceram, Timor. The area in question is 120-140 east and 5 north to 5 south with the gas belt having an average place of about 127 east on a slight northeast-southwest axis.

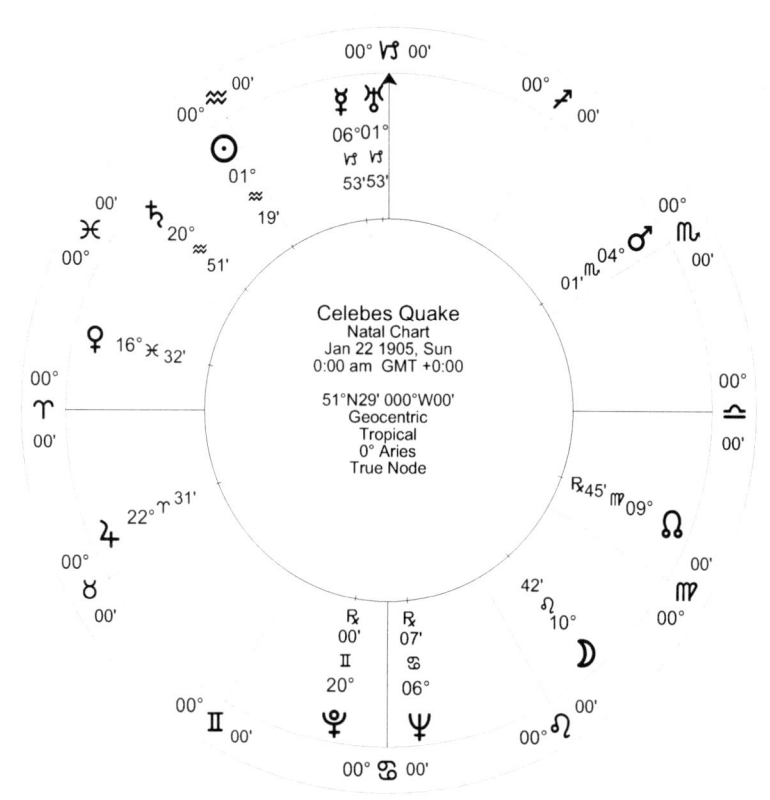

Dealing specifically with the locations nearest the Grand Pacific Circuit Belt and the above coordinates, the following observations were made:

- Broadly speaking, any of several signatures apply here, the grand cross, the cardinal T-square, fixed T-square, grand trines air, fire and earth as well as the universal water, and its well traveled cousin, the Cancer-Capricorn axis.
- A common signature involves generally two or three of the major signature components. That is, a major complex, specifically cardinal T-square. Grand trine water and fixed T-square miss one of their points.
- Libra and Aquarius are important signs. A common occurrence is a planet in Libra and Leo.

- A Gemini or Virgo stellium may also trigger an event here. Any stellium in the Celebes signature appears to be a component.
- Virgo is the most frequent mutable sign, but if there is not a planet there, one will be in another mutable sign.
- Venus-Mars-Jupiter integration and energizing is present but seldom spectacular in the chart. Venus often appears in a 15° type aspect to another planet, a position somehow pivotal in energizing. Jupiter is frequently in cardinal signs. The Moon usually appears to have made a recent strong aspect to Mars, probably approaching, and at least three times a conjunction to Uranus. In the random sample, lunar angles varied but never an event at the time of the New Moon. Perhaps because of the fractional signature components noted earlier on here, the Sun also has a more enhancing function that usual.
- The Sun is often in Pisces or Leo, water or fire, exceptions Taurus and Aquarius (fixity).
- Mercury is usually in degree, but it may be to any planet, Mars through Pluto. If it is not in degree, it has recently separated from some planet.

In assessing EM signatures, I work with signs, This includes the assessment of aspects where, unlike natal astrology, I'm more interested in sign (element and mode) and separation, than in orb (number of degrees from exact aspect angle).

In Celebes quakes there are at least two and often three conjunctions by sign. Where there are only two, one of the signs often has at least a third planet. While this is hardly rare zodiacally, there is no quake without it.

This area is quake prone and the vulcanism is indicated by one or more planets in early cardinal and/or the early degrees of the second decanate cardinal.

As a clearly third world area undergoes economic development with its subsequent gatherings of populations, in masonry structures, and the possibility of nuclear power planets, monitoring of the area's events will become more important. Because of this, I'm hopeful of some communication and integration between the fields of geology and astrology.

Sumarizing the Celebes signature:

- Any grand trine.
- Any fixed T-square.
- Any cardinal T-square.
- Components of any two or three of the above (two to three incomplete major aspect complexes.
- Mercury usually in degree or separated.
- Sun important in Pisces, Leo, water, fire.
- No New Moon. Sun and Moon enhance ``broken signatures.''
- Pairs of planets in two to three signs, not four or one; more than two planets in one of two signs, where only two involved.

Randomly Collected Sample

March 6, 1993	7.0R	Near San Cristobal
December 12, 1992	7.5 R	Flores Island
February 27, 1988	6+R	Indonesia-Celebes Islands
August 6, 1984	6.5R	Indonesia-Celebes Islands (Japan quake same day)
September 24, 1972	?	Banda Sea
August 6, 1969	?	Molucca Passage
February 23, 1969	?	Makassar Strait, Celebes, Indonesia

August 14, 1968	7R+	N. Celbes Islands
August 6, 1968	?	Molucca passage
November 2, 1950	8.1R	Banda Sea
June 30, 1943	6.8R	Celebes Sea
December 21, 1939	8.6R	Celebes Sea
June 29, 1934	6.9R	Celebes Sea
May 14, 1932	8.3R	Celebes Sea
March 14, 1913	8.3R	Molucca Passage
January 22, 1905	8.4R	Celebes Sea
September 30, 1899	?	Ceram, East Indies

The January 22, 1905 quake is a classic one. It has Grand Trine Water with Mercury at 6° Capricorn, Uranus in Capricorn 180° (opposition), and Neptune 6° Cancer. There are two universal signatures: Mercury in the degree of Neptune, plus cardinal T-square and fixed T-square.

45

The Signature of Eastern Indonesia

This location includes New Guinea and West Irian and the sea north of Australia. Its coordinates in round numbers are 0 to 15 south and 130 to 155 east. According to Churchward, this would be an area of intense seismic and vulcanistic activity with branches of the Great Pacific Circuit Belt running from approximately:

- Melville Island, North Australia to Ceram.
- Cape York, Australia across the Torres Strait into western New Guinea and through West Irian into Hamahera and up into Mindanao, Philippines.
- A parallel branch of the above lies to the north, running from Mindanao north of New Guinea (entire island) into the Solomon Islands to the east, passing the eastern end of the BismarcK Archipelago above the Solomon Islands.

The Pacific Cross Belt runs through Timor and the Arafura Sea, through the Torres Strait. It intersects the Great Pacific Circuit Belt branches near Melville Island, Cape York and just south of the Solomon Islands. Working from my random sample, there are differences between this area and Indonesia, though one similarity is a seeming variety of signatures. There is some inner cohesion which includes grand trines in all elements. The grand trines are probably in this order of frequency: fire, air, water, earth.

Apparently, and according to my sample, all grand trines are accessed (opposed) from one of their three positions. For example, water grand trines have planets in Capricorn, completing the universal signature, GTW and Cancer/Capricorn. The term "accessed" means that energy may enter or escape the grand trine complex by its nature being a closed circuit.

At least four, and up to seven, signs in sequence have planets. Virgo, Libra and Scorpio are the most tenanted signs. A stellium may appear in these or any two of them. Aquarius, Pisces, Aries and Taurus are the least frequent planetarily. When these signs appear they are necessary for completion of a signature.

- Aquarius, fixity and air trines.
- Pisces, water trine, head of GTE kite.
- Aries, Moon, fire, cardinal, fire trines.
- Taurus, earth trines, fixity.

Mercury may or may not be in degree, and if in degree, may be in that of any planet from Venus through Pluto, sometimes a degree earlier or later. Venus-Mars-Jupiter integration, average and various means. The Sun seldom appears alone—here in both instances in Capricorn. Other than Venus and Mercury, it is often with Mars, Saturn, Uranus. It may also form part of the noted stellia Virgo, Libra, Scorpio.

Planetary separation appears less than usual here. This perhaps is because of the belts, or the ready availability of vulcanism—or perhaps the trines indicate easily stored or infused energy. Rather than dwell on causality, it is probably better to simply note that matters mesh here. But in working these signatures, a grand trine with kite head (opposed), modest separation, modest Venus-Mars-Jupiter, and erratic Mercury in degree, is itself a quite complex signature. In terms of the above signature, the Sun always occupied an important place in the grand trine, the kite head, in the stellium with a heavy planet, etc. This is true of other locations as well.

A planet or planets often occur in early cardinal, especially Cancer or Libra, as befitting vulcanism.

Randomly Collected New Guinea Quakes

July 6, 1988	6.7R	Near Papua, New Guinea
October 17, 1987	7.8R	280 miles east of Port Moresby, New Guinea
October 3, 1985	6.9R	1,200 miles northwest of Brisbane, Australia; 100 miles southeast of Port Moresby
September 9, 1979	8.0R	New Guinea
August 19, 1977	7.7-8.4R	Eastern Indonesia
June 26, 1976	7.1R	New Guinea
August 17, 1972	?	New Ireland, east of New Guinea
July 26, 1971	?	New Britain east of New Guinea
January 10, 1971	8.0R	West Irian
October 21, 1970	?	Madang, New Guinea
October 1, 1968	General activity	New Guinea
January 13, 1916	8.1R	New Guinea
September 14, 1906	8.4R	New Guinea

46

The Signature of Indonesia

The main gas belt of Indonesia is the Pacific Cross Belt, here running through the western island of Sumatra, more or less along the northern coast of Java, through Timor and on through the Torres Strait, separating the entire island of New Guinea from Australia. Western New Guinea is now known as West Irian, a political entity, so the island will be designated, or not, according to the data. Pacific quakes are often of little importance and many are only vaguely located in the Western press and television.

The Pacific Cross Belt intersects with the Grand Pacific Circuit Belt east of Timor roughly around Melville Island. It throws off a complex of minor belts known as the Malay Belts. This complex runs up the Malay Peninsula just north of Ankara, about 18N near modern Chingmal in Thailand. Another minor belt runs from eastern Sumatra through the ocean into Vietnam ending near Vinh again about 18N. The belt running up the Malay Peninsula breaks back near the inland tip of the penninsula and cuts into Borneo near Pontianak, cutting beneath Borneo into the Celebes. This perhaps relates, in some way, to the confused signatures discussed in the previous chapter.

A branch of this branch, breaks to the northeast, roughly along the eastern border of Sarawak, North Borneo, another political entity. This branch runs through Palwan where it may or may not join the Grand Pacific Circuit Belt arcing through the Philippine Islands. This branch ends in Thailand, and Vietnam seems relatively quiet.

Of the land masses involved, the Malay Peninsula, Sumatra, Borneo and Palawan, Sumatra and Java are the more seismsically active. This seems appropriate to their being over the major Pacific Cross Belt. The other land masses are over branches known as the Malay belts.

A random sample of ten events was used. Some quakes were obtained without a Richter measurement, but the context indicates strong events. Absent is the grand trine water and the Cancer-Capricorn axis, that is the universal signature. There is always something in earth, usually two signs. Grand Trine Earth events occurred February 4, 1971 and February 1, 1938, this with an Aquarius stellium, Sun, Moon, Venus and Jupiter. In seven of the ten charts, Aquarius usually has a planet, excepting the stellium above. Noteworthy of those planets, the Sun and Mars.

Often a fixed square or T-square, with Leo the least frequent fixed sign. As usual with all quake signatures the wild card factor is present and July 23, 1943 shows a Leo stellium, Mercury, Jupiter and Pluto. The Moon is in

Aries and Mercury in the degree of Jupiter, 4° Leo, emphasizing fire and fixity. Mars in Taurus separates from the Leo complex.

Pisces appears only once in my sample in an 8.1R Richter, February 27, 1903, Java event with Sun, Moon and Jupiter there. (Please note the chapter on the rolling signature, under the same name.) As in all vulcanistic areas, there is often one or more planets in the first decanate cardinal, or the next degrees but not always. The Moon may appear in Aries. Venus-Mars-Jupiter, the energy triad show good integration. Venus has usually separated and Venus or Mars may conjunct Jupiter. Integration may be by the midpoints of two of these, to the third (Venus, Mars, Jupiter).

Mercury most often is not in exact degree but one or two degrees from the degree of Uranus Neptune or Pluto, the slow planets. Twice, not in degree at all, and once in degree of Sun, once in degree of Jupiter. An overall assessment of Mercury in degree here would be normal plus. Again, whether approaching or separating Mercury clearly is nearest to degree of the slow planets in those so noted.

Occasionally a planet is in early Scorpio and 16° to 17° Sagittarius may appear by midpoint. Up to 1943, there are four appearances of late Cancer, three times Pluto, once the Sun. Apparently, one way or another other, this may now be disregarded either as irrelevant or a rolling signature. (Check New Zealand Signature.)

Summary of Indonesia:

- At least two planets in earth signs.
- Some fixity always, Aquarius, noteworthy, Leo the exception.
- Sun or Mars may be in Aquarius
- Moon may be in Aries.
- Venus-Mars-Jupiter integrated, separation good.
- Mercury in degree of slow planets—Uranus, Neptune and Pluto usually, and not exact, with one to two degrees approaching or separating.

Randomly Collected Indonesian Sample

November 16, 1984	7.5R	Sumatra
October 5, 1984	6.5R	Java Trench
June 10, 1983	R?	Java
June 11, 1971	R?	Indonesia-Java
June 11, 1971	R?	Indonesia
February 4, 1971	R?	Sumatra (Grand Trine Earth)
November 21, 1969	R?	Sumatra
July 23, 1943	8.1R	Java
February 1, 1938	8.6R	Java (Grand Trine Earth)
December 28, 1935	8.1R	Sumatra
February 27, 1903	8.1R	Java

47

The Signature of the Marianas, the Caroline Islands and Bonin

At present I have no sample and note that they are fed by the Ladrone Belt, a branch of the Great Pacific Circuit Belt originating off Japan, running by Bonin then the Marianas, then the Carolines.

I would expect a Great Pacific Circuit Belt type signature with similarities to Japan plus local touches.

Geologically speaking, I'd cast an eye on this area following a prolonged increase of EM activity in the Japanese Trench.

One simple way to note future periods of increased EM in this area is to combine any early cardinal emphasis occurring at times with a planet or planets in Virgo. This combination occurs yearly, to some degree, when the Sun is in Virgo and Libra. Nearby Mercury and Venus will complete the signature.

48

The Signature of the Solomon Islands

The Solomon Islands are on a northern parallel division of the Grand Pacific Circuit Belt running north of New Guinea. (See belt details in New Guinea Signature.)

A small sample of Solomon Islands quakes, in terms of my random collection, does not permit a definitive assessment. General indications are clearly very much like New Guinea, though perhaps the grand trine shows up less frequently.

The two grand trines in the sample have the kite head in fire, Oct 4, 1971, Bougainvillea, S.I.

An interesting layout appears on July 14, 1971, 8.1R Solomon Islands where a grand trine air is interlocked with a grand trine fire, and all six points are accessed.

Again, Virgo, Libra and Scorpio are the most frequent signs. Cardinal squares and T-squares are frequent, as are mutable squares and air, fire and water trines. The importance of water and fire is indicated by lunar enhancement, and the Moon is also often cardinal.

Cancer may be more important here and the Sun appears three times each in Cancer and Libra accompanied by other planets. Other than Mercury and Venus, Saturn and Uranus appear here. As in New Guinea, the Sun is alone in Capricorn once.

Uranus appears with the Sun in Taurus, Libra and Scorpio, again sigificant given the small sample. Saturn often with another planet in sign, alone in mutable signs, or part of a cardinal T-square. Mercury by degree is unreliable and separation is moderate. Early cardinal degrees are regular, and as in New Guinea, I surmise that immediate vulcanism is a key factor in this. The Venus-Mars-Jupiter are moderate.

We might thus hypothesize that the above paragraph is indicative of unstable areas, e.g., islands on or immediately adjacent to ongoing vulcanism. The situation whereby there are two to three signs with two or more planets reappears. Where there are only two such signs, one may have a stellium.

Capricorn is one of the lesser frequented cardinal signs. The Sun, Moon and Saturn each appear once alone as a matter of enhancement, vulcanism and twice as part of a T-square, once to enhance the importance of Libra, indicate that an entry into mid-Capricorn may be noteworthy when matters implied by its presence there are lacking or needed, but other components are in place. Stated simply, Capricorn is an enhancement positon completing needed energy circuits here.

As one reads these Grand Pacific Circuit Belt signatures, one sees that they tie into the Ring of Fire and that there are similarities all around the Pacific. I've included Churchward's Belts to open minds to horizontal movements of propellant and magma within this giant system.

Summarizing, I'd say the highly unstable areas are defined by moderate or irregular signature components. Simply, when such an astrological signature appears, look to the geologically active archipelagoes of smaller islands.

Random Sample

Date	Magnitude	Location
September 27, 1985	6.5R	S.I.
July 5, 1984	6.8R	Bougainvillea, S.I.
November 5, 1978	7.5R	S.I.
July 20, 1975	7.9R	S.I.
October 4, 1971	?GTA	Bougainvillea, S.I.
July 14, 1971	8.1R GTA, GTF	S.I.
January 6, 1969	?	S.I.
April 30, 1939	8.1R	S.I.
October 3, 1931	8.1R	S.I.

By the time a Solomon Islands quake reaches a western news source, time is forgotten, OGMT for the calendar day was used on all S.I. quakes, this regarding lunar enhancement.

49

The Signature of Australia

Australia is a mighty land and my sample is small. The Great Pacific Circuit Belt runs underneath Australia more or less from Darwin (north) to Brisbane (east) as it heads for New Zealand.

The Pacific Central Belt runs north of Australia from Timor through the Torres Straits.

The sample of three includes one south, one west and one central event. Utter scarcity. Nevertheless, a couple of clues unveil themselves.

Despite the Great Belt running underneath Australia, it seems sensitive to Central Belt signatures, noting the Pisces, Aries, Taurus clues.

Earth is important, especially Virgo, 2 stellia, June 27, 1941, grand trine earth, Neptune, Saturn, Uranus.

Venus-Mars-Jupiter energizing above moderate, but not extreme.

- 15° type aspects important.
- Venus clearly relates to Saturn (3 of 3).
- Mars clearly relates to Neptune (3 of 3).
- Mutable T-square (3 of 3).
- Libra without planets (3 of 3).
- Moon enhances fire or water deficiencies (3 of 3).

I see this as a clear starting position and offer the suggestion that these smaller location samples be drawn up by the reader, enabling him to note the differences in location signature. There is a blurring in larger signature samples, both astrological and visual—wild card events, rolling signatures, small versus large events, etc.

Random Sample

June 20, 1969	Tremors	Victoria, SE Australia
October 14, 1968	7.2R	Meckering, W. Australia
June 27, 1941	6.7R	Central Australia

50

The Signature of Macquerie Island

This dot in the far South Pacific lies at about 55 south, 160 east and belongs to Australia. It lies south of the Great Pacific Circuit Belt, of which a branch may run to Macquerie and on to Antarctica. I suspect my single Antarctic event, which will follow, had an epicenter south of Macquerie.

The building blocks of my two Macquerie events are much the same as in New Zealand—mutable, fixed, fire, water, earth. June 6, 1924, has no earth.

Both have Libra planets with September 6 1943, having the sequence Virgo, Libra, Scorpio, and June 26 1924 having an exalted Saturn in Libra, no planets in Virgo or Scorpio.

Water is extremely important—fire planets in Pisces and Cancer June 26, 1924, and September 6 1943 have the Moon in Scorpio, lunar enhancement proving the need for water and fixity. Gemini, Leo and Libra positions occur in both. Early cardinal (vulcanism) in both.

- Saturn in air (2 of 2).
- Mars mutable (2 of 2).
- Sun negative (2 of 2).
- Moon in Mars sign (2 of 2).
- Mercury in degree of Uranus (2 of 2).
- Venus-Mars-Jupiter energy triad fairly strong.
- Venus separation good, relates to Uranus and Pluto.
- Mars in same sign as Uranus (2 of 2).

With a sample of only two events, it is almost certain that some of the above would show more variation, thus becoming secondary parts of the signature.

Random Sample

September 6, 1943	7.8R	Macquerie Island
June 26, 1924	8.3R	Sea quake southwest of Macquerie Island

51

The Signature of Antarctica

A geologist named Eiby, from a source I did not properly note, declared Antarctica a quake-free zone. As I've discovered astrologically, the paradigm of EM automatically includes the exception. A glance at the globe indicates that Antarctica would lie south of the Great Pacific Belt or the Pacific Cross Belt, but not both at a given point.

Since Macquerie Island is active, I'll guess the epicenter of my example as being south of Macquerie.

The event includes a loose grand trine earth, the stellium Neptune, Jupiter, Mars in Sagittarius. It contains the basic Grand Pacific Circuit Belt building blocks, mutability, fixity, fire, water, earth, and Libra and Scorpio in sequence. Refer to New Zealand and other signatures for further information.

Mercury, exalted at 0° Aquarius, had just been in 29° Capricorn with Pluto at 29° Virgo. Venus-Mars-Jupiter strong with Venus separated from the stellium, Neptune, Jupiter, Mars and arriving at 2° Capricorn, early cardinal for vulcanism.

The Sun-Mercury-Jupiter primary triad are strongly integrated.

Lunar enhancement is strong, with the Moon in its own sign, proving the need for water.

Sample

February 8, 1971   R?   Antarctica

52

The Signature of New Caledonia and the Loyalty Islands

I do not have a sufficient information, nor clarity, within this small sample. The lack of clarity itself is a major clue as this archipelago is more or less midway between the two belt systems, the Great Pacific Circuit and the Pacific Central. Keeping that in mind, a clear point for a beginning is indicated.

I suspect, that given a historical series or sequence of events, I'd continue to find muddy signatures indicative of the influence of one or the other, or both systems at a given time.

Stated inoffensively, this should indicate the direction of origin of the vulcanism, the Central Belt from the north, the Circuit Belt from the south.

I do not have a sample for New Hebrides to the north and I expect New Caledonia would be much the same.

53

The Signature of the New Hebrides Islands

The New Hebrides Islands lie east of Australia and the Loyalty Islands in the late teens of south latitude. A seismically active area, they are closer to the Pacific Cross Belt to the north, by a third of the distance between this belt and the Grand Pacific Circuit Belt to the south, located east of Sydney, Australia and south of Lord Howe Island. The Cross Belt runs east and west between New Guinea and Australia.

The signature incudes the following:

- A cardinal complex.
- A fixed complex.
- Air trines are emphasized over fire trines.
- Aquarius planetary positions more frequent than Leo.
- Fire strong.
- Planetary dispersion often bowl (180°) or see-saw (pairs of planets 180° apart, the opposition).
- The air stellium most frequent in Libra.
- Air and fire both strong.
- In forecasting, a slight preponderance of fixed over cardinal.
- Mercury close to the degree of Uranus, Mars, Pluto, Neptune, but not in the same degree.

Random Sample

July 8, 1981	7R	New Hebrides
December 28, 1973	7.6R	Banks Islands, New Hebrides
November 28, 1973	?Strong	Tanna Islands, New Hebrides
January 23, 1972	?Strong	Torres Islands, New Hebrides
October 27, 1971	?Strong	Espiritu Santo, New Hebrides
August 11, 1970	R?Strong	New Hebrides
December 2, 1950	8.1R	New Hebrides

54

The Signature of Fiji Island

The Fiji Islands are directly west of Tonga at about 177 east and 17 south. A small sample of three quakes indicates the signature is more or less the same as the Tonga Island and Samoa signature.

The Fiji Islands lie slightly to the south of the Pacific Central Gas Belt and clearly come under its influence. The Great Pacific Circuit Belt at that longitude has passed between North and South Island, New Zealand. A supplementary study of this volatile area, along with others where the sample is weak, will hopefully follow publication of this book. For the moment I'll continue to work with the random probability, which clearly indicates, but doesn't prove, a signature similar to that of Tonga.

Water and fire continue to be important and their trines respectively emphasize Cancer, Pisces and Aries, Sagittarius. Pisces has a planet or planets in three of three. In one, a Pisces opposition to a Virgo stellium is present. In one the Moon is with the Sun in Pisces. The principle of lunar enhancement would thus tend to confirm the importance of this sign for Fiji.

While this signature is akin to Tonga, it may have its own subtleties and the Pisces emphasis is probably significant. The chapter on California quakes will clearly demonstrate that specific signatures exist for small locations. That possibility should be kept in mind for all detailed, specific location research and forecasting.

In this mini-sample, Jupiter in Pisces 1, in Virgo 2, Saturn in Aries, Virgo and Sagittarius. Uranus too, shows a predilection for mutable (two) or cardinal (one) signs. Separation is moderate as is the Venus-Mars-Jupiter relationship. The Mercury degree perhaps should be illustrated here and will be included in the listing. Jupiter and Neptune are important. Early cardinal is always present.

Random Sample

January 9, 1987	6.4R	Fiji Islands Jupiter 18° Pisces, Sun 18° Capricorn, Mercury 15°Capricorn, Neptune 5°Capricorn
September 20, 1920	8.3R	Fiji Islands Mercury 5° Libra Jupiter 5° Virgo
February 22, 1909	7.9R	Fiji Islands Mercury 13° Aquarius Neptune 14° Cancer

55

The Signature of Polynesia

Polynesia is west of the international dateline, most of which is known as Polynesia, east of dateline being designated broadly as Micronesia. EM activity, both volcanic and seismic, decreases here.

Except for one or two Marquesan events, I'll simply note that it is under the influence of the Pacific Cross Belt and I would immediately compare known Polynesian events and differences. In areas that are relatively quiet, I believe that a historical perspective is as important as the current seismic reading.

An illustration of this exists with Mt. Pele, Martinique, French West Indies. Major eruptions have bene recorded since the late 17th century and including the May 8, 1902 eruption, numbers about five, the inference being that Mt. Pele is now overdue, since a greater time (91 years) has now elapsed than any other interval between her eruptions. Of course this can also mean centuries of dormancy. Or that 1976 venting there, and in neighboring Saint Vincent, offered safe and harmless release events.

Historians, geologists and astrologers really should attempt some mutual communication on these areas of sparse activity.

56

The Signature of Samoa and Tonga

This is the greatest concentration of small islands on earth spanning more than 60° of eastern longitude, from roughly 160 east to 137 west and zero to 20 south. I group these together because they are not on the Grand Pacific Circuit Belt but on the Pacific Cross Belt. To those who have closely read the signatures preceding this, in particular the last four chapters, or even gone further and charted the quakes, the difference will become immediately apparent.

This is the archipelago of archipelagos. Some are noted geographically or geologically, and others by nationality. It forms the most fragmented land mass on earth. It is heavily vulcanistic, whether dead, dormant or active. It may also be assumed to have certain acquired geological weaknesses as a result of this activity. At once one sees that the signs to the east—Capricorn, Aquarius, Pisces, Aries, Taurus, Gemini, Cancer—reappear. Actually, Cancer-Capricorn form the zodiacal divide between the two sides of the chart. In all vulcanistic locations, the cardinal signs are extremely important, by degrees, tenancy of planets, squares and T-squares.

The cardinal emphasis in these island groups is Aries and Capricorn, mutable signs and planets are always also important in vulcanistic locations. The emphasis here switches to include Pisces and Gemini, even while Virgo and Sagittarius more or less retain their status.

- Fire once again is important, but here Aries becomes the pivotal sign.
- In fixed T-square, Taurus and Aquarius reappear.
- Libra only has planets some of the time, ditto Scorpio.

As in the Solomon Islands, Mercury by degree, Venus, Mars, Jupiter and separation are vague, moderate, diverse an confusing, Please recall my comments on weaker land structure in vulcanistic locations as stated in the Solomon Islands Signature.

There is some evidence of the rolling signature effect, Cancer being more important in the first third of the century, now Aries, and with Uranus and Neptune in Capricorn in the 1990s we may expect another shift of cardinal emphasis.

Pisces, Aries, Taurus in emphasis replace their opposites (Virgo, Libra, Scorpio) as in the Solomon Islands in emphasis. However, these last three are present.

The Moon is often cardinal and often strong to the Sun by sign. When the Moon is mutable, it is clearly enhancing mutable, conjunct a lonely Mercury in Sagittarius January 1, 1919, square a lone Uranus in Sagittarius from Pisces January 4, 1903. The stellium may or may not occur.

Kermedec Island is probably influenced by the Grand Pacific Circuit Belt which passes through New Zealand roughly between North and South Islands and hits the Kermedec Trench. Note Tonga and Samoa are more or less directly north of Kermedec Island.

Random Sample

April 1, 1977	7.5R	Between Samoa/Tonga
October 11, 1975	7.8R	South of Tonga
April 14, 1957	8.0R	South of Samoa
April 16, 1937	8.1R	Tonga
May 26, 1932	7.9R	Tonga-Kermedec Trench
April 30, 1919	8.4R	Tonga
January 1, 1919	8.3R	Tonga
June 26, 1917	8.7R	Samoa
May 1, 1917	8.6R	Tonga
January 4, 1903	8+R	Tonga

A note to astrologers regarding June 26, 1917: a purported 8.7R, Jupiter 29° Taurus, Saturn 0° Leo, and Neptune 3° Leo form mutual antiscia or solstice points.

Moon in Virgo enhances mutability and earth and the Moon/Jupiter midpoint from Virgo and Taurus falls in Cancer, with Pluto 3° Cancer conjunct in vulcanistic early cardinal, with Sun separating.

Mercury and Uranus strong in their own signs and Mercury/Jupiter-Mars, another trigger.

Mars separates from conjunction to Jupiter. Venus is semisquare Mars, 2° approaching, but just separating from Mars Jupiter at 3° Gemini.

57

The Signature of New Zealand

Returning from our lengthy detour through the South Pacific archipelagos, known collectively as Micronesia and Polynesia, influenced by the Pacific Cross Belt, we move to New Zealand. The Great Pacific Circuit Belt passes more or less between North and South Island and the Pacific Cross Belt lies far to the north near Tonga and Samoa. Hopefully a clear signature can be isolated, especially in light of no converging belt influences and a good sample.

As I stare at the map, I see that New Zealand fits Australia with the extreme north tip of North Island about at Rock Hampton onto Brisbane. South Island, of course, follows complete with a perfect fit between Grafton and Newcastle. Tasmania relates well to Melbourne.

The above is not entirely irrelevant since the Great Pacific Circuit Belt exits Australia near Brisbane with the Darling River. Note that this corresponds to the point between North and South Island.

An analysis of the sample begins; it may be best understood in terms of the land masses involved.

- North Island.
- South Island.
- Kermedec Islands.

As noted, the Great Pacific Circuit Belt runs between North and South Island and the Kermedec Islands lie between the Great Pacific Circuit Belt to the south and the Pacific Cross Belt to the north.

In other locations, one indicator of the Great Pacific Circuit is the presence of planets in Virgo, Libra, Scorpio. This occurs in some of the Kermedec Islands sample clearly indicating its influence.

The question then becomes one of historical record, the record showing that some major events took place there between 1968 and 1976. What other areas activated at that time? Which were dormant, keeping in mind the constant shift of location emphasis in the Ring of Fire?

The astrological charts over such a short period of time, and the size of event show that periodically the islands receive great inputs of energy.

As noted, a grand trine is ripened, energized, accessed by a planet opposite one of its points. Most grand trine events have at least one such opposition.

On January 20, 1970, a major quake hit the Kermedecs. Unfortunately, I don't know the exact Richter measurement. A grand trine water was accessed by a grand trine earth. That is, all energy in each grand trine was made accessible, in this instance meaning a forceful increase of energy resulting in a quake.

On January 14, 1976, an 8.0R event occurred with mutual grand trine fire and grand trine air. The dynamics of the grand trine are the same in all elements as noted above. In both there was strong cardinal backup principally from Capricorn and Libra.

The sequence began in 1968 with two events (see list). I suggest their consecutive drawing the 0° Aries chart. The Virgo, Libra, Scorpio emphasis in the second event is classic Great Pacific Circuit Belt, and Jupiter has joined two slow planets, Uranus and Pluto, in Virgo.

As in other Circuit Belt and New Zealand quakes, the Kermedec Islands building blocks are cardinal, mutable, fire, water.

Mercury in or near degree of a slow planet or Venus. Venus-Mars-Jupiter integration strong. Mars is strong to Pluto, Jupiter and Neptune in the Kermedec Island charts by aspect and same sign.

Assuming that seismic activity is noted, the presence of planets consecutively in Virgo, Libra and Scorpio is indicative of activity in the Kermedecs, not New Zealand proper.

Random Sample

January 14, 1976	8.0R	Kermedec Islands GTFA
January 20, 1970	?strong	Kermedec Islands GTWE
September 26, 1968	7+R	Near Raoul Island, Kermedec Islands
July 25, 1968	?	Kermedec Islands

I'll start the signature of the North and South Island by a comparison to the last Kermedec Island paragraph above.

The New Zealand quake usually shows planets in two of the signs, Virgo, Libra, Scorpio, sometimes one, and seldom all three (September 26, 1985).

On June 16, 1968, a 7.8R event occurred at Bulber, North Island. The Moon was in Libra, enhancement of the missing factor, Libra, air and part of a cardinal T-square. The Moon's presence here confirms the importance of this position. My New Zealand sample is good and in only one are planets in all three signs Virgo, Libra, Scorpio. Only one has all three without a planet. Again this refers to North and South Island.

New Zealand represents a sizable land mass. There may well be several signatures covering various locations as well as a common thread throughout the area.

The presence of earth in the New Zealand signature varies considerably. Virgo is the most common. Keep in mind the possibility of special location signatures and the influence of rolling signature factors.

Random Sample (Earth Trines)

May 24, 1968	7.0R	Inangohua, New Zealand, Taurus Virgo
April 23, 1966	6.1R	Cook Strait, Taurus Virgo
December 23, 1963	5.2R	Northland, New Zealand, Taurus Virgo
May 10, 1962	5.9R	Westport, S.I., Taurus Virgo

May 24, 1960	7.0R	Fiordland, S.I. GTE
December 10, 1958	6.9R	Bay of Plenty, Taurus Virgo
August 5, 1950	7.3R	South of S.I., Taurus Virgo
February 5, 1950	7.R	South of S.I. Virgo Capricorn with Moon, Saturn in Virgo, Mercury inCapricorn
June 24, 1942	7.0R	S. Wairarapa, Taurus Virgo
September 16, 1932	6.8R	Wairoa, Taurus Virgo, Virgo stellium Sun, Mercury, Jupiter, Neptune, Moon in Taurus
May 5, 1931	6+R	Poverty Bay, GTE with GTF
February 3, 1931	7.9R	Hawke's Bay, Virgo Capricorn
June 16, 1929	7.8R	Buller New Zealand, N.I., only Taurus but GTF
June 19, 1922	R?	Taupo District, no earth but grand trine fire
June 19, 1921	7R	Hawkes Bay, Taurus Virgo
December 22, 1914	6.5R	East Cape Peninsula, Moon in Capricorn
August 9, 1904	7.5R	Castlepoint, Jupiter in Taurus, Mercury in Virgo
November 17, 1901	7R	North Canterbury, stellium in Capricorn, Venus Jupiter Saturn Moon
December 7, 1897	7R	Wanganui, Moon in Taurus

Several inferences or conclusions regarding earth arise.

- It is more common in New Zealand than some other places.
- As usual in the Circuit Belt, Virgo is the most important earth sign.

The Moon alone in earth, as noted in several events, indicates the need for earth in these specific places. The presence of Mercury alone in a sign probably indicates an enhancement or compensation factor. Earth must be present. As usual, a stellium will supply the necessary mode and/or element energy. Virgo will utilize either Taurus or Capricorn (see Hawke's Bay).

Of the grand trines, fire is frequent, air occasional, earth once. Oddly enough, grand trine water, our wandering bad girl, does not appear though most New Zealand quakes have some water, usually trines.

Again the basic components of a Great Pacific Circuit quake are cardinal, mutable, fire, water. If the reader draws September 29, 1953, 7.1R Bay of Plenty, whose planets cover more or less 120°, I cannot be sure of the Moon. At OGMT it is 24° Gemini and one will see how this recurring theme is covered. A high positive (air-fire) and air, are often part of the New Zealand signature, but again see the strong Virgo-earth with Venus and Mars in conjunction.

Note in this quake that the Moon chooses to enhance the Libra stellium. Like many stellia in Pacific quakes, four planets are involved including the Sun and Mercury, here with Neptune and Saturn. This clearly is the classic quake stellium. Sun and Mercury, sometimes Venus, move in with two slower planets in a sign. A little stellium of three planets may have any one of these not present. Often the fourth planet is nearby in an adjacent sign.

This fine example of major New Zealand quakes gives an interesting glimpse of the rolling signature. All quakes except July 13, 1897, 7R Wanganui, New Zealand from 1897 until June 12, 1955 have a planet in Cancer, making it the most important cardinal and water sign. It then seems to disappear from the New Zealand signature. In terms of my sample, it definitely did not show up in major events through 1966. It has not shown up in my incomplete sample since. This runs up to March 1986.

A semi-exception is just as interesting. Cancer planets are in two of four Kermedec Islands events, two without.

A further example of the rolling signature occurs here. The New Zealand Cancer quakes also had a three sign sequence centered on Cancer. Gemini-Cancer-Leo-Cancer-Leo-Virgo, which at times included Gemini through Libra for four sign, also disappeared.

Planets moved into the eastern signs, becoming more frequent in Aquarius through Taurus. While varying sequences appear, they do not seem to be as regular as the Cancer sequence of earlier years.

Aries and Capricorn have some more importance in this post 1955 signature. Libra continues to appear.

In the 1960s, three sign sequences of planets in the eastern signs appeared, Aries-Taurus-Gemini, Pisces-Aries-Taurus, Aquarius-Pisces-Aries. My last is May 24, 1968, 7.0R, Inangahua, Aries Taurus Gemini.

This partial signature reappears in the March 1986 Bay of Plenty quake. I do not have the day, but am quite sure Aquarius-Pisces-Aries was in place.

Regarding the potential of a precise location signature, I'll note March 1986 Bay of Plenty, "largest in 20 years," and March 5, 1966, Gisborne to the southeast of the Bay of Plenty, which is probably the reference.

Note three planets in Pisces, including the Sun in both. 1986 has Venus in early Aries, vulcanism with a strong Sagittarius, fire and mutability.

In 1966, Mercury is in early Aries and Moon is in Leo for fire. Both of these planets are performing enhancement, here for the lack of cardinal and fire. Mercury in an enhancement position appears periodically in New Zealand quakes. The important conclusions from this are vulcanistic early cardinal, cardinal in Aries and the need for strong fire.

Mutability must be strong. 1986, two stellia, one in Sagittarius of fire, in 1966 a mutable T-square with Jupiter in Gemini. A slow planet in Scorpio, Pluto 1986, Neptune 1966 in a fixed T-square. From these two quakes I have a hypothesis for a Bay o Plenty signature.

I move backward December 10, 1958, 6.9R Bay of Plenty. Very strong mutability with a five planet stellium in Sagittarius including the Moon.

No cardinal or air. These then become secondary criteria. Fire very strong, with Moon confirming fire, 1966 Moon in Leo, 1986 Pluto in Scorpio, strong fixity with the planet in its own sign, 1966 and 1958 Mercury in fire 1958 Jupiter co-ruler of Pisces with Neptune ruler of Pisces in Scorpio.

Pisces, mutable, fixed, probably T-square, water, fire.

September 29, 1953, 7.1R Bay of Plenty. The signature seems to disappear. Mutability strong, strengthened by Moon and Jupiter which provide trine to the stellium—three stellia in four events, all three with trines, but different element, this trine, air and Libra. Sun with Neptune will add a Piscean overtone. Polarity positive. Pluto in Leo yields strong, fixity. Venus-Mars-Jupiter strong but not at first glance. Mercury in degree two of four.

November 22, 1914, 6.5-7R, East Cape Peninsula adjacent to the Bay of Plenty. An apparently different chart confirms a key location signature and its components, Neptune is in Leo. Please draw these charts in a zero Aries wheel using only degrees and zero GMT.

The core essence of the Bay of Plenty quake is:

- Sun Leo, Neptune Pisces in some way related (5 of 5).
- Pluto or Neptune in fixed signs (5 of 5).
- A stellium (4 of 5).

- Sun in stellium (4 of 4) all stellia.
- All stellia and/or Sun positions trined (4 of 4, 5 of 5); all stellia squared (4 of 4).
- Strong fixity (5 of 5).
- Variable planetary dispersion pattern, both layout and signs (5 of 5).
- Variable mutable layout (5 of 5).
- Extreme cardinal variation—no planets to stellia in Libra and Capricorn - all four signs covered in five quakes (5 of 5).
- Mutable squares (4 of 5) 1914 exact Venus, Mars conjunctions 7° Sagittarius.
- Fire trines (3 of 5) but then Pluto in Leo in 1953, Neptune in Leo 1914; fire fulfilled.
- Early cardinal degree (4 of 5).
- Mercury in degree (2 of 5), one unknown (86) probably about half the time, not bad.
- Mars in fire one water two, earth two mutable three fixed two; Mars not in air or cardinal.
- Separation, Venus-Mars-Jupiter interaction, moderate to strong.

Consider the above a fine-tuned location signature for the Bay of Plenty.

Random Sample

March 16, 1968	used R?	Strongest in 20 years Bay of Plenty
March 5, 1966	6.2R	Gishorne, southeast of Bay of Plenty
December 10, 1958	6.9R	Bay of Plenty
Setpember 29, 1953	7.1R	Bay of Plenty
October 7, 1914	7+R	East Bay of Plenty

Some general comments on New Zealand end this chapter:

- Much general information about the signatures has been included in the more specific sections of this chapter.
- Planets in Pisces fit all three major sections, North Island, South Island and Kermedec.
- While I'm sure I've missed recent Hawke Bay events in my sample, a new signature, without planets in Cancer (see earlier comments) must be derived.
- Stellia occur primarily in the building block signs - mutable, fixed, fire, water, earth. Thus Pisces, Aquarius, Scorpio, Leo, Sagittarius, Virgo.
- Stellia in Libra also occur. Libra is part of the Great Pacific Circuit Belt three-sign sequence, Virgo-Libra-Scorpio, which usually has planets in any two of these three signs.
- The disappearance or major diminishing of Cancer as a planetary position in the New Zealand signature, as well as other Great Pacific Circuit Belt locations, circa the mid-fifties is indicative of possible major seismic changes in the area - note the word ``changes'' not events. Whether or not this is true, new signatures must be derived. Thus minor events deserve notice.
- Usually all five building blocks are present (see 4). This with the required conditions of the three sign sequence. Begin here.
- In meeting the conditions of building blocks, planetary dispersion becomes a secondary factor and the layout of the New Zealand quake charts vary considerably.
- The land mass is of sufficient size that an attempt should be made at location isolation with New Zealand proper, as I attempted for the Bay of Plenty.

The text of this chapter already includes most of the randomly collected samples.

58

The Signature of Chile

We move across the Pacific to the coast of South America and its more southerly country, Chile, to continue examining events of the Grand Pacific Circuit Belt. The Pacific Cross Belt has curved slightly northward as it passed beneath Polynesia, where, by and large, it causes few problems, though it has divided into two belts emerging at Central America. Passing beneath it, these divisions more or less bracket Guatemala and El Salvador as they enter the Caribbean. Here the belt loses its Pacific prefix and is known simply as the Great Central Belt. It crosses the Atlantic into Africa near Algeria and Europe, near northern Spain. Its continuation and branches will be picked up later.

The Great Pacific Circuit Belt probably hits Chile just north of whatever area is the most southerly active location. Another division forms and two belts run under the continent and one in the sea. At Central America, one under the land, two under the sa. They are parallel and do not run far into the continent, their influences usually not extending past the Andes.

Since Chile, a ribbon of a country, covers 35° of southern latitude, we may infer the possibility of specific location signatures within the country. Chile also utilizes the building blocks of the Great Pacific Circuit Belt, mutability, fixity, fire, water, earth. Cardinal varies widely, but often a planet in early cardinal, vulcanism. Libra appears in half the sample. Earth is at extremes, 15 events showing three grand trine earth events and one with no earth.

Beginning to deal with the above, August 8, 1987, 6.8R, centered on the Chile-Peru border (this event should be compared to Peru) has a grand trine fire with seven planets including a Sun-Mercury-Venus-Mars stellium in Leo (fire and fixity), and Jupiter in Aries with Saturn and Uranus in Sagittarius. The Moon in Aquarius enhances air and forms a fixed T-square. Water is deceptively strong. Pluto in its own sign Scorpio. Neptune in earth and early cardinal (vulcanism).

Three grand trine earth events occur:

May 21, 1960	8.9R	Concepcion "6:00 a.m."
January 25, 1939	? (strong)	Chillan, Chile
December 1, 1928	8.3R	Chile

Chillan is near Concepcion, but more inland. I suspect the epicenter of December 1, 1928 is somewhere near this area, but do not know.

Each event is with its variations, May 22, 1960, one of the great events of the century, variously estimated at 8.9R to 8.4R.

Along with GTE, it has a fixed T-square and fire trines. Neptune in Scorpio supplies water, Sun and Mercury and Gemini, air and mutability. Mars and Jupiter in early cardinal—vulcanism. Mercury one degree earlier than Neptune. Ann E. Parker used this as an example, noting its fulfillment of eclipse rules and geodetic degrees.

January 25, 1939, R?, Chillan, besides GTE it has a fixed T-square and GTF. It is unusual among quake charts for its lack of conjunctions, with only the Moon as a second planet in a sign. I'm not sure whether its in late Pisces or early Aries. However, without it both fire and water trines still exist. If the Moon is in early Aries, the signature of vulcanism is present, Mercury, one degree more than Venus.

December 1, 1928, besides GTE has a Cancer stellium of Mars, Pluto, Moon, water and cardinal. This is part of cardinal T-square and Cancer/Capricorn is the ``universal'' axis. Here Cancer is the head of the kite. Mars and Uranus early cardinal for vulcanism. Mercury not in degree.

June 17, 1971, R? strong, Chile Argentina border, which simply means under the Andes, has grand trine air. An anomaly here is the complete absence of water.

Uranus is stationary direct in vulcanistic 9° Libra, forming air trines to Gemini with Venus, Mercury and Sun. Mercury one degree higher than Mars.

Three weeks later, July 9, 1971, 7.7R, known as ILLAPEL Chile near Valparaiso, this approximately 10 degrees north of the grand trine earth area of Concepcion, this is another grand trine air, but with strong water, and a cardinal T-square formed by lunar enhancement in Capricorn, earth. Early cardinal vulcanism placements with Venus and Uranus.

November 11, 1928, 8.4R, Attacama, a GTW event, unusual with no earth. Also the grand trine was not accessed (no oppositions to its points, the kite head). Other than no earth, all Great Pacific Circuit Belt building blocks were in place.

Chile is definitely a grand trine location.

The Great Pacific Circuit Belt sequence, Virgo-Libra-Scorpio is present with usually any two signs with planets, then any one sign. Three signs with or without planets is rare.

Fixity is alive and well, occurring in any combination of square or T-square. Rare, the grand cross fixed (one) or the fixed stellium (two), one each in Leo and Scorpio. Of interest in the fixed signs is the tenancy of Aquarius, often rare in other Grand Pacific Circuit Belt locations. Appearing in the sample about half the time, it has Sun, Moon, Mars, Jupiter, usually alone. Note Sun-Mars-Jupiter are all fire and the Moon enhancement.

Mercury in degree is significantly better than average, appearing three times in the degree of Jupiter and the other usual variations, Venus, Mars, and the slow planets. Low cardinal—vulcanism 13 out of 14.

The Moon's Nodes are usually fixed or mutable. I have reason to believe the fewest major events occur when the Nodes are cardinal (see The Moon's Nodes). While I have not followed through on that observation in all of the signatures, I did notice it here.

Regarding the Valparaiso signature, I have two examples, July 9, 1971 and November 20, 1822, I'll just note the common signs as a point of beginning, Gemini, Scorpio, Sagittarius, Capricorn and Aquarius. Pluto in Pisces 1822, Virgo 1971. A third event March 3, 1985, 7.4R, Santiago has no Gemini. In the overall Chile sample, a planet is in Pisces two-thirds of the time.

How would I assign a Chilean event to the Concepcion area—earth emphasis and a planet in Cancer, but I'd want more events to examine.

I'll close with perhaps the largest event of the 20th century, January 31, 1906, 9R, Chile. This is the largest event instrumentally recorded according to *The Guinness Book of Records*. From the great era of quakes, it has Uranus at 6° Capricorn opposing Neptune at 8° Cancer. All planets to the east (Aquarius through Gemini, but no Aries—that is a bowl). Fixed and mutable squares, air, water, and earth trines, no great aspect complexes, just a simple bowl (180°) with interlocking squares and trines. It is an unusual planetary dispersion for Chile, but often occurs in California events.

Random Sample with Grand Trines (GT)

August 8, 1987	6.8R	Chile Peru Border—GTF
September 26, 1985	5+R	Chile (bowl)
March 3, 1985	7.4R	Santiago GTF
July 9, 1971	7.7R	ILLAPEL (Valparaiso) GTA
June 17, 1971	R? Strong	Chile Argentine Border GTA
March 28, 1965	7.5R	Chile
May 21, 1960	8.9R	Concepcion GTE
January 25, 1939	R? Strong	Chillan GTE Grand Cross Fixed
December 1, 1928	8.3R	Chile GTE
November 11, 1922	8.4R	Atalama GTW
August 17, 1906	8.6R	Chile stellium Cancer and Leo (8.3R same day in Aleutians)
January 31, 1906	9R	Chile
February 20, 1835	R? Strong	Chile GTA
November 20, 1822	R? Strong	Chile

59

The Signature of Peru

Peru lies north of Chile on the Pacific coast of South America. The divisions of the Grand Pacific Circuit Belt continue beneath Peru as in Chile (see The Signature of Chile). A similarity of signatures would be the guess, but the possibility of variations would be present.

The classic building blocks of the Grand Pacific Circuit Belt continue to be present. Those are fire-water, mutable-fixed, with variable earth and cardinality. The sequence Virgo-Libra-Scorpio is present, usually one or two signs, more seldom three, seldom none.

In these three signs a stellium appears most frequently in Libra. At this time the final position of the Moon may be Aries or Gemini.

The Sun may prefer Libra, Gemini, Leo and Sagittarius, then Taurus and Scorpio, seldom Aquarius and Virgo. The Sun seldom in Virgo is an isolating factor along the Circuit Belt.

Particular planetary relationships may be Jupiter-Pluto and Venus-Pluto as well as possible slow planet sequence Jupiter, Saturn, Uranus, obvious but not exact, and clearly showing accumulated stress (separation).

In a major quake, Venus and Jupiter usually form some aspect as energizers. The relationship, Venus to Pluto, here may be part of the earlier solar event signature. In this area of vulcanism (directly beneath the location as well as offshore) very early cardinal planets of 0° to 4° are present frequently (solar event, earth vulcanism, quake).

As in most Grand Pacific Circuit Belt events, six or seven occupied signs and most often two with more than one planet. Stellia are centered around the Sun and two slow planets in a sign.

The Sun and Mars may be together by sign, usually cardinal. They also are noted as square by cardinal signs, trine by water and one sign apart.

Mercury is good by degree, probably more than half the time, usually with the slow planets, especially Uranus, which is preponderant. If not in degree, there may be a strong conventional aspect to Uranus, e.g. square, but several degrees off partile either way. In the random sample, Mars, Saturn, Neptune and Pluto also show in the degree of Mercury.

Venus performs like a textbook example; good Venus-Mars-Jupiter including conjunctions with good separation and often an approaching major aspect or the exact 15° type indicating new infusion of energy into the system. Venus also appears in very early cardinal and involved with Pluto, here corroborative of a quake probably shortly after a major solar event.

Grand trines occur in earth and water. The axis Cancer Capricorn—a ``universal'' indicator, while rare, shows up with other factors present.

Summation, GTE, Libra stellium, Mercury with Uranus, Sun with Mars. Very strong Venus functions. The indication of a quick response to solar events and new vulcanism shown by 0° to 4° cardinal and Venus-Pluto. Jupiter-Saturn-Uranus may form a slow planet complex.

Random Sample with Grand Trines

May 29, 1990	5.8R	400 miles northeast of Lima GTW; Moon in Virgo on May 30 as well as Mars into 0° Aries creating GTE as GTW vanished. Seismic activity under under this GTE: 5-30, Romania, 6.5R; 5-31, Mexico 6.1R; 5-31, Mexico, a strong aftershock; 5-31, Peru, dozens of aftershocks; 5-31, quake off coast of Japan felt in Tokyo.
May 10, 1990	5.8R	400 miles Northeast of Lima GTW
February 5, 1988	6.6R	Northern Peru
October 9-10, 1987	3.4-4.8R	Three quakes Peru in three locations; Mars just into 0° Libra. Venus fully separated, Moon-Uranus; Sun involved in strong midpoint. A surge in vulcanism?
April 5, 1986	R?	Cuzco
August 2, 1985	5.7R	Chimbote, west coast seven fixed planets in T-square, Neptune 0° Capricorn, Mercury stationary direct, this often present at beginning vulcanism, makes an exact trine to Uranus (same degree).
October 3, 1974	7.3R	Peru GTW
December 9, 1970	?	Peru Ecuador Border GTE
May 31, 1970	7R+	Yungay, Northern Peru, CHIMBOTE
October 1, 1969	?	Huancayo
August 31, 1961	7.2R	Peru Brazil Border
November 20, 1960	?	Off Coast, Tsunami
May 21, 1950	?	Cuzco (damage to the pyramid at Sascachuan revealed its engineering)
November 10, 1946	7.3R	ANCASH
May 24, 1940	8.4R	Peru
December 18, 1921	7.9R	Peru

60

The Signature of Ecuador and Colombia

Ecuador lies north of Peru and Colombia north of it. My random sample is small but clearly shows itself with Grand Pacific Circuit Belt building blocks, fire, water, mutable, fixed, varying cardinal and the Virgo-Libra-Scorpio sequence, this last having planets in all three signs frequently, then two, then one. Only one example: January 31, 1906, 8.9R, Colombia. Ecuador has no planets in any of these signs.

Colombia at more or less the latitude of Medellin, may come under the influence of the Great Central Cross Belt (Atlantic name of the Pacific Cross Belt) which in two divisions passes under northern Costa Rica and northern Nicaragua as it enters the Caribbean Sea.

On September 27, 1987, a landslide following heavy rains occurred in Ecuador. I cannot trace a relationship except to surmise there may have been some tremors preceding September 27, 1987. Both charts are clearly Great Pacific Circuit Belt types.

On October 18, 1992, a 7.2 event lasting two minutes and the worst Colombia quake since December 12, 1979 occurred 185 miles northwest of Bogota, or slightly south of Medellin by latitude. Having just about circumscribed the Ring of Fire, and the Great Pacific Circuit Belt, I'm probably almost alone in knowing how rare the absence of both fire and mutable is.

The vulcanism behind this wake was massive, Jupiter 1° Libra, 75° Mars, Moon last over Saturn, Saturn stationary direct, Mercury, Mars-Saturn, vulcanism, Venus recently conjunct Pluto. Eight days earlier Jupiter entered Libra, the day after Venus was conjunct Pluto. Any reader with up-to-date records may check on solar conditions around this time (October 10-11, 1992).

Mercury is in the degree of Neptune. Separation excellent. Of note is tightening of aspects by midpoints, which deserves research by randomness and location history.

Finally I note January 31, 1906, 8.9R. This is the same quake noted in Chile, there at 9.0R. Obviously it was felt in Peru. Here it is noted as Columbia-Ecuador. Again this super event is a near perfect bowl and extremely well integrated. The Moon in Aries supplies fire and completes a cardinal T-square. Mercury at 26° Capricorn and Jupiter at 26° Taurus form a midpoint at Mars, 26o Pisces. In the previous week the Moon passed over all trigger planets by conjunction, that is Uranus, Mercury, Saturn, Mars. This too is unusual.

61

The Signature of Central America

Central America may pose interesting problems for the forecaster. This is the crossroads of the Belts. The Great Pacific Circuit Belt in one division runs directly under all Central America, including Mexico. A further division of this belt urns under Baja, California. Two divisions of the Great Pacific run parallel to each other and the overall Central American coastline approximately 200 and 400 miles offshore in the Pacific.

The northern division of the Great Pacific Cross Belt cuts across the two offshore divisions of the Great Pacific and enters Central America near the Mexico/Guatemala border. It again divides under the Yucatan Peninsula and Cuba. This division continues on through Haiti and the Dominican Republic to Puerto Rico and the northern Caribbean Islands.

The southern division of the Great Pacific Cross Belt divides just before the outermost division of the Great Pacific Circuit Belt, the upper division, subdividing on the other side of the middle vision of the Great Pacific Circuit Belt. These last divisions affect El Salvador and Honduras with the northern subdivision and Nicaragua with the southern subdivision. These two subdivisions enter Jamaica and rejoin their division, and in rejoining, create an eye shape. They continue on through the Caribbean slightly north of center. Meanwhile, where the southern division of the Great Pacific Cross Belt divided just west of the most offshore Pacific Great Circuit Belt, this lower section enters Central America more or less on the Costa Rica/Nicaragua border. This continues on through the Caribbean Sea and south of Haiti/Dominican Republic is rejoined by its own division. Thus, east of Haiti/Dominican Republic, the Great Pacific Central Belt is once again in two main divisions, one passing near the northern east to west part of the Caribbean chain, and the southern division through the middle of the north to south Caribbean islands. Obviously the southern division is more active since this involves the vulcanistically active Caribbean Islands of Guadeloupe, Martinique and St. Vincent. When these experience another active phase, the last a minor one occurring spasmodically from 1976 into 1978, we might infer some activity, or a lack of it, for Guatemala, Honduras, El Salvador,k Nicaragua and Costa Rica.

Note that Panama, with no central belt involvement, is without major vulcanism and is seismically more quiet than its neighbors. Note also that the Yucatan Peninsula, under the influence of the northern division of the Cross Belt, is also relatively quiet. Again it is this division that affects Cuba, Jamaica, Haiti, Dominican Republic, Puerto Rico and the northern Caribbean Islands, all of which are volcanically dormant.

Since I've elected to follow through with the random sample, which on review came up short, I took the roundabout means of closely assessing the belts.

One thing is clear. My overall Central American sample follows the overall signature of the Great Pacific Circuit Belt, indicating that it is more active than the Cross Belt.

That the Great Pacific Circuit Belt is more active is immediately confirmed by Mexico, where Mexico City, like several other cities (especially Ankara, Turkey; Tbilisi Georgia, FSU; and Tokyo, Japan) has significant seismic events at several year intervals.

Further proof of the strong influence of the Circuit Belt in Central American quakes is August 6, 1942, 8.3R, Guatemala. As I've noted elsewhere, a stellium may take the place of an aspect complex. Here the planets are distributed over 114° showing fully the bare bones of the Great Pacific Circuit Belt signature.

Overall in the Central American events, there is wide variation in fixity. Venus-Mars-Jupiter may be an indicator.

This is also clearly a grand trine water area and usually this has a Capricorn head. Grand trine water, Cancer/Capricorn, the universal signature here combined.

Of course some Grand Pacific Circuit Belt influences must be present—see previous chapters, but is there an isolating factor here? There appears to be some:

- A bunching of planets usually in four signs, usually Virgo through Pisces.
- Grand trine water relatively common and with Capricorn head.
- Planets often in Capricorn and Pisces.
- Usually cardinal T-squares and they seem more prominent than the mutable in a given chart.
- Early cardinal (vulcanism).
- Fixed emphasis varies widely.
- Jupiter has a cardinal preference.

Of most interest is subtle blurring of the Great Pacific Circuit Belt signature and the fact that the blurring is visible in such a small sample.

Random Sample

April 22, 1991	7.4R	Limon, Costa Rica
May 9, 1990	Swarms	Costa Rica GTW
March 25, 1990	5.5+6/9R	Epicenter 60 miles west of San Jose, Costa Rica; GTW
December 20, 1904	8.3R	Costa Rica—GTA
January 15, 1987	4R, 3R	San Salvador
April 3, 1990	6.5R	60 miles east of Managua, Nicaragua in Pacific
October 10, 1986	R	El Salvador
November 16, 1987	6.1R	Sea 50 miles off Nicaragua, felt in El Salvador
April 19, 1902	? Large	Central America—Grand Cross Mutable
December 23, 1972	7.5R	Managua, Nicaragua severely damaged. All slow planets integrate, Jupiter, Saturn-Uranus, then Neptune and Pluto with Sun. This one has Grand Pacific Circuit Belt signature.

62

The Signature of Mexico

Just above the Yucatan Peninsula the inner division of the Great Pacific Circuit Belt divides again. This easternmost division runs up through Mexico, entering the United States more or less near the Texas/New Mexico border. It runs north to Montana and may be said to define the limits of seismic activity in the western United States.

Mexico City is bracketed by this division. The middle Great Pacific Circuit Belt division as noted in The Central American Signature, runs close to the Pacific shoreline into the Gulf of California, which separates Baja, California from Mexico. The outer division of the Great Pacific Circuit Belt as noted in The Central America Signature divides off Guadalajara, Mexico, one division running under Baja, California, the other closely paralleling the Pacific coast of North America. It ends at Kodiak Island. Its last section is presently relatively quiet.

In a slight digression, Yellowstone National Park is influenced by the middle division (see Central America Signature) of the Great Pacific Circuit Belt, which cuts across both divisions of the inner belt division, which runs under all Central America. Clearly the venting action of Yellowstone is responsible in part for the EM calm of most of Canada. Yellowstone functions as a fumarole—a gas release system at the extreme end of vulcanistic activity in a belt.

In Mexico, earthquakes mean one thing: Mexico City, a mega-metropolis, is perhaps the most highly populated on earth. Not only is it bracketed by a belt division, it is built on filled earth of super seismic conductivity. The 8.1R quake of September 19, 1985 which caused massive destruction, took place off shore in the Pacific, its epicenter 250 miles from Mexico City. It passed inland through a sparsely populated region, causing little note, even geologically.

Mexico is influenced by three Great Pacific Circuit Belt Divisions, two under it and one close to the Pacific coast. These are in fact the eastern and middle divisions as noted in The Central America Signature. Quakes in Mexico show the qualities of the Great Pacific Circuit Belt events, mutable, fixed fire, water, some cardinal, air most usually through Libra, and the Virgo-Libra-Scorpio sequence. There is all the variety and sameness noted elsewhere in the Great Pacific Circuit Belt locations.

But Mexico is especially important. Mexico City is a seismic magnet due to its placement by the belts and its geological properties of seismic conductivity; its filled land creates deadly activity.

Can we be more precise? Fortunately I believe the answer is yes. The following is derived from the Mexico City quakes in the sample.

- There may be four pairs of planets by signs. If not, then two stellia, or Grand Trine Water.
- Planets occur in both Leo and Virgo. The only exception is the Grand Trine Water event.
- Pisces may be the substitute sign of importance.
- A Leo stellium is also noteworthy.
- Cardinal activity is standard for the GPCB, including at least one planet in early cardinal.
- The two and a half year transit of Saturn through Pisces which will occur with Pluto in Scorpio may significantly increase EM potential for Mexico when:
- Cancer is strongly transited (GTW).
- When planets are in both Leo and Virgo—in the immediate future only the fast planets, Sun through Mars.
- When a stellium in Leo occurs; again only fast planets in the near future.
- Increased activity in Colombia and Central America, in California and Yellowstone National Park, may constitute safety valves. This is especially true of Colombia and Yellowstone, this surely on the GPCB division that brackets Mexico City.
- Mercury in degree of Saturn 1985 Neptune 1949.
- In the general Mexican quake, Mercury relates often to Saturn in one way or another, approaching trine, conjunction, separating conjunction Mercury Saturn is a vulcanism indicator, in particular if involved with Mars.
- An event may occur just before the degree of Mercury reaches the planet in question (Mercury approaching). Various planets may fall in degree of Mercury in both the Mexico and Mexico City event.
- The September 1993 minor event felt in Mexico City may be premonitory.

Random Sample

May 31, 1990	6.1R	Epicenter 180 miles west of Mexico City
May 30		Romania 6.5R
May 31		Aftershocks Romania
May 31	6R+	Off Japan, note GTW
February 8, 1988	6R	Mexico
February 8-9		Caribbean minor
February 2-5		Northern Peru minor
May 5, 1986	5.4R	Mexico City
May 5		Turkey
May 4		Mt. St. Helen tremors
November 21, 1985	Tremors	Mexico City, Central America
November 21		Venting; rumbling in two Colombian volcanoes
October 29, 1985	5.7R	Mexico City
October 29, 1985		Puerto Rico
October 30, 1985		Challis, Idaho
October 20, 1985	4.3R	Mexico City
October 19, 1985		New Rochelle, New York, largest tremor in 30 years
September 28, 1985	5+R aftershock	Mexico City

September 20, 1985	Quake #2 7.5R	Mexico City, 7:37 p.m. CST
September 19, 1985	8.1R	Mexico City, the big one, 7:18 a.m. CST
July 14, 1984	5R	Mexico City, 3:04 p.m. CST
October 24, 1980	6.7R	Oaxaca
March 14, 1979	7.9R	Mexico City GTW and no Leo planet
November 29, 1978	7.9R	Mexico City
August 28, 1978	7R	Centered in Pueblo, Mexico
January 30, 1973	7.8R	Manzanilla and Colombia
July 28, 1957	7.8R	Guerrero and Mexico City, strong Leo stellium
July 30, 1949	7+R	Mexico City. Considered the most violent of the century prior to the 1985 event, its relatively small size corroborates the geological dangers and nuances of Mexico City.
June 3, 1932	8.1R	Central Mexico
April 15, 1907	8.3R	Guerrero, Mexico
January 14, 1903	8.3R	Guerrero, Mexico

63

The Signature of California

The Pacific Ocean, the Ring of Fire and Churchward's Great Pacific Circuit Belt have been almost circumnavigated. We began in Alaska and have reached California. Alaska was a point to begin, both geographically, geologically and alphabetically. The hands-on, rather eyes-on, examination of the entire sample of Pacific quakes yielded new insights with and without reference ot the belts. Recapitulating, there is a Great Pacific Circuit Belt general signature throughout the Pacific and this will apply to California.

Location nuances may appear in some of the events. There were indications of some rolling signature changes in the late 1950s. I felt that attention to the belt hypothesis was worthwhile. It gives a horizontal dimension to the matter of EM, not just the straight vertical general concept, and finally it at least raises the question of a propellant force and its nature in vulcanism.

The continuity of signature also infers the importance of noting events, major and minor adjacent to a location, or the absence of same.

Western North America is affected by five divisions of the Great Pacific Circuit Belt, that is three main divisions and two further divisions. In coming up the Pacific coast of South and Central America, I have used the term divisions, as did Churchward, to emphasize the parallel nature of their direction, as opposed to branches, more or less right angled.

Beginning with the three main divisions we start form the Pacific Ocean or western side. The western division skirts the coast of Baja, California. Hitting California proper, it clearly equates to the San Andreas Fault and follows through to the area of Yakima, Washington.

The middle main division runs under the Gulf of California between Baja, California and Mexico and enters beneath the continent again more or less at Hermisillo, Mexico, moving on to Yuma, Arizona, then into Nevada and Idaho. Yellowstone National Park is its fumarole complex. It may affect the California-Nevada events.

The third or eastern division enters the Untied States near the Arizona-New Mexico border, stays well to the east in Arizona, goes through the middle of Nevada and Idaho, moving on to the Spokane, Washington area. This is the belt that brackets Mexico City and the eastern subdivision enters the United States in line with Roswell, New Mexico and passes through Colorado and Wyoming. It too uses Yellowstone as a fumarole.

This covers the western United States as a quake and volcano area. The eastern United States is covered by the Appalachian Belt. Churchward notes it as beginning somewhere up the Mississippi which it follows to Lake Erie and Ontario, exiting the St. Lawrence Sea Way. The main branch hits the south of Greenland where we'll leave it for now. A division near Richmond, Virginia skirts the coast of the eastern United States, rejoining the main division at the southern tip of Greenland, again making an oval eye shape as noted in reference to the Great Cross Belt in the Caribbean.

Returning to California proper, it is clearly Great Pacific Circuit Belt signature, but with its own distinctions. Again the building blocks of this signature are mutable-fixed, some cardinal-fire and water strong, air and earth less accentuated Libra in air most important being also cardinal and part of the Virgo-Libra-Scorpio sequence. California is an important place. Major events at Los Angeles, San Francisco or a nuclear power plant would be devastating.

Fortunately I did come up with some observations and I'll move directly to them. Again the sample is random and the excellent sample of minor events covering ten years. It will prove valuable in estimating release and premonitory events. It also clearly notes the influence of the double universal grand trine water and Cancer-Capricorn axis not only in major, but also minor events. Here it may be seen as release event, blowing the fuse, instead of burning out the circuit, as it were. Grand trine water events will be noted in the sample, GTW.

- The California events love a stellium or two. The stellium may appear in any sign, but especially note Gemini through Capricorn and then Pisces.
- Pisces is important, both as an indicator sign and a water sign. The transit of Saturn in Pisces which begins in 1994 with the simultaneous transit of Jupiter in Scorpio with Pluto indicates an increase in California seismic energy, hopefully released in minor events. A glance at the ephemeris shows a planet in Cancer completing the grand trine water circuit from late May through September. At other times, the Moon in Cancer two and a half days per month will function. The roughest of calculations would indicate a 10 times increment of grand trine water energy by time, not examining the nuances of the Cancer planets.
- The Sierra region may be more sensitive to New Moon events, the San Andreas to Full Moon events. I read somewhere, unfortunately not noting the source, that parallel fault systems (slip faults) may be more sensitive to the Full Moon.
- California is sensitive to placements in Pisces.
- Ditto all water grand trines, which usually have a Capricorn head. This Capricorn head will be automatically in place for the next several years until Neptune leaves Capricorn on January 29, 1998.
- Venus-Mars-Jupiter integration is strong, by aspect and/or separation.
- Mercury is often in degree, of any of the planets. The slow planets are, as usual, noteworthy. Mercury also appears frequently in the degree of Venus, sometimes in conjunction.
- The midpoints of the Sun-Mer-

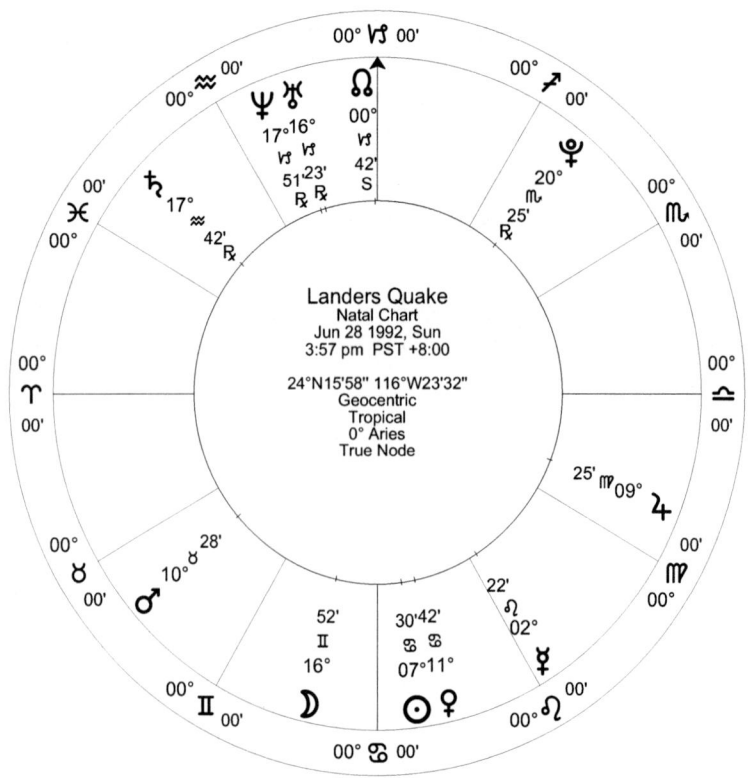

170

cury-Jupiter triad of initiatory energizers will often supply a missing Mercury degree.
- Like all Pacific Great Circuit Belt locations, the planetary dispersion varies widely as does the placement of fixed planets or fixed complexes.
- Finally, can anything be said about the great California quake? Fortunately, there are gleanings.

Using just four quakes the following may be noted:

June 28, 1992	7.4R	Landers, California
March 10, 1933	6.3R	Long Beach, California
April 18, 1906	8.3R	San Francisco, California
January 8, 1857	8R	Los Angeles, California

- A planet in Aquarius, all four.
- A planet in Cancer, all four.
- Strong Pisces, 1933, 1906, 1857.
- Venus-Mars-Jupiter interaction strong, all four.
- Venus conjunct Mars, 1906, 1857.
- Moon past Mars, conjunct Mars 1992, 1933.
- Moon past Uranus one sign+, 1906, 1857.
- Some interaction among Uranus-Neptune and Sun-Saturn.
- Splay dispersion, 1992, 1933.
- Cancer Capricorn bowl, 1906, 1857.
- If I had to pick a Mercury degree, I'd note that of Neptune (1906) but the Mercury degree varies.
- On May 21, 1960 a superquake of 8.9R hit the Pacific coast of South America centered in Chile. This was a splay layout with a grand trine earth, and Moon over Mars 12 hours earlier. California 1992 was also a GTE and California 1933 had a strong Virgo stellium. On January 31, 1906 the largest quake recorded on the Richter scale estimated at 9.0R and so noted in *The Guiness Book of Records*, was a cardinal bowl, much like the upcoming San Franicsco 1906, but without Aries planets. Again Moon last over Mars, Mercury in degree of Jupiter.
- All six events, California and Chile, had a planet in early cardinal.

Over the years I've read and noted many elaborate attempts at predicting the next big one in California. Somehow I feel some have missed the boat, often by including after-the-fact perspective involving angles or complicated procedures.

In fact, the "bowls" above (Peru 1906, California 1906, and California 1857) are simple, forthright and somewhat scary, precisely because of the deceptive simplicity of planetary dispersion.

Lunar factors, noted here in a lump, are interesting but inconclusive at 2° Gemini, 2° Virgo, 1° Taurus, 1° Aquarius (California, enhancement), with two early, two middle, two late (California) Moon last over Mars three, approaching 1° Mars one, last over Uranus two.

Sun Moon angles are totally inconclusive two last quarter 1992, 1906, two gibbous 1933, 1857, Chile 1960 last quarter, Chile 1906 first quarter. Lastly, to muddy the ground, clearly the Moon's Nodes are Chile 1960, Virgo; Chile 1906, Leo; California 1992, Capricorn, 1933, Virgo, 1906, Leo, 1857, Aries.

I have not noted the eclipses in most of this work. One has to draw a limit, but for the interest in and importance of the superquake and the California superquake in particulate we note:

- Chile, 1960, Mars in degree of past solar eclipse February 27, 1960, 6° Aries.
- Chile 1906, Uranus and Venus in degree of solar eclipse August 30, 1905, 6° Virgo. Uranus a trigger.
- California 1992, South Node 0° Cancer, Sun 7° Cancer, Mars/Jupiter, 9° Cancer, Venus 11° Cancer. On

June 30 a solar eclipse at 8° Cancer (Ann E. Parker notes future eclipses).
- California 1933, solar eclipse February 24, 1933 at 5° Pisces, Mars at quake time at 7° Pisces, Moon at 6° Pisces, and this with upcoming lunar eclipse March 12, 1933 at 21° Virgo. Uranus at the event was at 21° Aries.
- California 1906. This is not as clear but on February 23, 1906 a solar eclipse occurred at 3° Pisces with Saturn at 5° Pisces. Also of interest in the event is Mercury stationary direct in the degree of Neptune forming a perfect T-square for the Uranus 8° Capricorn (separated) opposition Neptune 7° Cancer. Mercury is a trigger. Note Uranus stationary direct September 30, 1993, India, 6.4R.
- California 1857. On November 29, 1956, a solar eclipse occurred at 6° Libra. While the quake data seems inconclusive, note Chile 1960, 6° Aries.

Eclipse data will prove important and I direct the reader to the work of Ann E. Parker (see bibliography). Her quake and forecast perspectives emphasize geodetic degrees and eclipses and I can do no better than defer to her in this area. It constitutes a system in its own right, which ultimately can only be complementary to any integrated astro-geological forecast process.

This is an unending process, so as I wrote this I noted:

- 29° Aquarius: California 1857, Venus; California 1906, Moon
- 21/22° Taurus: California 1857, Uranus; California 1906, Mars
- 6/7° Aries: California 1933, Mercury; California 1906, Mercury
- 7° Cancer: California 1992, Sun; California 1906, Neptune
- 8/9° Virgo: California 1992, Jupiter; California 1933, Neptune

Moving to the two superquakes of Chile:

- 7° Aries: Chile 1960, Mars
- 21° Taurus: Chile 1960, Venus
- In Chile 1906 the previous eclipse (March 6, 1905 at 14° Pisces) showed: 9° Virgo, North Node; and 21° Taurus, Mars in opposition at 21° Scorpio

The automatic note of California events by media afforded an excellent chance to collect a random sample of minor events. What became evident rather quickly was not only the grand trine water event of major proportion but also the grand trine water dispersion pattern acting in minor events. Whether in a premonitory event or aftershock, it is a release event. It will also prove a factor in assessing simultaneous events, for there is a twist to the conventionally held wisdom of the geological and astrological establishments (see Appendix I).

The second insight provided by access to a large sample of moderate events was the possibility of isolating a precise geographic location signature.

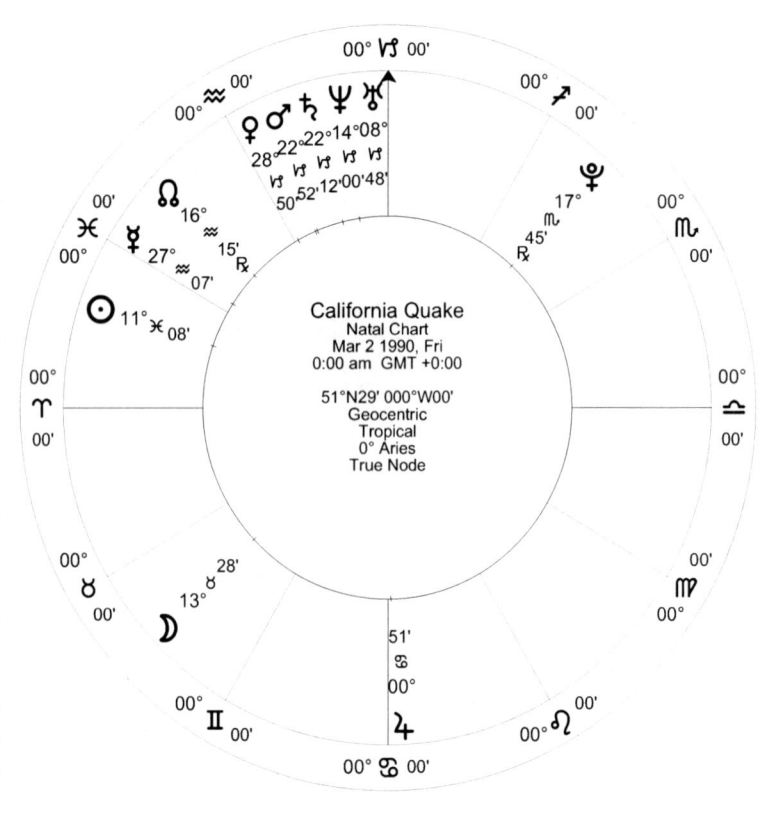

From the Earthquake Epicenter Map of California, Magnitude 5 and Greater Earthquakes, 1900-1974, I selected a random point south of Bakersfield, since it provided a suitable sample. The sample was of twenty quakes, half of them occurring between July 21 and July 25, 1952. I threw out the extras. The Moon was in late Cancer at the beginning of the sequence, in Leo in most events and on July 25 in Virgo. Briefly about 10, five plus events occurred at this time so I've chosen it as the main quake to refer to and a point to begin my signature search.

The first event, 7.7R, occurred at 11:52 a.m. on July 21, 1952 at 35N, 119W. A bowl with Mars in Scorpio, opposite Jupiter in Taurus, square a Leo stellium, Venus-Pluto-Mercury. Venus-Mars-Jupiter thus form a T-square, but relative to each other they are still approaching. According to the hypothesis of planetary separation, energy was still building, and this may explain the significant number of aftershocks.

This showed Uranus, Moon and Sun in Cancer with Moon over Uranus to Mars (15° type aspect). The Moon was thus classically involved with the heavy triggers. Sun/Jupiter gives the Mercury degree—(midpoints of the primary energy triad).

Saturn and Neptune were in Libra, Saturn at 9° Libra for early cardinal. Planets in Libra and Scorpio are part of the Great Pacific Circuit Belt signature Virgo-Libra-Scorpio. The GPCB signature is strongly built except for the absence of mutability. This is a wild card factor.

After 1919, a rolling signature factor took effect. There are always planets in Leo and Scorpio, however varied other fixed factors are. Water is usually strong with three to four planets, sometimes in stellium or trine, but no GTW. No planet ever appeared in Aries in the sample which must be viewed as pretty much complete.

The Mercury degree is most often found as a midpoint of the primary energy triad Sun-Mercury-Jupiter. There is a Saturn-Uranus connection, either Saturn approaching in terms of a classic aspect (30°) or within two to three degrees separating or approaching in the weather aspect (15°).

Mutability is never strong, though it varies. Virgo-Pisces is not as freqent a one would guess and Pisces alone does not appear. Planets in both Virgo and Pisces (2X) involve the Sun and Moon both once. Lunar enhancment may occur in Virgo.

The Grand Trine Water does not appear but grand trine earth and grand trine air do. The late degrees (24° on) of Capricorn and Cancer may have significance. Planets may or may not be in early cardinal. Whereupon we do have a Bakersfield signature.

Regarding the single large event, here used as a benchmark in beginning to search for an extremely local location signature, it maintained certain parts of the Great California Event; the bowl shape, Uranus and Neptune in cardinal signs as well as a very significant Venus-Mars-Jupiter, here the T-square itself.

The catalogue of events greater than 5R just south of Bakersfield at approximately 35 north and 119 west between 1900 and 1974 follows. Here it is the location that was randomly picked. It is worth noting that the astrological establishment has itself focused on major events and time. This is respectively a reflection of data circumstance and habit. The hypothesis to be tested is the consecutive collection of a particular location's events in order to determine if an extremely local signature can be noted. See Appendix B for San Francisco.

The implications of the Bakersfield sample are several.

- A signature for a specific location is a clear possibility.
- The geographic limits of the signature may be tested by moving outward from the chosen test location, here for example 35N, 119W.
- Knowing by definition that a very local signature must end in geographic terms, I would here hypothesize the cross faults more or less east and west as the probable points of signature change.
- The greater California quakes would have some overall similarities.

- The California signature must show indications of its GPCB origins.
- The grand trine water, even of moderate size, may be a release event in some locations, but not in others that are conventionally thought of as the same location, e.g. California.
- The charting of even lesser events (4R) held to an exact coordinate limit may aid even more in isolating a well-defined signature.
- The integration of location history and present geological indicators would be joined with astrology in both analysis and forecasts.

Bakersfield Random Sample

Date	Magnitude	Details
March 1, 1963	5.0R	00:25 Grand Cross Fixed, GTE
Novwember 15, 1961	5.0R	05:38
May 23, 1954	5.1R	23:52 GTA
January 27, 1954	5.0R	14:19 GTA
January 12, 1954	5.9R	23:23
July 25, 1952	5.0R	13:13
	5.7R	19:43
	5.7R	19:09
July 23, 1952	5.2R	18:31
	5.7R	13:17
	5.4R	07:53
July 21, 1952	5.5R	19:41
	5.1R	17:42
	5.1R	15:13
	5.3R	12:19
	6.4R	12:05
	5.6R	12:02
	7.7R	11:52 First event
February 16, 1919	5.0R	15:15
December 23, 1905	5.0R	22:53

California Random Sample

January 15, 1993	5.3R	Gilson
June 28, 1992	7.4R	Landers, 3:57 a.m. PST
April 6, 1992	4.0R	Palm Springs, GTW
April 4, 1990	4R+	San Diego
March 2, 1990	4.7R	California
June 12, 1982	4.5R	Near Los Angeles
December 15, 1982	4.8R	Palm Springs
December 3, 1988	5.0R	Pasadena
November 19, 1988	5R+	California
November 9, 1988	4.5R	North of San Jose

Date	Magnitude	Location
June 27, 1988	R?	"Wide area" California, GTW
June 20, 1988	4.0R	San Francisco, GCM
June 12, 1988	5.3R	10 miles west of San Jose
January 25, 1988	5-6R	60 miles southeast of San Diego
November 23, 1987	6.0R	100 miles northeast of San Diego, 5:53 p.m. PST
October 7, 1987	4.4R	Palm Springs
October 4, 1987	5.5R	Pasadena
October 1, 1987	6.1R	Pasadena, 7:44 a.m. PDT
July 31, 1987	5.5R	Eureka
February 21, 1987	3.3R	San Francisco Bowl, Moon in Aries
February 20, 1987	4.6R	AM Hollister, Moon in Aries
February 21, 1987	3.9R	PM near Bakersfield, Moon in Aries
February 1, 1987	3.3R	San Francisco Bowl
November 21, 1986	5.1R 6.1R	40 miles southwest of Eureka; Mt. Mihari Japan erupted November 21, quake felt in Tokyo, GTW
October 28, 1986	4.7R	San Diego
October 11, 1986	3.7R	San Francisco, Bowl
July 31, 1986	5.5R	Bishop, GTW
July 29, 1986	4.4R	California, GTW
July 20, 1986	5.5R	California/Nevada border, GTW
July 21, 1986	5.2R, 6R	Nevada, GTW
July 21, 1986	6R, 5.2R	Near Bishop, fourth, fifth GTW events; see previous two events
July 13, 1986	5.7R	26 miles offshore, GTW
July 8, 1986	6.0R	Southern California, GTW
March 31, 1986	5.3R	Fremont
January 26, 1986	5.2R	Hollister
October 3, 1985	R?	San Bernardino
September 3, 1985	2.6R	Los Angeles
August 4, 1985	6R+	Coalinga, GTW
May 10, 1985	Mild	Offshore
April 18, 1985	3.6R	Maryville
February 17, 1985		Used beginning, three minor events over three days, Coalinga
January 1, 1985	4.2R	Palm Springs
November 23, 1984	5.7R	Mammoth Lakes, wedge of 84°
October 26, 1984	4R+	Southern California, wedge of 73°
September 10, 1984	6.5R	Offshore 100 miles west, 7:01 GMT, Cape Mendocino
July 8, 1984	2.6R	Long Beach
June 10, 1984	Several 4R	California

April 24, 1984	6R	San Franicsco and environs, bowl fixed T-square, Taurus-Scorpio with Moon in Aquarius
April 21, 1984	Swarm 2.8/3.2R	Los Angeles, Santa Barbara, offshore
May 2, 1983	6.5R	Coalinga severely damaged, Saturn at 0° Scorpio quake degree, see-saw with trine opening both sides
January 15, 1981	4.5R	California
May 1980	Swarms	Owens, Mammoth Valley
January 26, 1980	4.4/5.2R	Mt. Diablo, Livermore, Virgo stellium
January 24, 1980	5.5R	Mt. Diablo, Livermore, Virgo stellium
August 6, 1979	R?	San Francisco bowl
October 3, 1978	Minor	Laguna Beach
August 13, 1978	Major offshore	Santa Barbara almost a bowl
June 20, 1977	4.2R	San Francisco bowl
December 7, 1976	5.0R	San Diego, Yuma, Arizona, quake actually in Gulf
August 1, 1975	6.1R	Oroville, said to be dam-related
March 21, 1971	4.6R	San Fernando
February 9, 1971	6.5R	Los Angeles, 6:00 AM PST, GTE
October 22, 1969	?	Channel Island
October 2, 1969	?	Santa Rosa
December 28, 1968	Swarm	Santa Barbara Channel
August 22, 1952	5.8R	San Fernando
July 21, 1952	7.7R	Kern County San Fernando fault, 4:21 a.m. PDT, 3:21 a.m. PST, see south of Bakersfield, bowl, fixed T-square
March 10-33	6.3R	Long Beach, 5:54 p.m. PST, unusual dispersion, Virgo stellium
October 22, 1926	R?	California, GTW
April 18, 1906	8.3R	San Francisco, 5:13 AM PST
January 8, 1857	Major	Southern California, Los Angeles

As I went through these again one by one, the bowl is clearly the most frequent dispersal pattern in California events, both major and minor. Rather than a statistical or random approach, it would simply have the largest piece of the pie and should be just one consideration. A Cancer-Capricorn or Taurus-Scorpio influence is significant.

Finally a word on some faults, gleaned randomly and needing some further corroboration.

- Central San Andreas Fault—more Pisces, Gemini and air trines.
- North San Andreas Fault—general California rules apply, but also cardinal and mutable grand crosses as well as the wedge dispersion (90°).
- Santa Ynez Fault—Cancer, Cancer-Leo-Scorpio stellia, grand trine water.

64

The Signature of New Madrid

The Appalachian Belt is clearly a branch of the Great Central Gas Belt. It enters beneath the United States from the Gulf of Mexico near the mouth of the Mississippi River and pretty much follows the river to the northeast, exiting near Buffalo, New York where it follows the course of the Saint Lawrence River through its gulf to the south tip of Greenland.

A minor division occurs near Charleston, South Carolina, arcing along the coast quite closely, in the familiar oval eye shape, and rejoins the main belt at the south tip of Greenland after arcing beneath Newfoundland. The reunited belt then crosses beneath the middle of Iceland, midway beneath the middle of the Scandinavian Peninsula, beneath the southern tip of Finland, north of the Gulf of Finland, beneath the Russian subcontinent, arcing slightly south more or less near Sverdlosk where we will leave it for now.

As usual, all belt directions and designations are Churchward's. In the sense that this is a manual, I'll note that Churchward does not clearly delineate the eastern reaches of this belt. Implicitly, it would link up with the Great Pacific Circuit Belt on the Kamchatka Peninsula. This belt would function in shunting magma and gases/steam to the more stable equatorial regions (see Chandler Wobble).

The history of New Madrid is more important than its brevity. On December 16, 1811, 2:00 AM LMT and 2:15 AM CST, two quakes of 8.6R wreaked the continent from an epicenter of 90W, 36N. On January 23, 1812, and February 7, 1812, similar events occurred. The geological structure of the continent enhanced the destructive power of these quakes and earth changes were three dimensional, up, down, sideways. The course of the Mississippi was altered and Reelfoot Lake was created.

A previous event probably occurred in 1683 as noted in a missionary journal. If one were to draw a conclusion, a major New Madrid event is overdue. Nevertheless, this would not be a necessarily correct conclusion. These events are related to vulcanism and if one notes ``extinct'' or ``dormant'' volcanoes, even thousands, not hundreds of years become a possibility. Conversely, this belt energy may be continuously venting itself elsewhere, both along its course, as noted above, and even in a contributory fashion to the Great Pacific Circuit Belt feeding the Ring of Fire if it were to reach its extremes.

At this time both United States divisions of the belt probably remain clear. It is this belt that would relate to any New York quake of major proportions.

The original event is shown in chart form. While I must be careful in drawing conclusions, some are nevertheless evident. The quake was a grand trine water event with the Capricorn head, Cancer/Capricorn axis, that is that two universal quake configurations were in place together. This alone is highly significant since the three water placements were slow planets. Jupiter in Cancer, Uranus in Scorpio, and Pluto in Pisces.

Not knowing the month or day of the 1683 event, a glance at Michelsen's *Tables of Planetary Phenomena* notes that in 1683 Pluto was in Cancer, water, and Uranus was in Taurus, polar opposite of its 1811 Scorpio position. Neptune was in late Aquarius (see 1811 Mars), Jupiter was in both Leo and Virgo over the course of the year, Virgo being the polar opposite of the upcoming 1994 Saturn in Pisces position, when Pluto also remains in Scorpio.

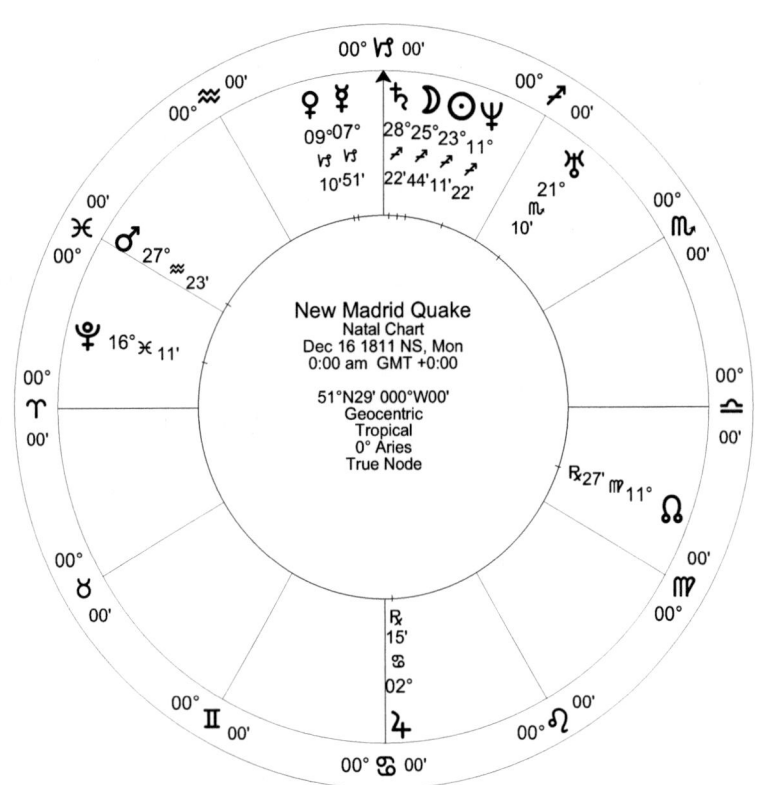

The Moon had just moved into Capricorn, enhancing earth and cardinal. Mercury in degree of Venus. The midpoint of the Mars/Uranus triggers is on Venus. The midpoint of Venus/Mars energizers is at 3° Aquarius, 150° from Jupiter.

A byproduct of isolating quake signatures was the information linking vulcanism and quake activity, for vulcanism is a direct cause in the Ring of Fire quakes and a secondary cause in lateral slip events, because vulcanistic heat drives the plates. The evidences of vulcanism are clear in this chart:

- Jupiter in early cardinal.
- Sun and Moon around Saturn.
- Mercury, Mars, Saturn integrated by Moon.
- Moon last over Saturn.

How did vulcanism cause an event well away from any volcanoes? Restated in belt theory, where did the propelled magma and gas come from and why did an event occur at New Madrid?

Since land disturbance was three-dimensional, we may hypothesize a massive explosion, probably arising from some form of blockage. The eastern division of the Appalachian Belt may have been created at this time. Conversely, magma from the southern division, for example a massive flow form Iceland, may have encountered a blockage at this point in the main (St. Lawrence) division.

In short, what were other events just prior to the 1811 event? A sequence of quakes indicate an east to west activation or movement of magma and gas of the Great Central Gas Belt. Note the immediate sequence in this direction of earthquakes.

October 9, 1808	Severe	Iran
December 16, 1808	Severe	Iran
December 7, 1809	Severe	Iran

February 10, 1810	Severe	Greece, Crete
March 20, 1810	IX	Canary Islands
October 1810	Moderate	Cuba

Since the American Revolution, only one other major quake has hit the eastern United States: August 31, 1886, 9:15 p.m. EST, a IX Mercalli known as the Charleston quake. To the east, it was felt in Boston. Like New Madrid and many European quakes, it is geologically most noteworthy as covering a wide area with its intensity.

The main layout or dispersions the same, 120° minus in water here Scorpio/Cancer. It is not grand trine water, and Neptune is slightly outside the main formation, creating a bowl instead of the Jupiter handle New Madrid bucket.

Both events show the Sun between Saturn and Uranus. The Moon is also cardinal and strongly linked with Jupiter, in Charleston by conjunction. Mercury recently over Venus. Scorpio remains the sign common to both. Here Leo/Virgo replace New Madrid's Aquarius/Pisces. Vulcanism is clearly indicated by a major stellium in early cardinal, Moon, Jupiter, Uranus in tight conjunction, astrological dynamite.

While the direction flow in the Great Central Gas Belt is not quite as neat, Greece, Italy and Iran again figure with major events in Greece. This is the most common factor with multiple severe events on August 27 and 28, 1886 in Greece and one in Turkey. On February 27, 1887, severe quakes truck Italy and France. I have no records of volcanoes.

On June 10, 1987, a minor 4.5R quake, struck in the New Madrid area with its epicenter at Lawrenceville, Illinois, across the river.

It was felt in 16 states, which is all of the northwest except the upper New England states and the New York area. They were: Illinois, Iowa, Missouri, Tennessee, Kentucky, West Virginia, Pennsylvania, Ohio, Indiana, Michigan, Wisconsin, Virginia, North Carolina, South Carolina, Minnesota and Kansas.

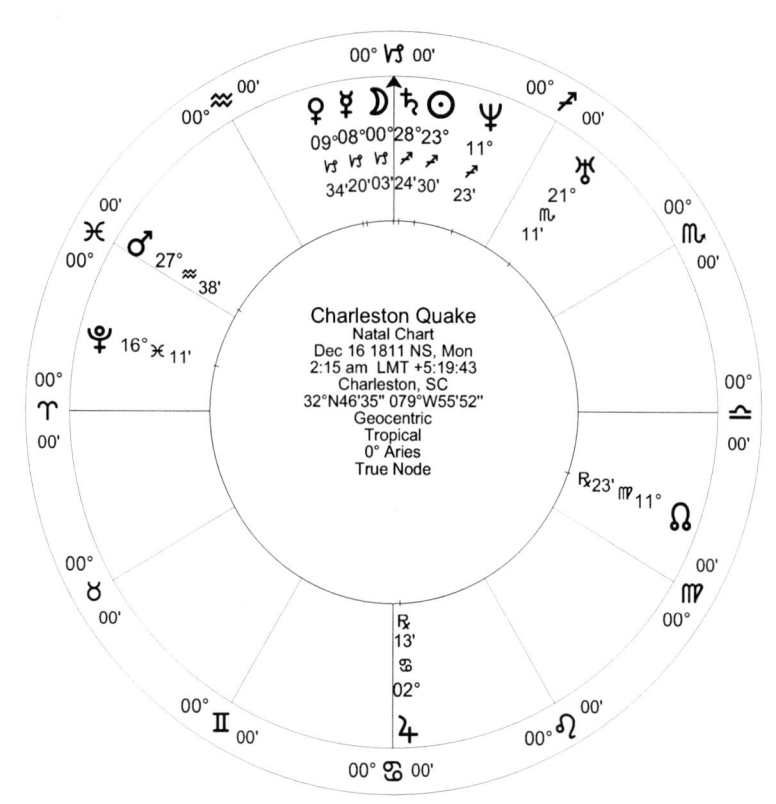

Since New Madrid and Charleston were felt in New York and Boston, we might define the north and east boundaries of this event in terms of its strength. The south and west boundaries would appear to be based on geological conditions and wave direction into Kansas. This minor event shows the vulnerability of the eastern Untied States to a major event. History clearly records that nations recover from the economic damage and loss of life from quakes. Both cities and villages tend to rebuild on the same site after quakes and/or volcanoes.

My premise is the true damage of future great events on population centers will come through pollution, a thoroughly modern phenomenon.

On October 15, 1993, the Gannet News Service noted in an article written by Ken Miller that "forty-one million Americans live within four miles of the nation's 1270 Superfund (pollution) sites. . . ." Some weeks later Moscow acknowledged more than 800,000 were exposed to serious radiation from Chernobyl. Unfortunately, both statistics are undersized, each reflecting only present levels of acknowledgement by the respective governments.

Returning to our subject, using New Madrid and Charleston as benchmarks, we will continue to see if a signature may be unraveled.

The main body of the sample comes from the area's more notable, but nevertheless minor events. The AP report on the Lawrenceville quake gave a list and it will constitute the bulk of the example.

I show the chart for a minor event, March 2, 1990, 3.4R, southern Illinois, AM. A signature emerges as related to New Madrid and Charleston.

- Grand trine water with a Capricorn stellium (New Madrid).
- Jupiter in Cancer (New Madrid).
- Jupiter and Pluto in water (New Madrid).
- Mercury in degree of Venus (New Madrid, related Charleston).
- (Moon) forms Taurus-Pluto axis (Charleston).
- Planet at 27° (New Madrid).
- Sun/Mercury midpoint at 27° Leo, a quake degree (Charleston).
- Neptune 27° Taurus (Charleston).
- Venus-Mars-Jupiter strong (New Madrid, Charleston).
- Sun mutable (New Madrid, Charleston).
- Saturn-Uranus-Neptune (New Madrid and Lawrenceville, not as tight or clear with Charleston).

In the California signature delineation, grand trine water also serves as a venting mechanism, being universally present in both major and minor EM, though some locations appear to respond to it more than others.

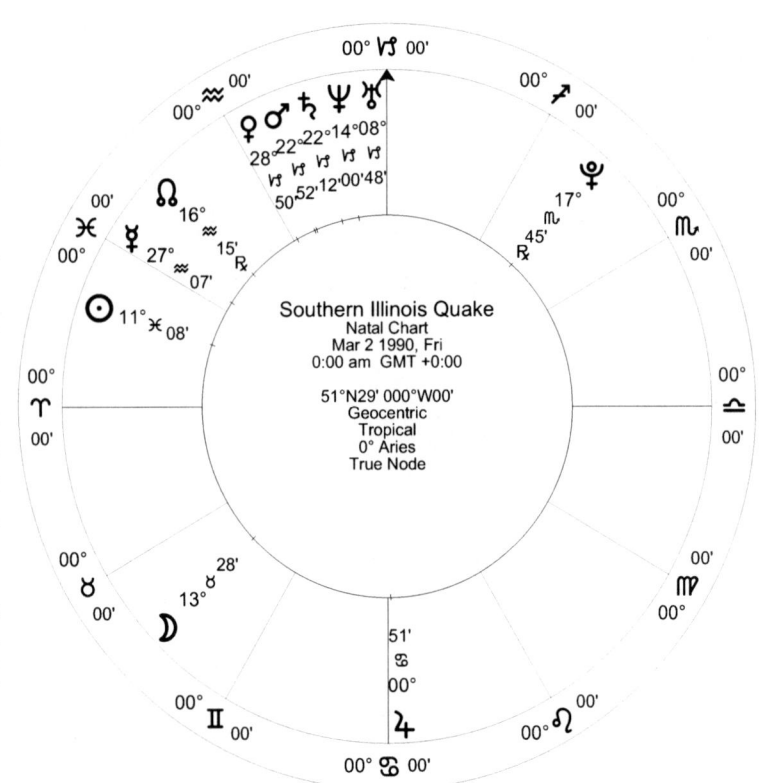

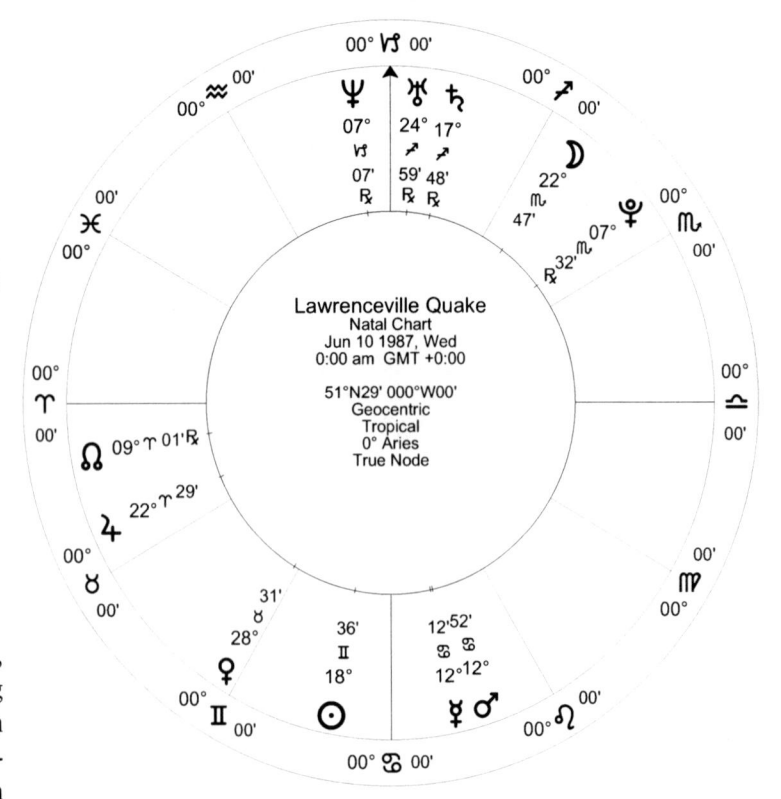

Since the trine is astrologically symbolic of flow and the grand trine is a closed energy system, we might call it a safety valve. In a major event we might say it became stuck or overloaded.

The widespread Lawrenceville event September 27, 1987 had Saturn in Sagittarius (New Madrid) and Moon conjunct Uranus (Charleston) also in Sagittarius. In this event the Moon is near the Sun's degree of New Madrid and the Sun is near the Moon's degree of Charleston.

Notable once again is the less than general 120° planetary dispersion, here with the cardinal Jupiter handle (New Madrid). Here I'll note a strong early cardinal in the four events and clearly bring us up to date on Jupiter.

- New Madrid, 2° Cancer.
- Charleston, 8° Libra.
- Southern Illinois minor, 0° Cancer.
- Lawrenceville, 27° Aries.

We thus have Jupiter twice in water and four times in cardinal in two major events and two minor events. In both these vents the Moon is related to Jupiter, 45° southern Illinois, 120° Lawrenceville. This Moon-Jupiter relationship continues and early cardinal degrees of vulcanism are present, as noted with minor events. Again, working with the minor events, the eastern United States shares the New Madrid signature.

65

The Signature of the Caribbean

The entire Caribbean comes under the Great Central Gas Belt, which moves directly east in two divisions in this region. Churchward maintains that the northern division is older and shallower and that the southern division is newer and deeper. He links this directly to the sequential sinking of Atlantis from north to south. Whether legend or reality the final sinking probably encompassed an area east of the Caribbean archipelago between about 22N to 2N.

The northern division runs just south of Cuba and just north of the east to west part of the Caribbean archipelago including Hispaniola. At the Azores it divides into the familiar almond or eye shape, the lower section in southern Iberia, the northern more or less on the France-Iberia border forming the corner of the eye where Spain and France meet at the Mediterranean Sea. It then crosses to Italy, this northern belt being the Vesuvius connection where we will leave it for now. The southern division passes more or less midway through the Caribbean Sea and the north to south section of the archipelago. Heading across the Atlantic it reaches the Canary Islands and hits Africa at mid-Morocco. It crosses Morocco and Algiers to Sicily. Somewhere beneath Italy proper it reconnects with the northern belt and the reunited belt crosses the Adriatic. Passing beneath Greece it enters Turkey about midway. A minor eye is formed as the belt passes between Morocco and Algiers. A squinting eye, it is probably only good for distinguishing minor events.

It is worth noting that Edgar Cayee connects Italy and the Caribbean in his famous countdown sequence to cataclysmic EM, India, Japan, Vesuvius Italy, Caribbean in particular Mount Pele and finally California.

Great quakes and major eruptions are extremely rare in the Caribbean, but minor ventings and tremors remind us that this area is anything but dormant or dead. Most Caribbean tremors take place in or along its trenches and plate junctures. At present several things may be said about this.

First, it would seen that this entire area may at present function as a safety valve between the highly sensitive belt junctures of Central America and the seismically sensitive area of Greece and Eurasia with its many branches and two divisions of the Great Central Belt.

During the eighties there were minor offshore volcanoes venting in the southern Antilles. Changes in current (heat) were noted by NOAA during the 1980s.

The question of rising temperature has been hypothesized in various local coral "bleachings." During the mid-1980s, shortly after Pluto entered Scorpio, there was a Caribbean-wide die-off of the spiny black sea urchin. While the astrologer might note that Pluto in Scorpio may be an indicator of plagues, it is also worth noting that the course of the die-off was never satisfactorily explained and the gradual resurgence of the urchin put a potentially embarrassing question on the back burner, much in the way of magma propellant.

The benchmark Caribbean events are Port Royale, Jamaica, June 7, 1692, and Kingston, Jamaica, 7R+, January 14, 1907, and November 18, 1867, St. Thomas USVI and Puerto Rico.

The 1907 event, which destroyed Kingston and took some 1400 lives, has the universal signature, GTW and Cancer-Capricorn, or when it is with the GTW, the Capricorn kite head. It also has a loose opposition on the Gemini-Sagittarius axis.

The Moon's North Node was at 2° Leo. The early and late fixed degrees are quake degrees. In Taurus, Leo and Scorpio, Aquarius they also have one antiscia or solstice point relationship to each other. The stellium occurs in Capricorn.

In 1692, Port Royale was an active port. Ostensibly mercantile, nevertheless much of its finance involved piracy and slavery, themselves true businesses of the era.

At 11:43 a.m. LMT on the late spring morning of June 7, tragedy struck in the form of a great quake with a strong aftershock or two and perfect geological hit. Port Royale vanished beneath the sea. The subsidence involved was approximately 20 feet and divers and marine archeologists today routinely view the ruins.

The Port Royale event corroborates the 1907 event. There was no planet in Scorpio, but Pluto was in Cancer; thus, according to Vedic astrology, reflecting in Capricorn. This Cancer/Capricorn axis as noted is a universal signature and one important to Caribbean events. Two slow planets are in various two of the water signs in both events. In 1692 the Moon enhances water, appearing with Neptune in Pisces.

In 1907, the stellium occurs in Gemini. Sagittarius is also present. Venus is at 2° Leo in the placement of 1907 North Node, and Mars in Leo supplies some fixity to the chart. Note that Mars, while part of the GTW in 1907, was also in Scorpio a fixed sign.

Saturn was in Jupiter signs: 1692 in Sagittarius, and 1907 in Pisces. In both 1907 and 1692, Venus-Mars-Jupiter perform their integrated functions as energizers more fully than noted at first glance. Integration and separation reveal themselves through the Venus Mars midpoints in both events. Almost always a planet in early cardinal (Vulcanism).

I'll succinctly list my descriptive notes on the Caribbean event. Of interest in terms of the random sample is the large number of minor events. I live in the U.S. Virgin Islands and minor events are reported on radio and in local newspapers.

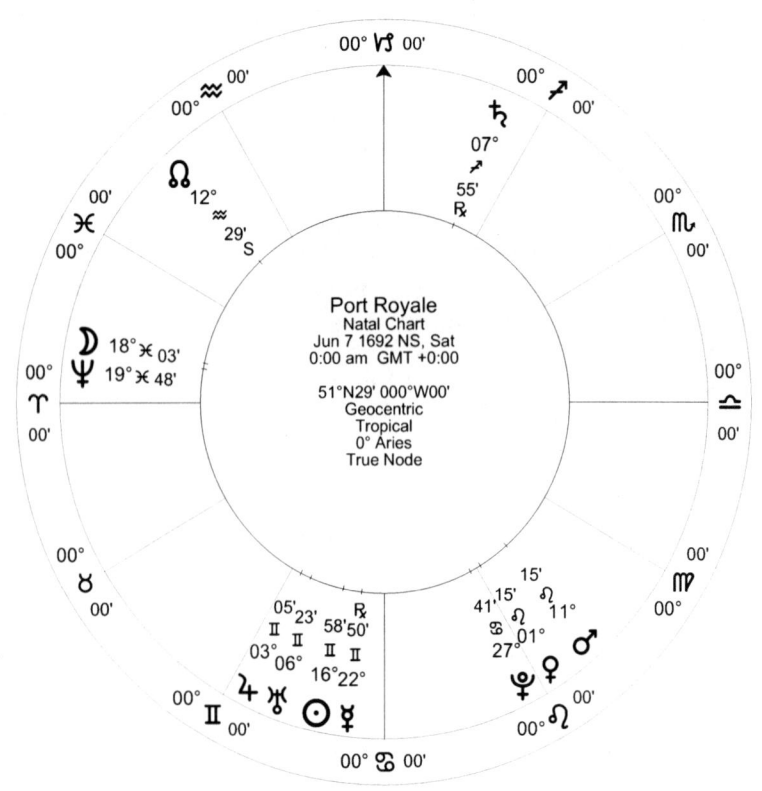

On September 8, 1615, a major quake struck the Dominican Republic. This was GTW with no Capricorn, but a Virgo "head" opposition Pisces. Saturn in Aries supplied Fire. Venus is in early fixed at 0° Scorpio and Venus/Mars perform well as noted by midpoint. Some notes on Caribbean events:

- Cardinal Capricorn/Cancer or Capricorn/Libra.
- A planet in Scorpio.
- Gemini/Sagittarius.
- A three or four planet stellium, usually but not always in Cancer, Scorpio, Sagittarius or Capricorn.
- Jupiter may well be in one of these signs.
- Often a water emphasis which varies.
- Sun/Moon midpoint often Leo, Scorpio or mutable.
- Sun more widely separated from Jupiter when in major aspect, e.g. opposition as compared to the semisquare of 45°.
- Mars often strong to Neptune.
- Sun strong to Mars in major aspect, usually just separated.
- Mercury or Venus to Saturn.
- Wedge (120° spread) and handle (180° bowl with planet 90° to it), dispersions common.
- Mutable squares.
- Fire or earth trines.
- The Sun is usually with another planet in the same sign. This often involves planets other than the companion planets Mercury and Venus.
- The Sun usually has separated from this planet, e.g. Mars. Regarding the sometimes faster Mercury and Venus, he also holds a higher zodiacal degree
- Mercury is often one degree approaching or earlier in making its Mercury degree.
- In quakes over 5R, Sun-Mars-Saturn are often well integrated.
- Ripeness or integration, separation is not well shown in events under 5R.
- Sun/Saturn is often a significant midpoint.
- Cardinal squares are the predominate mode, followed by more or less the same amount of fixed and mutable. Mode signs, as well as squares or T-squares, vary widely.
- Fire is usually present.
- Grand trines water may show Cancer emphasis.
- If a cardinal opposition is involved, Cancer/Capricorn predominate.
- A stellium complex substitutes for a deficiency of the mode and element involved. Restated, the stellium is a complex in itself with compensatory properties.
- Almost always a planet in first decanate cardinal.
- In a major event, Venus and Mars may well be within 30° of each other.
- The Dominican Republic minor event of 5R may show a bowl dispersion, based on Taurus Scorpio or Aries Libra rims.
- The Jamaican event is water based. January 13, 1993, 5.3R Kingston was GTW. Venus is often semisquare the Sun or at its furthest point. Mercury may be in the degree of Uranus or Neptune or in the same sign as Uranus. In a 4.6R event, September 2, 1988, the Mercury degree fell near the midpoint of Uranus/Neptune.

The Puerto Rican event confirms the Caribbean signature as noted through the Jamaican events. A major event of October 11, 1918, which caused a tidal wave and 116 deaths, struggles to duplicate the basic signature components. A stellium in Libra. Another major event September 27, 1906 has the GTA and GTW with Capricorn head! The moon is in Aquarius enhancing fixity and air of which the Puerto Rican event may require more than the Jamaican event. A planet in Aquarius is frequent.

A major event December 28, 1875 also includes a hodgepodge of signature components by both presence and absence. Major quake, November 28, 1846, has fire stellia in Aries and Sagittarius, Gemini Aquarius Trines and Mars in Scorpio. Again Venus and Mars are in adjacent signs. In 1906 and 1875, they are sextile by sign. Major quake, September 15, 1787 confirms the above and also has GTA. Moon enhances water and fixity from Scorpio.

The American and British Virgin Islands directly east of Puerto Rico share the Puerto Rican signature. The greatest event was the 7.5R+ of November 18, 1867, which sucked the harbor of St. Thomas dry and then hit it with a tsunami, for which it is remembered. Felt also in Puerto Rico, we can thus say that in major events the Virgin Islands share the Puerto Rican Signature.

Finally the signatures of Puerto Rico and the Dominican Republic vary slightly from benchmark Jamaica and each other but a common thread may be seen all through Caribbean events, these of the Great Central Gas Belt.

The Dominican Republic end of Hispaniola is more quake prone than the Haitian end. St. Croix of the US Virgin Islands is a geological anomaly and is less quake prone than St. Thomas or St. John and the directly eastward British Virgin Islands.

West Indian Random Sample

March 2, 1989	54R	Off Dominican Republic
November 3, 1987	5.1R	D.R. epicenter 25 miles
September 2-3, 1987	5R event	D.R.
December 28, 1985	5.3R	D.R.
September 8, 1615	Major	D.R. with hurricane
January 13, 1993	5.3R	Jamaica
November 11, 1988	5 Mercalli	E. Jamaica
September 2, 1988	4.6R	Jamaica
June 10, 1983	R?	Kingston
January 22, 1907	R?	Jamaica
January 14, 1907	7R+	Kingston destroyed, 1,400 dead
June 7, 1692	7R+??	Port Royale 11:43 a.m. LMT, subsidence
November 23, 1992	4.7R	NW Puerto Rico
February 19, 1990	4.4R	SE of Humacao
June 27, 1989	Swarms to 2.5R	Cabo Rojo
June 18, 1989	4.8R	120 miles SW of San Juan—rattled island
April 27, 1989	4.3R	75 miles SE of San Juan
April 14, 1989	3.5R	Between St. Croix and Virgins
March 2, 1989	5.5R	Between P.R. and D.R.
December 15, 1988	4.9R	West of P.R.
November 3, 1988	5.4R	80 miles north of Aquadilla
June 5, 1986	4R	20 miles southwest of Ponce GTW
November 29, 1985	3.7R	6 miles off southeast coast
October 29, 1985	4.3R	North of Mayaguez
September 20, 1985	Swarm 3R	Puerto Rico
August 14, 1985	4.4R	North of Mayaguez

July 21, 1985	5.4R	Between P.R. and D.R.
March 16, 1985	6.6R	290 miles SE San Juan 9:54 a.m. AST Taurus-Scorpio with Mars 0° Taurus and Pluto 4° Scorpio (quake degrees early Taurus Scorpio)
March 6, 1985	4.5R	Mona Passage
March 7, 1985	4.0R	Mona Passage
October 2, 1984	4.3R	SW P.R. in sea
June 24, 1984	6.5R	Mona Passage felt in D.R. and Haiti
October 11, 1918	Strong	Mona Passage
September 27, 1906	Strong	North of P.R., GTW
December 28, 1875	Strong	Ponce, Grand Cross Fixed
December 8, 1875	Strong	Ponce, Grand Cross Fixed
November 28, 1846	Strong	Mona Passage
September 15, 1787	Strong	P.R.
December 28, 1992	4.8R	Tortola BVI
April 27, 1990	4.0R	St. John, USVI
February 19, 1990	Tremors	St. John
February 3, 1990	5.0R	St. John
January 16, 1990	3.5R	N of St. Thomas
January 9, 1990	4.8R	65M west of St. Thomas
December 26, 1989	Tremors	St. Thomas
September 18, 1987	4R	N of Anegada, BVI
June 26, 1985	5.5R	N of St. Thomas
November 18, 1867	7.5R	St. Thomas, P.R. with tsunami
July 12, 1990	5R	Martinique
May 31, 1990	3.5R	St. Lucia
March 1990		Under sea Vulcanism off Grenadines
March 21, 1990	5.2R	Caribbean coast of Venezuela
April 29/May 3, 1989	Seismic Storm	Near eastern Cuba
October 26, 1988	Swarm, avg. 4.5R	St. Kitts, BWI
March 9, 1988	6.9R	50 miles southeast of Port of Spain, Trinidad, 11:37 p.m. Local, strongest since January 23, 1910 of 7.2R
February 8, 1988	4.8R	St. Martin, St. Barts
February 9, 1988	4.0R	St. Martin, St. Barts
June 11, 1986	Strong	Off coast of Venezuela, felt in Trinidad
March 9-10, 1986	8 tremors	Dominica
December 25, 1969	Strong	Leeward Islands
August 4, 1946	8.1R	West Indies
January 23, 1910	7.2R	Trinidad Grand Cross cardinal Capricorn Aquarius, Pisces; signs in common with March 9, 1988

66

The Signature of France

I did not achieve a randomly collected sample for France, which is under the influence of the northern division of the Great Central Gas Belt, and probably a branch or two of this. The belt, in two narrowly separated subdivisions, more or less follows the Franco-Iberian border. One-third of the way across this border from the Atlantic, a branch arises into the Alps ending up arcing down into Yugoslavia. An inner arc moves from the Swiss Alps into Italy, connecting with the divisions that join at the foot and ankle.

At the time of this writing I have a copy of *The Catalog of Significant Earthquakes 2150 BC-1991 AD* and I will analyze the severe events listed there in an appendix according to this system.

France presents some special problems for future major quakes. One has not taken place there since February 23, 1887, 5:23 GMT, a X Mercalli, an untimed shock of IX Mercalli accompanied this. The coordinates were 43N9, 8E1. In 1887, with the exception of several major cities, France was largely agrarian. Today she is not only a highly developed industrial nation, but also has the most nuclear power facilities in Europe, and the most anywhere in the world within a comparable land mass area.

A full scale history is not the scope of this work, but astrology notes that nations have their own character. Part of France's is its intransigence and the general inability to see itself as possibly being wrong. The Treaty of Versailles, the garrisons of Dien Bein Phu and its Pacific nuclear testing are listed here to show a facet of national character. Extrapolating from this, I do not see much in the way of nuclear caution or foresight.

Many of France's nuclear power reactors, like most of the world's, were made during the 1960s and 1970s, in a time of nuclear optimism. The return of transiting Saturn to its place is hard, not only on human beings but on the institutions, accomplishments and buildings. A certain number of these facilities will weaken or fail around their thirtieth year. With more than 60 plants in 1986, it is an ongoing process.

What can be said geologically about France? I would pay special attention to the locations adjacent to the belt lines as noted in the beginning of this chapter.

The intervals between severe events, as noted in *The Catalog of Significant Earthquakes 2150 BC-1991 AD*, are in years beginning in 1227, when we may assume they have been listed sequentially: 224, 129, 198, 80 to 1644, 67, 39, 67, 70 to 1887.

Looking at this we may infer two things. Between 1227 and 1644, some extreme events may not be listed in that volume. In terms of the clearly known times since 1644, France may be considered overdue. The latitudes for the severe events were 43 through 45 north, not 46 north but then 47 north. The longitudes east were 0, 0, 5, 6, 7, 8. The perimeters of France, 43 to 50 north, and 0 to 8 east.

Since the whereabouts or intensity of the next severe quake are unknown, crude assessments are as good as any. In terms of the whereabouts I think 4 east appears safe so far, as do 46, 48, 49, 50 north. It is then a matter of punching in the nuclear sites. Two other facts deserve juxtaposition. France's nuclear sites have never been subject to a 6R event.

The Catalog of Significant Earthquakes 2150 BC-1991 AD lists:

April 5, 1959	5.5R
April 25, 1962	5.3R
August 3, 1967	VIII
September 7, 1972	5.6R
February 13, 1991	3.8R

The second consideration is that some western European quakes, like the U.S. New Madrid, are capable of affecting large areas. In a word, they may not be localized. In three words, nuclear emergency teams?

67

The Signature of Italy

It is now time to move across the Atlantic following the Great Central Gas Belt. Mid-Atlantic quakes are not as frequent as in the Ring of Fire, for the linear distance of plate juncture or separation, is also considerably less.

The Great Central Gas Belt is followed across the Atlantic in the beginning of the chapter on The Caribbean Signature. Southern Europe, including the Iberian Peninsula, France and Switzerland form one grouping. Italy, Greece, Turkey and Iran form a second, and Algeria forms a third. All are fed by divisions and branches of the Great Central Gas Belt.

The following chapters deal with the second grouping and attempts to isolate both a common signature for this area as well as local or country variants. Quakes in Italy, Greece, Turkey and Iran are historically frequent, deadly and recurring in the same locations. Geologically their impact is generally quite localized, as in California. This differs from those strong and infrequent Iberian Peninsula, French and Swiss events, which, *a la* New Madrid, seem to cover a wide area geographically in both impact and damage such as Lisbon 1755.

Finally, the Algerian events occur directly above the southern division of the Great Central Gas Belt and, while they are localized, at least one, El Asnan, October 10, 1950, 7R+, involved considerable subsidence in the sea. This is also true of Lisbon, November 1, 1755, the European equivalent of New Madrid. Other subsidence quakes are Port Royale 1692, Honshu 1923 and New Madrid. Alaska 1965 had both subsidence and uplift. This also occurs frequently, and to a lesser degree, in minor Nevada quakes.

Subsidence poses special problems. It does not occur everywhere and only occurs infrequently. Late in the 20th century it poses special problems regarding shoreline nuclear facilities and skyscrapers as in New York and Tokyo. Most subsidence occurs in the sea, (El Arnan and Honshu) and subsidence involving land, geologically speaking, is just a nibble (Port Royale and Lisbon). The relative scarcity of quakes involving major subsidence is the surest thing known about it. Belt theory would call for some form of collapse in the belt or chamber. All areas noted here are close to the belts—over them as defined by Churchward. (perhaps this in some way corraborates his belts).

Italy, itself a country that differs from city to city, shows a widely varying signature. A small random sample shows that Italian quakes follow some common universal signatures.

- Grand trine water, both examples with the Capricorn head
- Cancer/Capricorn axis
- Taurus/Scorpio axis

Beyond this, earth trines are frequent and the majority of the sample shows a predominance of earth and water, or negative polarity.

Finally, other grand trines such as earth and air are present. Italy-Greece, March 27, 1636 and Calabria-Sicily June 26, 1505 both have grand trine fire. One event is predominately air and fire and one shows no planet in early cardinal or even any cardinal at all. This last is of interest since both Italy and Sicily have respectively the live volcanoes, Vesuvius and Etna.

Mercury often not in degree, when in degree seems to prefer Uranus and Saturn followed by Pluto and Jupiter. Jupiter, often in the same sign as another slow planet, makes aspect to other slow planets.

Water is important in the Italian or Sicilian event and 1994 with transiting planets Jupiter in Scorpio, Saturn in Pisces and Pluto in Scorpio may have a significant event. In forecasting, I'd especially note the Taurus Sun, Cancer Moon, and Cancer Sun, Taurus Moon times for what by now should be obvious dispersion patterns to the reader. These two solunar combinations provide the grand trine water and the Taurus/Scorpio axis. Remember the Capricorn head, now Uranus and Neptune stay in place for any grand trine water events in 1994 and 1995, indeed until early April 1996. While we speak of Italy, please note that these are components of the universal signatures, here blended into a whole. The widespread but relatively minor 6R quake that hit Naples on May 5, 1990 shows the integration of these aspect complexes.

In forecasting for Italy I would integrate the records of quake prone cities with eclipses prior to the event to seek the confirmation, and the prior activity of Vesuvius and Etna, a geological confirmation for geologists and astrologers. Mode and dispersion with a mode varies widely.

Random Samples

Date	Magnitude	Location/Notes
May 5, 1990	6R	Naples seashore GTW, GTE, Cancer/Capricorn, Taurus/Scorpio Moon creates GTE from Virgo
May 12, 1984		Near Rome Taurus/Scorpio
April 29, 1984	?	Italy, Taurus/Scorpio
November 23, 1980	Serious	Naples, eight planets positive
May 6-8, 1976	6.9R	Friull, Bolzano, "worst since 1915," Taurus/Scorpio
February 6, 1971	?	Tuscany GTE, GTA
March 1970	?	Pozzuoli, uplift involved, Taurus/Scorpio
July 2, 1969	Tremors	Tolfa, Taurus/Scorpio
June 12, 1969	?	Mediterranean, Taurus/Scorpio
July 23-25, 1930	?	Naples
January 13, 1915	7.5R	Avezzano, Cancer-Capricorn, Mercury in degree of Saturn
December 28, 1908	7R+	Messina, Sicily, Italy, GTW
September 8, 1905	7.9R	Calabria
January 15, 1968	6.1R	Sicily, GTW
March 27, 1636	Major	Italy, Greece, GTF
June 6, 1505	Major	Sicily, GTF

68

The Signature of Greece

The Great Central Gas Belt reaches Greece as extensions of both divisions that reached Italy. The main belt divisions, north and south rejoined in southern Italy, and a northern branch of the north division affects southern Yugoslavia, Bulgaria and Greece. In the familiar eye shape it branches off the northern division near the Franco-Iberian border from a more westerly position.

Just as in southern Italy, the southern division of the Great Central Gas Belt rejoins the northern division in southern Greece. The reunified gas belt immediately redivides, a northern section crosses the Black Sea somewhat to the north and continues inland, crossing under the Caspian Sea at its midpoint, where we will leave it for now, noting that the Central Gas Belt here begins a southward arc through Afghanistan and India. This section of the belt probably also affects western China. Branches of the Great Central Gas Belt affect the subcontinents of China and the former Soviet Union. The southern division (the immediate redivision formed in southern Greece) sweeps through Turkey and Iran. Based on the belts, the following inferences may be made:

- There may be at least two major types of Greek signatures, or more realistically the astrologer will see them as varied.
- Turkey and Iran probably share a similar signature.
- At least some of the Greek events should be similar to those of Turkey and Iran.
- The same may be said of Italy.
- Italy, since its belt situation is similar to Greece's, may also have more than one signature.
- As noted in the Great Pacific Circuit Belt, areas of much division and branching are seismically active. They also will have an active volcano area (Central America, Italy).
- Truly local signatures should be isolated on the basis of those cities involved in major events (Ankara, Turkey for example).
- Since much of this area is highly populated, the attempt at establishing truly local signatures should be made carefully, from a series of sequential events for a specific location. Again, for example, major events in Ankara.

Since my random sample will not fulfill the last four inferences, I'll confine myself to some general observations.

There are several main dispersions of planetary patterns; the bowl, about half the chart; the splay, widely scattered, and semi-splay, and often highly cardinal, including the early cardinal of vulcanism.

Venus-Mars-Jupiter, the energy triad, are usually quite well integrated. The Mercury degree varies, present or not. Planets in Cancer and Virgo may be the most consistently present.

The slow planets consistently involve interaction among Jupiter, Uranus and Pluto. Often the semisextile (30°) and the quincunx (150°) are involved in this. Grand trines in the random sample occur in all four elements, often completed by the Moon (lunar enhancement). Mars may prefer Aries, Pisces and Leo, this clearly inconclusive.

Compensation, most often the stellium, involving strong planetary combinations, occurs in the Greek event, perhaps especially when the Taurus/Scorpio axis is involved.

Using the 0° Aries chart, degrees only, I invite the reader to draw May 13, 1895, Greece-Turkey, and April 17, 1893, Greece, directly from the ephemeris.

Random Sample

June 17, 1990	5.6R	Athens
August 20, 1989	5.9R	28 miles west of Peloponneus
October 16, 1988	6.4R	150 miles west of Athens in Ionian Sea
June 20, 1978	7.0	Salonika, bowl
July 9, 1956	7.7R	Santorini, GTW
March 18, 1953	7.2R	Northwest Anatolia
December 26, 1939	7.9R	Anatolia, splay, GTF
August 11, 1903	8.3R	Thessaly, GTW
January 22, 1899	? Serious	Southwest Greece
May 31, 1893	? Serious	Greece-Turkey
April 17, 1893	? Serious	Greece
January 31, 1893	? Serious	Greece, GTA
April 6, 1514	7-8R	Zante, Greece, GTW

Sneaking at look at *The Catalog of Significant Earthquakes 2150 BC-1991 AD*, areas of seismic emphasis are 20, 21, 22 east and 38 and 39 north. This basically encompasses Yante, then east to Athens, all in the area of the Gulf of Corinth. Crete and the Dodecanese Islands are also exceptionally active. This written in regard to present and future nuclear power plants as Greece continues to westernize.

69

The Signature of Turkey

A southern division of the Great Central Gas Belt crosses the Aegean and enters Turkey more or less near Izmir and continues south of Ankara into Iran, curving gently to the south. Some detail is at the beginning of The Signature of Greece.

The northern division, or redivision, arcs across the northern Black Sea. Turkey is clearly under the influence of the southern division.

In passing the Caucasus, including Georgia and its quake-prone Tbilisi, Azerbardzhan and Armenia lie more or less midway between the divisions.

I consider my 12 examples inadequate. The most noteworthy observation is the possibility of planets in Taurus for the more recent and upcoming events (see Rolling Signature). There is always a planet in fire and the pattern of planetary dispersion, like Greece, varies.

There is usually a planet in early cardinal, indicating vulcanism. This question arises: which way is the belt magma and gas flowing? With only one belt, I'd look to recent events, east or west of Turkey, for some clues.

Since the late 1980s, Turkey has been undergoing an economic renaissance and is enamored of development. There are indications that the urge to develop may overcome good judgment. In regard to nuclear power facilities, Istanbul is less quake-prone than Ankara.

Glancing at *The Catalog of Significant Earthquakes 2150 BC-1991 AD*, I get the impression that many earlier events were simply assigned to, or claimed by, Ankara. That is, Ankara was probably not the epicenter for many events now referred to as Ankara.

In modern times the last direct hit on Ankara, epicenter, was April 3, 1872, 36.2N, 36.2E, and listed as severe (damage). If one errs on the side of caution in terms of the country's historical reputation, it is overdue for an event. In EM, overdue is a most general term encompassing tomorrow or a century. Historically, Turkey is clearly a quake-prone nation. I hope discretion is used in nuclear power plant decisions.

70

The Signature of Iran

The southern division of the Great Central Gas Belt under Turkey moves on into Iran. The divisions rejoin in Afghanistan, and thus are located in the same area. Churchward notes the southern division as newer and deeper. Thus Iran may well have a signature similar to Turkey.

Cardinality is always present. In 19 of 23 events in the sample, this included early cardinal. Since 1970, the Aries-Libra axis has received more emphasis. I have noted a couple of other location signature changes occurring about this time. The early 1960s were under the influence of the Uranus-Pluto conjunction, an event occurring about every 115 years; the rolling signature may have taken a change at this time. There is usually air; Tabas, August 30, 1987 was an exception.

Iran, too, is subject to the universal grand trine water event and this with an earth stellium. Tabas, March 24, 1990, occurred with Capricorn, the universal head; Buyin-Zara, September 1, 1962, had Virgo.

The Mercury degree is above average, as are Neptune, Uranus, Mars, and Venus, and especially Neptune. The Moon may aspect Venus, having just aspected Mars. Stellia do not occur in Aquarius or Pisces, and only once in Leo. The Sun does not appear in Libra or Pisces, but frequently in Aries and Virgo.

Always some fixity appears in various combinations. The single Leo stellium, present in the sample, was all the fixity present, an example of compensation, as periodically noted in this work.

As in Greece, where I noted the influence of two belts might make for some signature distinction and thus, forecast problems, grand trines are present in all elements. This in a sample of only 23 randomly collected events. This implies to me, with the two belt divisions crossing over each other and separating that the grand trine of any element may be part of location signature for this general area; Italy, Greece, Turkey and Iran.

Random Sample

June 21, 1990	7.4R	Resht, Gilan
March 24, 1990	5R+	Tabas
September 28, 1988	4.6R	Southwest Iran

August 23, 1988	Beginning of swarm	Iran
August 30, 1987	5.0R	Tabas
February 4, 1985	5.4R	Southern Iran
September 18, 1984	6.4R	Tabriz
August 15, 1984	Two small quakes	Southern Iran
September 16, 1978	7.7R	Tabas, Moon trine Mars, Venus, Uranus by sequence
March 22, 1977	7.0R	Iran, GTF
August 31, 1973	7R	Iran, Libra stellium
April 10, 1972	?	Jahrom, GTA
July 30, 1970	?	Damghan
November 7, 1969	?	Southeast Iran
September 1, 1962	7.5R	Buyin-Zara, GTW
June 11, 1961	6.75R	Lar
December 13, 1957	7.2R	Iran
July 2, 1957	? Serious	Iran
May 1, 1929	7.1R	Shirwan
January 17, 1895	?	Khorasan, Persia

I have three events centered at Tabas. I truly believe that refined forecasting will end up using geology and the charts of sequential events, including minor, intermediate and failed events for specific coordinates (see The Signature of California and The Signature of Tblisi).

The three events are:

March 24, 1990	5R+	Tabas
August 30, 1987	5.0R	Tabas
September 16, 1978	7.7R	Tabas

The signature is as follows with reference by number:

- A planet or planets in Aries (1+2) or Libra (3).
- Strong water includes Moon (1, 2,+3)
- Earth stellium Capricorn (1), Virgo (2+3).
- Moon in Pisces (1+3) Moon in Scorpio (2).

Tabas, March 24, 1990, 5R was a grand trine water event with a strong Capricorn head Saturn, Uranus and Neptune being there. Here is where Richter size sequence, geology and astrology blend into a coherent whole. The planetary energy was peaked in this chart and since it only evoked a 5.0R event, we may assume that sufficient energy for a major event had not yet built up and that all built-up energy was dissipated. Tabas will be quiet for a while. This was a release event, the benevolent face of the universal grand trine water quake.

Iran is somewhat larger than Turkey and less developed, outside of a few major cities and areas. Events of the 1980s and early 1990s, especially the Iran-Iraq War and the continued theocracy, have hindered development.

A glance at the coordinates does not show safe areas. It seems any area may be subject to a significant event. While a fated mindset may indicate extremes of caution or recklessness, here it is clearly the latter and the future development of nuclear power may be considered risky.

71

The Signature of Tblisi

Tblisi, Armenia, lies between the redivided belts of the Great Central Gas Belt. Tblisi is unusual in having had several significant events over an extremely short period. They are:

October 24, 1992	6.7R	55 miles northeast of Tblisi
April 29, 1991	7R	44E55, 41N55
December 7, 1988	6.9R	Tblisi epicenter

The sequence of these events and their magnitude does not permit the use of any form of aftershock theory. In fact most aftershocks occur while the Moon is still in the same sign as that of the event (see *The Catalog of Significant Earthquakes 2150 BC-1991 AD* and Appendix I here. Los Angeles 1994 is an anomaly with strong aftershocks and one 5R event as of two weeks later.)

In belt theory we may surmise a blockage periodically tested under new conditions of vulcanism or the transferal of extreme amounts of heat through some secondary conduit. Tblisi lies between the two belt divisions.

The Catalog of Significant Earthquakes 2150 BC-1991 AD reveals that occasionally a given location may be subject to two or more major events in a short period of time. Like truly simultaneous major event occurring in the same Moon sign, it is a relative rarity.

The question here is of a Tblisi signature.

- All three charts were predominately negative, 1992 and 1991 with seven negative planets or 3+ to 7-.
- The Moon made a recent major aspect ot Jupiter, 1992 conjunction 16 hours earlier, 1988 opposition 14 hours in the future, but the Sun/Moon midpoint would be an energy of separation.
- New Moon one sign away, 1992 and 1988.
- Recent Full Moon 1991.
- 1992, 1991, Mars in Aries past square to Uranus. In all three, Mars involvement with Neptune is also close—1992, 4° separating; 1991, 2° approaching; 1988, 1° approaching.
- 1992, 1991, Mars in Cancer just past opposition to Uranus.
- Mercury degree1992, Mercury 1° separating from Pluto; 1991, Mercury closest to Venus, 25', 1° plus

earlier than Pluto, 1° and later than Neptune, Mercury at 17° Aries 59'; 1988, Mercury separtes 2° from Venus.
- Air trine or fire trine, 1991 both.
- No planet in Virgo/Pisces—all three, this significant.
- Strong fixity, 1992 four planets; 1991, largest event, five planets; 1988, four planets.
- Either or both Sun and Moon fixed.

Definitely there is hope of a Tblisi signature. Here the magnitude of three events, when noted in time, is indicative of different geological conditions than that of the Tabas-Iran sequence.

In 1992, early cardinal indicates vulcanism in progress. 1991, the major event broke after a recent infusion of energy by Mars at 14° Cancer at the time of the event. In 1988, vulcanism is clearly building with four planets—Mars, Saturn, uranus, Neptune—in the first decanate cardinal.

The basic signature can replicate itself in 1994, including under grand trine water conditions.

In working backward with my sample, I would assess the aspect relationship of the five slow planets, that by major aspect (by sign) as usual manage to integrate among themselves.

For those wishing to verify this signature or note differences, I give the dates of the major event and two previous ones (not included in sample) in the area.

J	anuary 9, 1925	5.R	41.1N, 42.4E
	October 21, 1905	7.5R	42N, 42E
	April 29, 1991	7.5R	Major event of this sequence, 41N45, 44E55

72

The Signature of Afghanistan, Hindu Kush and India

Churchward becomes vague about the belt lines in this region, as he does with the Appalachian Belt once it hits the Ural Mountains. The Appalachian Belt probably crosses the former USSR fairly uneventfully at about 60N latitude. It reaches the active volcanoes of Katchamka where it may vent itself in an active eruption or merge quietly into the Ring of Fire, the Great Pacific Circuit Belt system.

The Ring of Fire is the safety vent for most of the earth's vulcanism, along with its smaller Atlantic Ridge counterpart. The belt system is now integrated, for another probable feature is its shunting of northern latitude magma to more southerly latitudes; more precisely, the shunting of higher latitude magma to the equatorial regions stabilizing the Chandler Wobble, etc. (see Chandler Wobble).

The northern division of the Great Central Gas Belt cuts across the USSR and is responsible for most of its quakes, which lie on latitudes 38 to 51 north. We left it recently at Tbilisi. It obviously cuts across the continent and funnels into the Japanese volcano system, where once again it is integrated with the Great Pacific Circuit Belt. This northern division also is responsible for the quakes of Mongolia and northern China.

Finally we come to the southern division of the Great Central Gas Belt. Following the same line of reasoning we know that it influences the seismic signature of Afghanistan, the Hindu Kush and India. Ultimately, it too must find a system of volcanoes. A branch belt probably moves south around the longitude of Burma, connecting with a Great Pacific Circuit Belt branch that moves up the western coast of Sumatra.

It may also be inferred that the main southern division of the Great Central Gas Belt crosses the Asian continent at somewhere around 25 north latitude, reaching Taiwan where it joins the Great Pacific Circuit Belt and quickly moves south to reach the volcanoes of the Philippine Islands.

Activity in Taiwan, the Philippine Islands and Sumatra may thus indicate intensified activity in the Indian subcontinent as well as Burma and southern China. Conversely, it may signal release for this area or a period of relative seismic dormancy. Astrology and geology would both be needed to assess which possibility is the more probable. The quakes of this area would seem to bear the same signature.

- There are usually planets in all four elements.
- Grand trine water.
- Grand trine fire.
- Cardinal grand cross.
- Mars-Saturn conjunctions common.
- Usually Saturn conjuncts something.
- Usually Jupiter aspects Uranus.
- Cancer and Libra are important signs. A stellium may form in another sign of the same element (compensation). The presence of the Moon corroborates their importance (see next item).
- On June 12, 1897, 8.7R Assam, no planets were present in Cancer or Libra but Moon, Saturn, Uranus were in Scorpio and Pluto, Neptune, Sun in Gemini.
- There is usually a planet in the first decanate cardinal (vulcanism). However, June 12, 1897 had no cardinal at all—a wild card factor.
- The Taurus/Scorpio axis appears to be active about one-third of the time.
- Some earth is present in most of the major events, its importance again corroborated by the Moon in earth signs, at times only the Moon in earth signs (lunar enhancement).
- Mars is usually in air or water, especially Libra, Aquarius, Scorpio.
- Mars often approaches Jupiter except with the opposition.
- Venus-Mars-Jupiter, the energy triad, are usually fairly strong. Separation among these three planets varies. On August 15, 1950, 8.7R Assam, they are the three planets forming the grand trine water.
- Mercury in degree a little above half the time—good. In particular, Mercury may be in the degree of Saturn and may relate to midpoints of the primary triad Sun-Mercury-Jupiter and may be separating from Uranus.
- Mercury in degree best functions as the final near-term event indicator, separation, planetary patterns and geological indicators being in place. Again, Mercury is perhaps the most important trigger planet as well as the final one.
- The Assam Quake has relatively little cardinal and planets in Leo, Virgo and Scorpio.
- The Hindu Kush may prefer a planet in Pisces, this corroborated by Mars in Pisces in one of the Afghanistan events.

Random Sample

July 1, 1984	5.5R	Afghanistan
June 9, 1956	7.7R	Kabul, Afghanistan, GTW
August 21, 1988	7.5R+	Mountains of Nepal and eastern India
August 6, 1988	7.3R, 6.3R	India-Burma border, GTF
March 23, 1970	5.1R	Gujarat, India
August 15, 1950	8.7R	Assam, GTW
November 27, 1945	8.3R	Seaquake, Indian Ocean
May 30, 1935	7.5R	Quetta, Pakistan, GTW
January 15, 1934	8.4R	Bihar, India
March 29, 1928	8.1R	Indian Ocean
November 15, 1921	8.1R	Hindu Kush
July 7, 1909	8.1R	Hindu Kush
April 4, 1905	8.4R	Kangra
June 12, 1897	8.7R	Assam

73

The Signature of Assam, India

I collected the major events of 1897 and 1950 randomly and filled in the others from *The Catalog of Significant Earthquakes 2150 BC-1991 AD*. The signature for a precise location is sought from an exact sequence of major and moderate events. This sequence is made up of three major and two minor events.

December 30, 1984	5.8R
August, 15, 1950	8.7R, GTW
July 29, 1947	7.9R
August 14, 1932	Moderate
June 12, 1897	8.7R

- 1950 grand water trine; 1984 and 1947 water trines; 1897 Scorpio stellium; 1932 Cancer stellium.
- Saturn and Pluto relate conjunction, same sign, semisextile (30°) separating opposition, 165°.
- In three events, Sun with two slow planets, one with one slow planet and one with Mercury.
- In five of five events the Sun approaches Jupiter by classic aspect 10° to 13° distant and in three of these by 12°.
- The axis 3° Virgo/Pisces is sensitive; 1984, Mars 3° Pisces; 1950, Jupiter 3° Pisces; 1932, Jupiter-Neptune midpoint 3° Virgo; 1947, the exception with no planets in Virgo or Pisces; 1897, Jupiter 3° Virgo.
- Jupiter and Neptune are slow planet factors, Jupiter usually separating, one year plus or minus.
- In three of five, Mars in water, one air, one fire.
- Mercury in degree (3 of 5).
- Mercury recently conjunct or opposite Uranus (3 of 5).
- Planets in Leo (4 of 5).
- Saturn negative polarity (4 of 5).
- Mars conjunct Uranus, 75° twice, approaching square and approaching trine each once.

All of this is more than enough to begin an Assam signature. Again, I believe forecasting gold lies in a sequence of events, including moderate ones, at the same coordinates. There is some indication of chart similarity in both major and moderate events when this is done.

Both astrologers and geologists have, by and large, failed to emphasize the moderate event so I'll here define it as part of the location sequence. It has value in defining the level of energy buildup or release, thus showing itself as a premonitary event or a prelude to dormancy.

It is worth noting that 1947 and 1950, both major, show the potential for a major quake occurring after a relatively short time. However, it must also be noted that the designation Assam does not mean exact coordinates but a couple degrees variation in latitude, longitude or both.

At first glance the 5.8R event of December 30, 1984 is innocuous both astrologically and geologically. At first glance! In fact, by midpoint the entire chart moves to Capricorn, either between Sun/Neptune in first decanate Capricorn or conjunct Jupiter, third decanate Capricorn. The Moon in Aries adds cardinality, fire and squares the first decanate complex.

Midpoints in EM are a relatively undeveloped field. I have begun to use them and believe in their judicious use (see Midpoints). This chart, however fascinating, is not that rare, though the series of close orbs is above average. Herein lies the clue to the intensity of wedge quakes (120° minus). Here only the Moon is outside and definitely enhances the concentrated early Capricorn.

Once seen as an extreme chart, I'd then say it released most of the energy that had built up and that Assam should go a while without a major event.

Can the new energy be assessed? I would say by assessing the occurrence of grand trine water patterns and first decanate cardinal intensity periods, as well as eclipse paths, etc. with the geological knowledge of minor events, that it is possible. This would be of value regarding locations where an event is overdue, for example Mt. Pele, Martinique, or where there is premonitory activity.

74

The Signature of China and Russia

The Belts of Churchward were extrapolated for these two giant countries in The Signature of Afghanistan, Hindu Kush and India. That was done in keeping with showing the belt environment beyond the location in question.

Northern Russia would be under the influences of the Appalachian Belt. Southern Russian and northern China would be under the influence of the north division of the Grand Central Belt.

I consider my random sample of these events woefully inadequate.

As noted elsewhere in the text, I'd begin here with specific locations as I did with Tokyo, Tblisi and Assam, and I'd begin with those quake-prone locations that have nuclear power plants.

75

An Overview on Vulcanism

As with the earthquakes, the primary motive is to forecast major eruptions. As I charted eruptions I became aware of a degree sequence, the much-noted first decanate cardinal.

Late in the 20th century the importance of vulcanism as a life process for the earth is generally recognized. Nevertheless, parts of it remain understudied, in particular its horizontal movements and the source of its superheated steam, trapped and heated under basic laws of plumbing and physics.

Vulcanism has a greater role in climate regulation than it is given credit for, maintaining an absence of ice in the ocean depths and affecting its currents as well. Major currents originate from these areas of the North Atlantic and the South Pacific. The Gulf Stream and El Niño are the two best known. Note the instability and variation of the latter, being in a more vulcanistically active zone.

I have proposed that the Chandler Wobble is related in the main to vulcanism. Changing patterns and intensity of vulcanism give greater wobble. This can be corroborated quite simply with the ephemeris and ongoing records. The wobble is normal. The earth changes in relationship to the ecliptic. It is not a perfect sphere and its vulcanism changes with planetary circumstances and seasons. Intensity, flow and locations are also variables.

Once again the Chandler Wobble can show its variations with eggs—raw, poached, hard boiled. Ultimately the Chandler Wobble will be found to have a normal range. Major increases in wobble would be due solely to vulcanism, the shape of the earth—not perfectly spheroid, being a constant, and the earth's relationship to the ecliptic giving seasonal and recurring changes for a variable norm.

Astrologers have studied the weather for centuries. It is perhaps the most difficult area in astrology requiring, in terms of the Quarter Moon, 52 or more charts and the solar ingresses of the seasons adding another four. These must then be related to a given location by planetary angles. Weather astrology is also an ongoing process, this requiring a single-minded type of dedication or a lot of time. Weather astrology uses exact aspects, including those based on 15°, which are not as frequently used in other astrological fields.

In April 1946, RCA Communications hired John Henry Nelson, an engineer. He was given an assignment: forecast clear and unclear (static) times for radio. Neither an astrologer nor an astronomer, he designed a heliocentric system of astrology and by 1951 had achieved, according to RCA, some 85 percent success.

He noted that hard planetary angles forming exact aspects of 0°, 90°, 180° caused solar disturbances and that furthermore this was felt on earth almost simultaneously as radio static.

In short, solar weather, which also incudes solar EM, had been given a direct time relationship with events on earth, in this instance for all practical purposes, simultaneously. Of course weather astrologers had known this too, but they were not mapping solar events; rather, solar and lunar phases in the solunar cycle.

On March 23, 1940 a major solar magnetic storm lasting several days occurred. Sun 2° Aries, Venus 16° Taurus 75° Pluto 0° Leo. Saturn was at 0° Taurus and Uranus at 19° Taurus. Thus Venus 15° separating from Saturn and 3° approaching conjunction with Uranus. Mars at 23° Taurus had recently done the same. Mercury at 18° Pisces formed a midpoint with Uranus 19° Taurus at 18° Aries conjunct Jupiter 17° Aries.

The reader by now recognizes the integration of the primary triad. Sun-Mercury-Jupiter and the energy triad Venus-Mars-Jupiter. What is important here, however, is not the triad but the early cardinal degree and the relationship of Venus to Pluto, here at 75°, one of excess.

I mapped some more solar events and often enough I was able to find in solar events:

- Extremely early cardinal
- An aspect, not always classical, of Venus to Pluto
- Partile aspects

Meanwhile I continued charting volcanoes and quakes. All of the above is to illustrate an observation that allows for the formation of a timing sequence.

- Solar Events: Planets in extremely early cardinal degrees, exact aspects, Venus to Pluto.
- Vulcanism on Earth: This would have been stimulated almost simultaneously.
- Volcanic Eruptions: Planets in first decanate cardinal, often several, separations in aspects often present.
- Earthquakes: While many show planets in the above early cardinal positions, other planets are now in the later cardinal positons. Separation is pronounced.

A timing sequence was present:

- Solar event.
- Vulcanism.
- Eruption.
- Major quake.

This sequence follows the increase in cardinal degrees. While at first glance there is overlap in all this, it is afterall an ongoing process on both the sun and earth; nevertheless the timing is there in the charts.

Mercury and Venus orbit close to the Sun in terms of the zodiac. Vulcanism increases on both the Sun and Earth as the Sun enters the cardinal signs of the tropical zodiac. At these times Mercury and/or Venus may also be with the Sun in these early cardinal degrees. The Sun might also encounter a slower planet there.

Such an extreme period occurred at the winter solstice 1993. You may see it at a glance in the ephemeris, the increase in solar and earth vulcanism. There is a steady buildup with possible eruptions or quakes increased during 1994, respectively at times of early cardinal activity and when planets enter Cancer completing the grand trine water circuit.

Again, vulcanism causes quakes. Heat damages, melts, swells and displaces rock. Without vulcanism, most quake activity would not be possible. We'd also not be here, the planet being dead.

The amazing stellium which peaked with the entrance of the Moon into Capricorn on January 10, 1994 would already have stoked the furnaces of the earth. The stage was now set for some major quakes. Some of these may well occur on February 21, 22, 23 with the Moon in Cancer. On February 21, Mercury would be in the degree of Pluto. Based on lunar theory as a step-down transformer, quakes are more likely on the latter two days in particular after the Moon has opposed Mars and Uranus.

The quake would occur as a grand trine water event with a Capricorn head. In short, a truly universal signature. The event could occur anywhere from an astrological point of view. However, there are clues. Astrologically, the likely locations could well have been under recent eclipse paths or those with afflicted angles in recent ingress and lunation charts.

The passage of January's Capricorn planets through the early and late degrees of Aquarius may also have caused some premonitory events. These degrees in fixed signs are quake degrees.

To my knowledge this is the first presentation of a method to time a sequence of these various events which, in terms of the earth, are an overall process for renewing itself.

Its primary purpose would be to note major increases of vulcanism, then to follow through on them with both geology and astrology for the subsequent eruption and quakes.

The next chapter examines some forecasting possibilities for the major event, an eruption.

76

Forecasting the Volcanic Eruption

A perspective on the volcano may help. Astrologically it responds to one signature which is based on planets in early cardinal positions. We may infer that it is part of a single system. That in fact active volcanoes are surface features of a worldwide distribution system for magma and superheated steam, a circulatory system for planet earth.

Science at this date has chosen not to think of vulcanism in terms of horizontal distribution. This only proves that they have not looked for it, not the existence or non-existence of such a system. Such a system was put forward by James Churchward, who did not claim credit, saying it was ultimately of ancient origins, most recently from Tibet.

The Sun, under early cardinal and Venus-Pluto influences, produces solar disturbances and concurrently Earth increases its vulcanism. Eruptions follow, then quakes, this all noted by the cardinal sequence of planets. Overlapping of events are natural to the process as is augmentation of energy over a long period of time and the release of energy. (Verification for the hypothesis may be shown by weighing—simple addition—the cardinal degrees and number of degrees of separation of aspects in an event using a reasonable number of events for a sample. Cardinal and separation totals would be lowest in solar events, midway in volcanoes and highest in quakes.)

Since vulcanistic energy builds up constantly it must be released constantly. The rift system of the Atlantic Ocean and the Ring of Fire perform this function as well as that of continental drift or tectonic plate activity. Systems of fumaroles exist in Alaska, Siberia and beneath the Pacific. This last system recently discovered by the U.S. Navy and NOAA was described as volcanoes.

Churchward's belt system would allow magma from extreme latitudes to move towards the equator where its effects would be less destabilizing in terms of the Chandler Wobble.

So just what then is a volcano? A large amount of magma reaching the point where it can go no further becomes simply a boil on the skin of Earth.

The Uranian quake goes off suddenly. A truly Uranian quake of major magnitude is comparatively rare since most give some warning. The truly Uranian event as a volcanic eruption probably does not exist. There is warning of a volcano, it is known to be active. An active volcano becoming more active in geological terms such as seismic swarms and venting or swelling is the place to begin your forecast.

- Early cardinal planets are important at the premonitory event signalling intensification.
- Early cardinal planets will be important at the eruption.
- The eruption can be forecast for periods of early cardinal activity in the near future and for periods of early cardinal intensity at the next solar ingress into a cardinal sign.
- At these times, certain components of the quake chart should be in effect, notably the integration of the primary triad Sun-Mercury-Jupiter and the energy triad Venus-Mars-Jupiter. Separation would be less on the average than that of a major quake. For a major event there may be a Mercury degree as noted with quakes.
- Aspect complexes, a well-integrated chart (many aspects and all planets involved) and strong outer planet activity, are required as in major quakes.
- Slow planet relationships probably have some effect on location selection, but I do not have sufficient data which could only be the sequential eruptions of a given volcano. I do believe substantial data is available to verify this.
- The eruption follows venting in from six weeks to a little less than a year. The forecaster must note cardinal intensification and assess whether this results in buildup or release.
- Grand trine water periods probably relate to intensification and some eruptions have grand trines of various elements.
- The triad Mercury-Mars-Saturn may have special meaning in vulcanism.
- The Moon may last pass over or aspect Saturn before a major eruption.
- Lunar enhancement functions as in a quake, and the positions of planets not in cardinal may well aid in defining location.
- Duration between eruptions is extremely unreliable, but again there may be slow planet significance and the significance of planets in signs other than cardinal.
- Finally, volcanoes offer an excellent opportunity for geology and astrology to cooperate in forecasting as summarized below.
- The next period of early cardinal intensification with as many other signature factors present as possible, narrowed by a Mercury degree and lunar enhancement. Particularly strong aspects at this time also are indicators, whether closely approaching or recently separated.
- Should the forecast fail to materialize, an assessment of continuing buildup or sufficient release must be brought forward to the next early cardinal emphasis period while looking for an increase or decrease of geological and astrological indicators. Usually the event would occur in less than a year.

From my collection of randomly collected volcanic eruptions, I noted those involving grand trine water and grand trine fire in the Grand Trine Fire Volcanoes Appendix.

These same events may be used to illustrate anything in these two chapters. What follows has not to my knowledge appeared in any astrological text. The dates of the premonitory and major events are noted in a randomly collected sample of major eruptions. Notice the elapsed time and Mercury-Mars-Saturn connections. The reader will note that this complex received little note in the text. It became noticeable here. As usual, erect an Aries Ascendant chart. Take just the degrees form the ephemeris. I offer the suggestion that if the charts are quickly erected at one sitting you'll notice more. By hand is also suggested as the mind can scan every planet as it is drawn.

Volcano	Awakening	Eruption
Mt. Pele, Martinique	April 24, 1902	May 8-02
Mt. Agung, Indonesia	February 18, 1963	March 17, 1963
Krakatoa	May 20, 1883	August 26-27, 1883 (major 11:15 a.m., August 27)

Mt. St. Helen	March 20, 1980	May 21, 1980
Mt. Bezimianny,	October 22, 1955	March 30, 1956
Nevada de Ruiz, Colombia	December 12-15, 1984	September 11, 1985 (first major eruption since 1955, November 13, 1985, Helen type blowout lava flow kills 20,000)
Mt. Piñatubo, P.I.	April 2, 1991	June 15, 1991

Mt. Tacana awakes and erupts April 18, 1902. A Uranian event, note strong Mercury-Mars-Saturn (volcano triad) through Sun and strong Venus-Mars-Jupiter (energy triad) by midpoint Mars/Jupiter, Mt. Pele awakened six days later.

At awakening, Mars and Pluto may be the Mercury degrees. At eruption, the Mercury degree varies or may not be present in the degree of another planet.

At awakening, the triad Mercury-Mars-Saturn may be strong. At eruption the energy triad Venus-Mars-Jupiter is stronger. At awakening, Mars-Jupiter is not notable. At eruption in these major events Mars Jupiter may be in conjunction, trine or separating from a trine. In the Mt. Bezimanny eruption Mars-Jupiter are 150° or quincunx.

As always, think "joker is wild" in all EM forecasting. I have not been able to isolate a single signature factor that is always present at the time of a major eruption. However, one factor is a "more or less" relationship of the Sun to both Saturn and Uranus. Separation and aspect vary, but in terms of a human natal chart one might say that the Sun loosely aspects both.

The volcanoes of this sample were major events. The occasional absence of first decanate cardinal in either an awakening or an eruption might be likened to a volcanic type of planetary separation. Pressure has continued to build or the containment system weakens under the swelling. Once again the balloon image come to the rescue. An overfilled balloon is left up and eventually breaks instead of slowly deflating.

I do not have a sample involving a series of eruptions in several volcanoes over a long period of time. I hesitate to draw too many conclusions from Kiluea as this has a couple of special properties, being over a hot spot and not subject to explosive high altitude eruption or *nuee ardiente*.

My several forays into quake charts of the same geographic location, that is quakes on more or less the same coordinates, shows some promise. There may be similar promise if the same volcano is examined at different eruptions. Mt. Vesuvius of Italy and Etna of Sicily come to mind. That is, given that the volcano signature is universal or common to all volcanoes there may be a repetition of secondary factors for the awakening and eruption of a given volcano.

Two of the most likely secondary patterns involve the aspects between particular slow planets or the presence of a particular slow planet in the vulcanistic first decanate cardinal.

Similarly grand trines of various elements may serve to isolate certain volcanoes or areas. The presence of transiting Saturn in Pisces in early 1994 for two and a half years, as well as Jupiter in Scorpio in 1994, with Pluto already there, emphasizes grand trine water events.

April 1996 with both Saturn and Pluto in fire will increase the number of grand trine fire events. Saturn in 1996 is in Aries and into March 1997 it also forms a slow planet in first decanate-cardinal-Aries factor.

A listing of randomly collected GTW and GTF volcanoes as well as some Jupiter and Saturn placements are present as appendices (see Grand Trine Fire Volcanoes Appendix).

Last, to belabor the obvious, eruption forecasting begins with an awakened volcano. It is then usually a short term matter of when. When generally covers a period of two weeks to somewhat less than a year. The sample of events showing both awakening and eruption illustrates this principle clearly. Volcano prediction hasn't hit the ground floor yet. Kiluea is a special case and perhaps should be thought of as a giant fumarole.

An awakened volcano should prompt a look at its adjacent sisters. This may involve consideration of the belts. Their locations can be noted in the chapters on quake signatures for the locations in question.

In an increasingly developed world, nuclear power plants should be placed clear of volcanoes. This is an easy exercise. There is no such thing as an extinct volcano. Several hundred years plus between eruptions is common enough to require caution. Piñatubo had been dormant for more than 600 years.

Appendices and Comments

Appendix I

Simultaneous Events As Related to Lunar Enhancement and the Universal Signature

This study grew from the observation that a Mediterranean quake varied in planetary dispersion from a South American event. It became a matter of Chinese puzzle boxes, and leaving much undone, I wish to draw the matter to a close.

Along the way I dealt with the occurrence of several quakes in widely separated areas (see Simultaneous Events) and came up with the concept of lunar enhancement as a geographic isolator (see Lunar Enhancement). Recognizing that much of the work needed further corroboration, in the main I've presented it as a series of working hypotheses.

In September 1993 I secured a copy of *The Catalog of Significant Earthquakes 2150 BC-1991 AD* and was able to weave the fact of simultaneous events and the concept of lunar enhancement into a definitive and corroborated conclusion.

Originally, I noted as simultaneous events those occurring within a week Sunday 0° GMT to Sunday 0° GMT. (It was particularly convenient to frame a 0° GMT Sunday chart.) Over a week I collected various events exactly as in the current Earthwatch column. Over a week the Moon may appear in four signs, certainly in three. I noted the appearance of the one-plus major quakes and a couple under 6R as sometimes noted, plus some major weather events and volcanoes. Using plus/minus three days, I even had some forecast hits. Then I had the concept of lunar enhancement, utter simplicity, the Moon by sign designating particular areas and with its collected planetary energies supplying needed factors of mode, element and aspect complex. It ripened certain areas, providing that all the energizing factors had accumulated, and the final ones were present at this two and a half day period of the Moon in a sign.

At present, worldwide earthquake monitoring records all major quakes. The annual number of 6R+ events is consistently about 80 to 100.

Again simplicity, as I went back 250 years and began the search for simultaneous quakes. The conclusions were immediate and clear.

We know that major quakes do not occur at every Moon sign change, about 150 annually, since there are only about 80 to 100 6R+ events. Furthermore, *The Catalog of Significant Earthquakes 2150 BC-1991 AD* lists the events and the conclusions were clear.

- Simultaneous quakes of 6R+ occurring with a two and a half day period are rare.
- Their occurrence probably signifies areas responding to like signatures.
- It corroborated thus indirectly the concept of lunar enhancement.
- Since it is known that certain signatures occur over wide areas, e.g. Grand Pacific Circuit Belt or Ring of Fire, it confirms the need for lunation and eclipse reading as put forward by traditional work and the new work of Ann E. Parker.

The true simultaneous quakes of 6R+ for the last 250 years are listed. Since I do not have an ephemeris for all of this period I will simply assume the obvious for the entire period. That is that some of these quakes involved the Moon in adjacent signs. This further reduces and thus further validates the concept of lunar enhancement and the relative rarity of major (6R+) simultaneous quakes. Though I've noted them, I eliminated most border events. I noticed further corroboration of lunar enhancement. Major aftershocks of major quakes usually occur on the same or following day, again indicative of the same Moon sign.

True simultaneous major quakes, as noted in *The Catalog of Significant Earthquakes 2150 BC-1991 AD* starting at 1750 (where two days are used, note country sequence):

April 24, 1771	Japan, Taiwan
August 14-15, 1784	Iceland plus, Spain plus
December 29, 1820	Indonesia, Greece
December 28-29, 1828	Japan, Indonesia
September 10, 1837	China, Venezuela
January 24, 1852	India, Mexico
October 11-12, 1856	Greece, Egypt, Greece
August 21-22, 1859	Turkey, Italy
June 9, 1863	Philippines, France
January 2, 1866	Mexico, Albania
April 3, 1868	Hawaii, Kazakkstan plus
August 14-15, 1869	Albania, Ecuador
March 26-27, 1872	California, Mexico
May 18-19, 1875	Colombia, Philippines
August 26-28, 1881	Greece, Iran
July 17-19, 1883	Balkan, Mexico
August 26-27, 1883	Malaipia, Indonesia, Indonesia Sunda Strait (Krakatoa)
October 15-16, 1883	Greece, Iran
May 13-14, 1895	Albania, P.I. Greece
May 3-15, 1897	Philippines, Italy
May 20, 1897	Peru, Philippines
June 27-29, 1898	Italy, CIS
November 23-24, 1899	Katchamka, Japan
August 9, 1901	Vanuatu, Japan, Loyalty Island, Gemini
January 4, 1907	Indian Ocean, northwest Sumatra, close events
November 6, 1908	Italy, Kuril Islands, Aries
December 12, 1908	Japan 26W, 97E, off Peru 12S, 78W. Both at 12:08 GMT and both 8.2R. A true simultaneous event, Leo. There was a second 8.2R in Peru and Burma.
May 11, 1909	France, China, China untimed, France, Aquarius
October 21, 1909	Pakistan, Italy, Capricorn
December 9, 1909	Marianas, Santa Cruz Islands, Scorpio
February 18, 1911	Tajikistan, Greece-Albania, Scorpio

The 1907 events up to February 18, 1911 are the simultaneous events that occurred under the Uranus-Neptune opposition transits of the early century. In terms of EM, this opposition ended on January 30, 1912. On January 31, 1912, the faster separating Uranus moved into Aquarius. It briefly reappeared as Uranus returned by retrograde to 29° Capricorn September 6 to November 12, 1912. The Moon sign is listed for each entry.

April 24, 1916	Dominican Republic, Puerto Rico 7.2R, severe Nicaragua, Capricorn
August 28, 1916	Taiwan, China-Tibet, Virgo

July 30-31, 1917	China Sichuan 28W, 104E; northeast China 42N, 131E; Sagittarius
December 16-17, 1920	China, Ganson, Shanxi Provinces; Mendoza, Argentina; Pisces
December 6-7, 1922	Afghanistan, Hindu Kush; Japan, Shmabara; Cancer
November 23-24, 1927	Italy; China, Yunan Province; Cancer
March 8, 1928	Italy, Iran, Libra
April 17, 1928	Mexico, Bulgaria, Pisces
December 7-8, 1930	Central Italy, Taiwan, Cancer
January 27-28, 1931	Albania, Burma, Taurus
February 1-2, 1931	Italy, New Zealand, Cancer
November 2, 1931	Mexico, Japan, Cancer
December 14-15, 1935	Mexico December 15; Papua, New Guinea; Solomon Islands; Leo
April 1, 1936	Indonesia, eastern China, Leo
December 23-24, 1937	Mexico, Peru, Virgo
November 21, 1939	Turkey, Afghanistan
January 29-30, 1943	Northwest Balkans; Bosnia Herzegovina; January 30, Peru, Scorpio
September 14, 1943	Kermedec Islands, Loyalty Islands, Pisces
August 5-6, 1947	Iran, Algeria, Pisces
October 6, 1947	Greece, Italy, Gemini
June 27-28, 1948	Yunan, China; June 28, Fukkui, Japan; Pisces
August 5-6, 1949	Ecuador, Tonga Islands, untimed Ecuador in Sagittarius, Tonga?
December 14, 1950	Mexico, Pisces; Tonga Islands, untimed, Aquarius or Pisces?
April 13-14, 1955	Greece, China, Capricorn
March 8-9, 1957	Italy, Alaska, Gemini
August 18, 1959	Solomon Islands; Montana, U.S.; Aquarius
July 5-6, 1964	Vanuatu Islands, Esperitu Santo Islands, July 6 Mexico, Taurus
March 7, 1966	Turkey, China, Virgo
August 13, 1967	Spain/France, 22:08 GMT; Papua, New Guinea, 22:15 GMT; Scorpio
July 30-31, 1970	Iran, Peru widespread, Cancer
July 14-15, 1971	Italy; Papua, New Guinea and Bismarck Sea, Aries
July 26-27, 1971	Papua, New Guinea and Bismarck Sea Rabaul July 27 Peru, Virgo
March 27-28, 1975	Turkey; Idaho, U.S.; Virgo
April 8-9, 1976	Uzbekistan, Ecuador; Cancer
March 11-12, 1978	Sicily March 12, Russo China border, Kyrgistan-Xiniang, Sagittarius
October 16 and 18, 1981	Chile, northern Venezuela/Colombia, Gemini
January 11-12, 1982	Philippines, Honduras, Leo
January 24, 1983	Mexico, Indonesia, Gemini
February 25-26, 1983	Northwest Balkans Afghanistan near former Soviet Union, Leo
April 2-3-4, 1983	CIS Turkmenistan April 3 southeastern Costa Rica, Panama 7.3R; April 4 Indonesia, Sumatra. All moderate in damage, Sagittarius
August 6, 1983	Pakistan, Greece, Cancer
November 8-9, 1983	Belgium, Italy, Capricorn

December 22, 1983	Papua, New Guinea 5S, 151E; Koumbia, Guinea, 11N, 13W; Cancer
October 18, 1984	Turkey, Wyoming, U.S.; Leo
March 16-17-18, 1985	Antilles, Leeward Islands Guadeloupe, March 17 Chile, March 18 Philippines Islands, Aquarius
October 10-11, 1986	El Salvador; Turkey; Capricorn
April 25, 1987	Philippines, Indonesia, Aries
September 3-4, 1987	Macquarie Island, Italy, Capricorn
November 3, 1988	Guatemala, Puerto Rico, Virgo
March 10, 1989	Turkey; Papua, New Guinea; Aries
May 3-4, 1989	Iran, Venezuela (both Great Cross Belt), Aries
June 26, 1989	Hawaii, Azores, Aries
October 18, 1989	California; China 40N, 114E widespread, severe; Gemini
November 20, 1989	China, Iran, Cancer
March 25, 1990	Costa Rica, CIS Tajikistan, Pisces
April 18, 1990	Indonesia, Iran, Aquarius
May 30, 1990	Peru, Romania, Leo
June 8-9, 1990	Costa Rica, Peru, Sagittarius
December 13, 1990	Italy, Sicily, Taiwan, Scorpio

Conclusions

- With more than 68 true simultaneous major quakes, they occur, on an average, less than once a year, but some years have several (e.g., 1900).
- I eliminated about 34 simultaneous events which involved adjacent Moon signs.
- I did not include ``border events'' indicated by coordinates, but did include several marginal dates.
- I believe there were only two dates involving three locations in major events.
- Most severe aftershocks occur, most of the time, in the same Moon sign and usually within 24 hours.
- The longitudes of these major truly simultaneous events usually differed. Regarding the geological isolating band of longitude formed by lunations, eclipses and ingresses, the following conclusions were reached:
- Different lunations, etc. were in effect.
- A major event may be independent of lunations, et. due to other factors:
- Everything else in place allowing.
- The Uranian event.
- Geologically speaking we are again pointed toward vulcanism with its universal signature, especially since neither are simultaneous events necessarily on the same gas belt, and lunar enhancement offers a sound explanation, peaking the energy of a given location to the bursting point as evidenced by the astrological chart where it precisely shows its enhancing properties of element, mode, aspect complex, etc.
- The tabulation for lunar placements is:

Aries	4		Libra	2
Taurus	1		Scorpio	5
Gemini	5		Sagittarius	5
Cancer	12		Capricorn	5
Leo	7		Aquarius	3

        Virgo   5   Pisces   5

There is no combination of three signs greater than those involved in the grand trine water (21) or in two signs great than Cancer-Capricorn (16), both the universal signatures. Together in 27, they are also greater than any other four signs.

Here, by random probability, is absolute proof of the GTW, Cancer/Capricorn, and GTW with Capricorn head as the universal indicators.

This was an unplanned surprise for we have now:

- Understood simultaneous major events.
- Corroborated lunar enhancement.
- Proven GTW, Cancer/Capricorn, and GTW with Capricorn head as universal signature.

There is no combination of three signs greater than those involved in the grand trine.

Appendix II

The Cancer/Capricorn Axis

On December 21, 1904, transiting Uranus moved into Capricorn. Neptune was already in Cancer. Uranus remained in Capricorn until January 30, 1912. Note that Cancer-Capricorn is the integrating axis between the two universal patterns grand trine water and Cancer-Capricorn axis. A question remains about the quakes of these years. Was it the integration potential of the trine and square complexes, or Uranus and Neptune in opposition, or both? I incline to the latter.

Regarding the 1993 Uranus-Neptune conjunction, will this be as strong as the opposition. As of June 1, 1993, this would not seem to be the case. It would seem that the connective factor between the two patterns, grand water and Cancer-Capricorn is more important. But as noted elsewhere, a few serious possible times exist in late 1993 and 1994. From January 9, 1906 until March 19, 1908, Saturn was in Pisces. It also was there on April 14, 1905 through August 19, 1905. The combination of a grand trine with a planet 180° form one of its points is often called a kite. Here I emphasize grand trine water and the Cancer-Capricorn axis. In this instance, Capricorn is the head of the kite.

A grand trine can exist in all four elements—fire, earth, air and water—and squares exist in the three modes—cardinal, mutable, fixed. The combinations are thus four times three or 12. All grand trines integrated with squares are powerful energizers if a planet in the square complex falls 180° from one in the grand trine to form the kite.

Here I note the grand trine water as connecting with the Cancer/Capricorn axis through Cancer. It moves around. Thus I have designated GTW and Cancer-Capricorn axis as the two universal signatures. As I move through the location signatures, perhaps their kite (Capricorn head) is in fact a super aspect complex. It does not matter. However, in any location note if the grand trine, whatever element, has a head (planet or planets 180° from one point) at the time of the event.

Those Cancer/Capricorn axis quakes listed below that involve grand trine water are designated with GTW.

November 25, 1988	Q6R	Quebec
August 22, 1949	Q8.1R	Alaska
January 22, 1907		Jamaica, GTW
January 23, 1910		Trinidad
August 17, 1906	Q8.3R	Aleut, Alaska
September 19, 1907	Q6R	San Bernardino, San Andreas Fault
April 18, 1906	Q8R	San Francisco
December 22, 1906	Q8.3R	Sikiang, China, GTW
January 2, 1905	Q8.4R	Celebes Islands, GTW
March 14, 1913	Q8.3R	Molucca Islands
September 14, 1906	Q8.4R	New Guinea, Eastern Indonesia, GTW
January 13, 1915	Q7.5R	Avezzano, Italy
December 28, 1908	Q7+R	Messina, Sicily, GTW

January 15, 1968	Q6.1R	Sicily, GTW
September 8, 1905	Q7.9R	Calabria, Italy
June 15, 1911	Q8.7R	Bekuyu Island, Japan
April 12, 1910	Q8.3R	Bekuyu Island, Japan
March 13, 1909	Q8.3R	Honshu, Japan, GTW
January 21, 1906	Q8.4R	Honshu, Japan
July 30, 1949	Q7R+	Mexico City
April 15, 1907	Q8.3R	Mexico
January 14, 1903	Q8.3$	Mexico, GT air
November 17, 1901	Q7R	N. Canterbury, New Zealand
February 25, 1925	QR?	St. Laurence Valley, Quebec, GTW
June 10, 1987	Q5R	Midwest U.S., Mississippi to West Virginia
June 29, 1984	Q4R	Illinois
December 16, 1931	Q?R	Northern Mississippi, U.S.
September 30, 1930	Q7R	Ohio, U.S.
December 18, 1916	Q?R	Hickman, Kentucky, U.S.
May 26, 1909	Q?R	Illinois, U.S.
November 4, 1903	Q?R	St. Louis, Missouri, U.S., GTW
June 28, 1925	Q6.75R	Montana, U.S., GTW
October 3, 1915	Q7.75R	Nevada, U.S., GTW
July 12, 1986	Q4.2R	Northern Ohio, U.S., GTW
May 22, 1910	Q6R	Salt Lake City, Utah, U.S.
November 14, 1901		Salt Lake City area, Utah, U.S.
July 1, 1984	Q5.5R	Afghanistan
September 1, 1954	Q6.75R	Orleansville, Algeria
December 23, 1972	Q7.5R	Managua, Nicaragua
November 27, 1988		Chile?
December 1, 1928	Q8.3R	Chile
August 17, 1906	Q8.6R	Chile
January 31, 1906	Q9R	Chile
March 16, 1906	Q7.1R	Taiwan
August 5, 1949		Colombia, Ecuador
May 14-42	Q8.3R	Ecuador
January 31, 1906	Q8.9R	Colombia, Ecuador, Chile
February 4, 1976	Q7.5R	Guatemala City, GTW
February 11, 1975	Q7.5R	Guatemala, GTW
August 21, 1988	Q7.5R+	Nepal, India
August 15, 1950	Q8.7R	Assam, India
January 15, 1934	Q8.4R	Bikar, India
July 7, 1909	Q8.1R	Hindu Kush
April 4, 1905	Q8.4R	Iran

August 23, 1988	Tremor sequence	Iran
February 4, 1985	Q5.4R	Iran
September 1, 1962	Q6.75R	Iran, GT earth
May 1, 1929	Q7.1R	Shevrian, Iran
January 7, 1895	Q strong	Khorosan, (Persia) Iran
May 4, 1959	Q8.25R	Katchamka
November 4, 1952	Q8.4R	Kathchamka, GT earth
May 1, 1915	Q8.1R	Katchamka, GTW
June 26, 1926	Q8.3R	Rhodes, Dodecanese Island, GTW
February 22, 1909	Q7.9R	Fiji Islands
November 22, 1975	Q7.4R	Hawaii, U.S., GTW
June 16, 1910	Q8.6R	Loyalty Island, Hawaii, U.S.
December 28, 1974	Q6.2R	Pattan, western Pakistan, GTW
February 18, 1955	Q6.75R	Quetta, Pakistan
May 30, 1935	Q7.5R	Quetta, Pakistan, GTW
August 21, 1985	Q5.7R	Peru?
October 3, 1974	Q7.3R	Peru, GTW
May 24, 1940	Q8.4R	Peru, Ecuador
April 14, 1924	Q8.3R	Philippine Islands
August 21, 1902	Major	Philippine Islands, Mindanao

Appendix III

Grand Trine Water Quakes

In natal astrology the trine is considered beneficial. The transferral of this mindset to EM has hidden its significance in EM. That is, astrology has little noted it or maintained silence, since a major quake is not good.

Precisely, a trine may be either good or bad even in natal astrology. Trines don't ask questions. They just are...pure, flowing, directed, and inherent energy.

The grand trine in whatever element—fire, earth, air water—has at least one planet in each of the three signs ruled by the element in question. In natal astrology the question of orb might be considered. In EM, the sign itself is of first importance. Orb, the planets involved and separation are important but secondary considerations.

The grand trine constitutes a closed circuit of extremely powerful energy. It cannot be destroyed. Energy may enter or leave it through a planet opposite one of its points. This yields a kite formation, looking exactly like the classic kite with this outside planet at the head of the kite. This planet, often enough, has planets square to it and the classic general signature of quake squares integrated with trines in effect.

The grand trine has a common element and a common polarity. Both of these factors isolate location. Grand trines of all four elements figure in location signature.

The grand trine water indicates that an event can occur anywhere. One must move immediately to other indicators in the effort to narrow down the times and locations.

General considerations would be intensity, integration, nodal positions and separation, as well as planetary grouping, etc. Specific location indicators might be slow planet placement, eclipse paths, particular sign or aspect emphasis, and variations in the rest of the chart, other than the grande trine water.

In late 1992 and early 1993, transiting Mars entered Cancer on one of its long stays, which occur every few years. For about five months Mars was in Cancer and Pluto was in Scorpio. Any planet falling in Pisces completed the circuit. The Sun in Pisces allowed one month. Venus and Mercury extended this and of course the Moon in Pisces each month other than Sun in Pisces added another two and a half days. That this grand trine water caused little EM I attribute to the position of the Moon's Nodes, which were in a gathering phase (see On the Moon's Nodes).

Since Pluto is in Scorpio for years the least possible amount of time that the grand trine water could operate would be five days - Sun in Cancer, Moon in Pisces, Sun in Pisces, Moon in Cancer. That is purely an illustrative extreme, for surely the passage of the fast planets Mercury and Venus through Pisces and Cancer extend this minimum time. The operative word here is illustrative.

Following a tentative entry into Pisces in May-June, 1993, Saturn retrograded into Aquarius and returned to Pisces on January 29, 1994. On November 11, 1995, Pluto moves into Sagittarius and the grand trine water emphasis is broken.

During this time the transit of any planet into Cancer will complete the circuit. Using our limited illustrative example of the Sun and Moon, we come up with one month—Sun in Cancer plus about 25 days of Moon in Cancer (the other 11 months). Again we ignore the presence of Mercury and Venus in Cancer. Note how the presence of a second long-term planet in water automatically extends grand trine water periods tenfold.

I forecast at this point a major increase in EM for 1994. This is also premised on the Moon's Nodes being in release phase (see On the Moon's Nodes). This will continue into late 1995, at least until Scorpio leaves Pluto.

Since the grand trine water, when transited by a planet opposite one of its own can both give and receive energy, a great deal of energy will also be stored for subsequent release. This will include some of the same areas still in release phase, areas in buildup phase (remember grand trine water is universal), as well as new areas.

With the spring equinox of 1996, the Sun moves into Aries, followed by Mars into Aries March 25, 1996 and missing only a day as Mars hits 10° Aries with Saturn entering Aries on April 8, 1996.

This will begin a period of unprecedented solar activity as well as general Earth vulcanism, supplying pressure and friction heat, as well as creating resistance and containment.

During the two years following spring 1996, the first year until spring 1997 may be considered a period of unprecedented volcanic activity worldwide. Saturn, a vulcanistic planet, will trine Pluto, the vulcanistic planet. Energy will be free-flowing and reciprocal.

Again, vulcanism in general responds to a common signature. Worldwide is the keyword.

At this time too, exactly as in the grand trine water example, two slow planets remain in fire: Saturn in Aries and Pluto in Sagittarius. Grand trine fire energy will increase tenfold. I'll list some probable locations here, noting that with all such grand trines the locations nearest to areas of vulcanism deserve constant monitoring because of spring 1996 to spring 1997 energy storage.

The list below is of grand trine water EM.

October 30, 1988	5.1R	60 miles northwest of Homer, Alaska, U.S.
July 9, 1986	5.7R	40 miles southeast of Adak Islands, Aleutians
June 29, 1925	6.3R	Santa Barbara, California, U.S.
April 6, 1990	4R	San Francisco, California, U.S.
February 25, 1980	5.5R	Yucca Valley, California, U.S.
March 15, 1979	5.2R	Yucca Valley, California, U.S.
November 22, 1975	7.4R	Hawaii, U.S.
December 18, 1811	8.9R	New Madrid (Cancer/Capricorn)
February 23, 1887	7R+	Riviera, France (Pisces stellium)
January 30, 1969	R?	Mindanao, Philippine Islands
April 1, 1955	7.6R	Lanao, Philippine Islands
February 28, 1969	7.9R	Atlantic off Portugal
November 1, 1755	8.9	Lisbon quake (Cancer-Capricorn, Jupiter and Moon in Libra)
May 30, 1990	6.5R	100 miles northeast of Bucharest, Romania
April 20, 1935	7.1R	Taiwan
March 28, 1906	R?	Turkey
August 19, 1966	6.9R	Varto, Turkey
March 5, 1990	7.1R	Near Vanuatu
February 11, 1987	6.6R	Vanuatu
September 8, 1615	?	Santo Domingo (with hurricane)
January 14, 1907	7R+	Kingston, Jamaica
January 22, 1907	?	Kingston, Jamaica
February 19, 1990	4.4R	Humacao, Puerto Rico

June 5, 1986	4R	20 miles southwest of Ponce, Puerto Rico
September 27, 1906	? major	North of Puerto Rico
December 28, 1992	4.8R	Epicenter Tortola, VI
April 20, 1990	4R	St. John, U.S. Virgin Islands
February 19, 1990	4R	St. Thomas, U.S. Virgin Islands
July 12, 1990	4+5R	Martinique
May 12, 1990	3.5R	St. Lucia
May 19, 1990	4.6R (first event)	St. Lucia
August 22, 1988	5.3R	Off Bermuda
June 11, 1986	Strong	Off Venezuela, felt in Trinidad
June 9, 1956	7.7R	Kabul, Afghanistan
March 25, 1990	5.5R-6.9R	60 miles west of San Jose, Costa Rica
May 9, 1990	Swarm	Costa Rica
November 11, 1922	8.4R	Atucana, Chile
July 9, 1956	7.7R	Santorin, Greece
August 11, 1903	8.3R	Thessaly, Greece
February 4, 1976	7.5R	Guatemala
February 11, 1975	7.5R	Guatemala
August 15, 1950	8.7R	Assam, India
May 31, 1935	7R+	Quetta, India (60,000 dead)
November 15, 1921	8.1R	Hindu, Kush
March 24, 1990	5R+	Tabas, Iran
September 1, 1962	7.5R	Buyin-Zara, Iran
February 3, 1923	8.4R	Katchamka Penn, USSR
May 1, 1915	8.1R	Katchamka Penn, USSR
August 11, 1969	?	Kuril Islands, USSR
June 10, 1965	7.2R	Kuril Islands, USSR
May 20, 1990	7.5R	Southern Sudan
June 26, 1926	8.3R	Rhodes, Dodecanese Islands
October 14, 1968	7.2R	Meckering, West Australia
December 28, 1974	6.2R	Pattoan, Pakistan (Cancer-Capricorn, 6,000 dead)
May 29, 1990	5.8R	400 miles northeast of Lima, Peru
May 10, 1990	5.8R	400 miles northeast of Lima, Peru
October 3, 1974	7.3R	Peru
February 18, 1911	7.7R	Ferghan Parmir, Afghanistan
July 23, 1905	8.7R	Southwest of Lake Baikal, Siberia
July 9, 1905	8.4R	Southwest of Lake Baikal, Siberia
January 15, 1993	5.3R	Gibson, California
April 6, 1990	4.0R	Palm Springs, California
March 2, 1990	4.7R	California
June 27, 1988	5.2R	North of Santa Cruz, California

June 27, 1988	R?	Over wide area, California
November 21, 1986	5.1R	40 miles southwest of Eureka, California
July 31, 1986	5.5R	Bishop, California
July 29, 1986	4.4R	California
July 20, 1986	5.5R	Nevada border, California
July 31, 1986	5.7R	26 miles off Oceanshore, California
July 8, 1986	6.0R	Southern California
August 4, 1985	6R+	Coalinga, California
October 22, 1926	R?	California
June 27, 1966	5.5R	Central San Andreas Parkfield Fault
November 28, 1974	5.1R	North of Bear Valley, California
June 29, 1925	6.3R	Santa Ynez, California
November 24, 1927	7.3R	Santa Ynez, California
April 17, 1986	6.3	W. Yunan Province, China
February 4, 1975	7.3R	Anshan, Leanoning Province, China
February 3, 1975	9.0R	Kiachen, China (One or two events? Secrecy about hundreds of thousands of dead)
December 22, 1906	8.3R	Sikiang, China
March 6, 1993	7.0R	San Cristobal/Celebes Islands
March 27, 1969	R?	Halmahera, Mollucas
January 22, 1905	8.4R	Celebes Islands
December 28, 1935	8.1R	Sumatra
July 6, 1988	6.7R	Near Papua, New Guinea
September 14, 1906	8.4R	New Guinea
May 5, 1990	6R, but	Naples, Italy; widespread
December 28, 1908	R?	Messina, Italy; 75,000 dead
January 15, 1968	6.1R	Sicily
January 15, 1993	7.5R	Hokkaido, Japan
May 31, 1990	6R+	Off coast of Japan
February 20, 1990	6.6R	Sea, 70 miles south of Tokyo (felt in Tokyo)
June 16, 1964	7.5R	Nigata, Honshu, Japan
March 4, 1952	8.6R	Hokkaido, Japan
September 1, 1923	8R+	Honshu, Tokyo, Japan
March 13, 1909	8.3R	Honshu, Japan
December 31, 1703	8R	Odowara, Japan
May 31, 1990	6.1R	180 miles west of Mexico City
March 14, 1979	7.9R	Mexico City
January 20, 1970	R?	Kermedec Islands, New Zealand
June 24, 1970	R?	Queen Charlotte Island, Canada
March 21, 1925	6.7R	Quebec, Canada
February 25, 1925	R?	St. Lawrence Valley

March 20, 1990	3.4R	Southern Illinois
November 22, 1974	R? Damaging	Charleston, South Carolina
November 5, 1926	R?	Southeast Ohio
October 28, 1923	R?	Marked Tree, Arkansas.
November 4, 1903	R? Serious,	St. Louis, Missouri; widespread
June 28, 1925	6.7R	Montana
December 16, 1954	7.1R	Nevada
October 3, 1912	7.7R	Nevada
July 12, 1986	4.2R	Northern Ohio
March 27, 1975	R?	Salt Lake City, Utah
August 16, 1966	R?	Salt Lake City, Utah

During 1994 and 1995 there will be a tenfold increase in time (and thus energy) for grand trine water. Note Uranus, conjunct or near Neptune in Capricorn, supplies great energy solely by virtue of its conjunctive powers and is also in the universal Cancer-Capricorn axis.

As indicated in Methodology of EM Sample, the sample is random. I have certainly missed recurring grand trine water quakes in a location and I've missed grand trine water quakes in other locations.

In going through my entire sample to list these grand trine water quakes, it became clear to me that these locations also often have an affinity for water and may have water trines or water stellia. One sign of three will show up less frequently in some cases. In 1994 and 1995, the water constant is Saturn in Pisces and Pluto in Scorpio. Since both Saturn and Pluto are slow planets, a slow planet signature is also present, Saturn-Pluto by aspect, water by element, mutability (Saturn) and fixity (Scorpio). In late 1993 and much of 1994, Pluto and Scorpio were accented by Jupiter in Scorpio. As Jupiter moves to Sagittarius for most of 1995 it will aspect Saturn by square. At writing (1993), Jupiter is square Uranus and Neptune. The dance of the slow planets is unending. While slow, the partners change.

Appendix IV

French Earthquakes

The French events are partially noted from *The Catalog of Significant Earthquakes 2150 BC-1991 AD*. Dates form 1660 forward are sequential as recorded. In only two events was the time available. Earlier events were major.

To note a signature, erect charts for noon GMT, Greenwich, more than close enough, as without time, coordinates are valueless. Convert these charts to 0° Aries charts. Noon GMT will provide clear knowledge of the Moon by sign or whether alternative signs cloud the issue. Even in that instance, other planets must be true by sign.

Coordinates are noted for geographic or location isolation. More than one signature is a possibility (California). And what of the rolling signature?

June 21, 1660	IX	43N0E
May 12, 1682	IX	48N6E
August 14, 1708	IX	43N5E
October 6, 1711	VIII	47N0E, Severe
May 24, 1750	IX	43N0E, Severe
June 1772	VIII	44N4E
January 25, 1799	VIII	46N2W
March 23, 1812	IX	43N5E, Severe
February 23, 1818	VIII	43N7E
July 20, 1854	?	43N0E
December 12, 1855	VIII	43N06
June 9, 1863	VIII	44N6E
July 19, 1873	VIII	44N4E
February 23, 1887	IX	43.9N8E
February 23, 1887	X	43.9N8E, Extreme

Earlier severe events by year: 470, 1003, 1227 extreme. No dates given.

October 18, 1356	X	47N7E
July 20, 1564	X	44N7E
July 20, 1564	X	44N7E
July 20, 1564	X	44N7E, Extreme

Even an incomplete listing shows a disturbing pattern:

- Severe or extreme events are 44+N6+E
- Two to three quakes occur on a day, the second or third being the worst.
- France may have no significant events for more than 20 years, then two or three over several years.
- France, according to *The Catalog of Significant Earthquakes 2150 BC-1991 AD*, is overdue.
- France has had only one 6.2R event this century, June 11, 1909, 43N5E.

Appendix V

Grand Trine Water Volcanos

My sample of volcanoes is 30 percent that of my quakes. I have 16 GTW volcanoes and 118 GTW quakes. If the sample were more equal I would have 50 GTW volcanoes on the premise that my collection is random.

All matters being equal there are twice as many GTW quakes as volcanoes. This corroborates geological and astrological differences between the two types of events. On the other hand it also corroborates the relatedness of vulcanism and quakes, for some quake charts look more like volcano charts and vice versa.

The GTW quake list also includes some minor events, but I do not feel this alters the results. The volcano chart has constants indicating more variation in quake charts. Many of the minor GTW quakes are significant by being Uranian (sudden events without warning). In both the minor and Uranian events, the analogy of a disruption—an electric power surge comes to mind—a sudden infusion of more power than the system can handle.

In flipping through all the volcano charts, I again found that water trines involving two signs were common and for those locations, one water sign seemed less common. This is noteworthy since both Saturn and Pluto will remain in water signs for 1994 and 1995, creating the tenfold water trine energy release.

Appendix VI

Volcanoes: Grand Trine Fire, Saturn in Pisces, Jupiter in Pisces, Jupiter in Scorpio

I will also list grand trine fire volcanoes. These four lists are of special importance because of the position of Uranus and Neptune in Capricorn. As noted, the Cancer-Capricorn axis will form a square by sign with Saturn when it enters Aries, a volcano sign.

Grand Trine Fire Volcanoes

March 25, 1988	Nevada de Ruiz, Colombia (Cancer-Capricorn)
January 14, 1993	Caleras, Colombia
March 2, 1955	Kiluea, Hawaii
July 18, 1986	Kiluea, Hawaii
November 21, 1935	Kiluea, Hawaii
March 30, 1947	Mt. Hekla, Iceland
July 12, 1966	Mt. Aw Sangi Talaud Island, Indonesia
September 11, 1950	Mt. Stromboli, Sicily
November 21, 1986	Mt. Mihara, Oshima Island, Japan
May 28, 1970	Mt. Swuanosezima, Japan
February 19, 1975	Mt. Ngauruhoe New Island, New Zealand
March 14, 1990	Mt. Redoubt, Alaska
March 9-10, 1990	Mt. Redoubt, Alaska
February 2, 1993	Mt. Mayon Legaspi, Philippines
July 5, 1966	Mt. Taal, Philippines
September 28, 1965	Mt. Taal, Philippines
August 12, 1971	Mt. Hudson, Chile
October 18, 1948	Villa Rica, Chile
September 3, 1985	Kiluea, Hawaii
March 20, 1980	Mt. St. Helen, Washington (awakens)
March 27, 1980	Mt. St. Helen, Washington (first venting)
August 24, 1928	Rokatinda Poloewch Islands, Dutch East Indies
April 6, 1971	Mt. Etna, Sicily (GTF not present in other eruptions)
July 14, 1973	Mt. Tiatia, Kuril Island, USSR
March 20, 1956	Mt. Bezimianny, Katchamka Peninsula; five cubic miles of ejecta; largest single event of the 20th century: Sun 0° Aries trine Saturn 2° Sagittarius, Pluto 22° Leo, Jupiter 26° Leo
April 4, 1982	El Chichen #2, Mexico
April 15, 1941	Colima, Mexico
May 3, 1971	San Cristobal, Nicaragua (activity)
July 19, 1973	Curacoa Reef, American Samoa
July 12, 1973	Mt. Langila, New Britain, Papuas, New Guinea

October 4, 1927   Falcon Island, Tonga Group
December 4-13, 1951   Camiquin Island, Philippines

About the same number of events as the GTW. Note GTFs figured in two major events, Bezimianny and Helen.

This is based on my entire volcano sample.

Volcanoes—Saturn in Pisces

November 21, 1935   Moana Loa, Hawaii
July 12, 1966   Mt. Awu, Sangi Talaud Island, Indonesia (Saturn retrograde stationary)
April 18, 1906   Vesuvius, Italy
March 28, 1907   Ksudatch, Kamchatka Peninsula
July 5, 1966   Mt. Taal, Philippines
September 28, 1965   Mt. Taal, Philippines (minor and sudden)

This from a volume of 211 volcanic events, again randomly collected. I would emphasize possible location over low probability.

Based on seven and a half years of Saturn in Pisces in the 20th century, or 1/14 of the time, I might have expected to collect twice as many samples, say 14 volcanoes with Saturn in Pisces.

Such general terms are correct as I'll demonstrate with Jupiter in Pisces, an event which has occurred seven times in the 20th century, for a total of about seven years. From the same collection:

Volcanoes—Jupiter in Pisces

January 22, 1987   Mt. Picayu, Guatemala
July 18, 1986   Mt. Kiluea, Hawaii
October 5, 1986   Mt. Helen, Washington (tremor and venting)
May 4, 1986   Mt. Helen, Washington (tremors)
February 19, 1963   Agang, Bali, Indonesia
September 11, 1950   Stromboli, Sicily
November 21, 1986   Mt. Mihara Oshima Island, Japan, GTW
February 19, 1975   Mt. Ngauruhoe North Island, New Zealand
March 27, 1986   Augustine volcano, on island 170 miles from Anchorage, Alaska, U.S.
May 22, 1915   Mt. Lassen, California
October 4, 1927   Falcon Island, Tonga Group
January 18-21, 1951   Mt. Laurington, New Guinea

While more correct by rates than Saturn in Pisces, it does not come from a conclusive sample. Again, it is perhaps most valuable as a geographic indicator. Note the volcanoes are not the same. Mt. Kiluea is of course extremely close to Moana Loa.

Volcanoes—Jupiter in Scorpio

December 1970   Erta'ale, Ethiopia
December 14, 1970   Nyirancongo, Zaire (activity)

December 2, 1970	Coast of Colombia, Colombia Lakar
August 12, 1971	Mt. Hudson, Chile
August 26, 1970	Rincon de Vieja, Costa Rica
January 7, 1970	Pacaya, Guatemala
August 14, 1971	Kiluea, Hawaii
March 30, 1947	Mt. Hekla, Iceland (GTW with strong Pisces)
September 18, 1970	Akita Komagatchi, Japan
April 21, 1970	Mt. Aso, Japan
January 29, 1970	Myojinsho, Japan
April 4, 1982	El Chichen #2, Mexico
March 28, 1982	El Chichen, Mexico
March 30, 1970	Chaparraspique, El Salvador
August 18, 1970	Telica, Nicaragua
April 4, 1970	Masaya, Philippine Islands
April 24, 1970	Mt. Malinas, Philippine Islands

Again the value appears as a geographic indicator. Jupiter by nature expands and Scorpio is the natural sign of volcanoes. What is noted here is activation or awakening of multiple volcanoes within a system or area—Central America, Japan and Philippines Islands.

Other than Japan, there are no Pacific volcanoes in this sample.

I would tentatively forecast activity for Mt. Hekla, Japan, Philippine Islands and Nicaragua, as well as some other events in Central America for 1994, Jupiter in Scorpio with Pluto, etc.

Appendix VII

The Semantics of Prediction

This chapter first appeared in *Today's Astrologer*, April 21, 1993, Vol. 55, No. 4 under the title Understanding Prediction. It is illustrative of my beliefs and techniques. I hope that it will clarify understanding of the predictive process for both astrologers and geologists which in EM is forecasting.

Winter 1959 in Vermont. We returned to senior English class and were hit with a bombshell. Mr. Brodine, who had given up driving after chasing rabbits across fields in his car, informed us that henceforward we would learn semantics. It turned out to be the most influential experience of my formal education. Quite simply, if you understand what a word means, you are in power of its circumstances. If you don't you will be manipulated by it, or without power. Much of the latter condition exists in astrology regarding predictive use.

Prophecy

Prophecy means implicitly or explicitly, from a higher power through a religious or psychic channel. Often, prophets live apparently humble lives, the children of Fatima or Edgar Cayce. They are generally without learned predictive tools (astrology) or knowledge related to the subject of their prophecies.

Prophecy should be 90 percent sure, let's say, but often we're told we can change circumstances - true of both Cayce and Fatima. An event will foretell the coming of the major events. One or both may detail a prophetic event into the future, even many generations.

Prophets are not around to deal with their failures. A cynic might call this astute. After a time frame is given, again Fatima and Cayce, the time frame sometimes fails. Cayce's great quotes involving land rise and subsidence fall in the late category. through they may begin tomorrow. Perhaps in Cayce's case he tuned in to our collective millennium induced visions. While there is some consistency between Cayce and Ruth Montgomery, another seer, they're both still late.

What is known is that the last two millennia had their own prophetic scenarios but passed uneventfully.

Nostradamus, often called a prophet, was an astrologer who also scryed, that is saw visions in a reflective surface believed to be a basin of water. Since he was a master of both arts he probably used either to induce or augment the other. Like most astrologers he needed another trade to make ends meet. He was noted for his medical versatility and his personal bravery in treating plague victims.

I also suspect that he didn't take himself as seriously as we do. He would be extremely proud of some of his hits, for example the capture of Louis XVI and Marie Antoinette, and would shrug his shoulders at some of his misses and confusing verse, "Eh bien." He'd probably not call himself a prophet, which was a word of simpler times when anyone who forecast or predicted was held in awe or conversely ridiculed and persecuted.

Finally, the record of prophets probably comes up well short of what some would have us believe, a situation that also exists among those who predict or forecast.

Prediction

Prediction sounds a little more dignified than forecasting and should be a little more spectacular in timing and content. It implies abilities learned and possessed by the predictor, e.g. astrology. These are more important than knowledge of the subject. The success rate is admittedly below prophetic standards and should be above forecast standards. Let us say 70 percent success rate. Note that Nostradamus fits this description.

Furthermore, I believe that in prediction a great hit is like a home run. You've struck out in five games but this one landed in the upper stands. In some way it stands on its own and should not be part of the problem.

Personally I could not have seen Trujillo waylaid and assassinated on the way to see his mistress. As they say, Nostradamus did good, but he did have psychic abilities beyond astrology.

Forecasting

Forecasting implies outright that it will not call them all, and thereafter deals with an ongoing sequence of the same type event or condition—the weather, ball games, handicapping the horse or football.

The forecaster makes an astonishing mental move; he learns his subject. Knowledge of his subject is his primary tool and he uses anything else he can. He lives on narrow survival margins since he must clearly define his position. The 1982 winner among football handicappers in the Las Vegas annual awards had a score of 57 percent.

I like to think of myself as somewhere between predicting and forecasting. The discipline of horary work, and the need for knowledge of a subject in mundane work, bring about this mindset when applied to natal astrology. Its just amazing how one's predictions improve when he knows if he's speaking to a butcher, a murderer or a surgeon. Remember the old court astrologer made it a point to know the king very well. His life depended on it.

Fortune Telling

Fortune telling is primarily binary, yes/no, and astrologically speaking relates to horary. The idea that horary principles do not relate to the natal chart would be rejected out of hand by an astrologer prior to the 20th century and in a rage by Evangeline Adams.

Casting fortune involves a bit more content, usually arrived at by assessing luck, or lack of it, as related to different areas. It is an effective way to predict eventualities, e.g. a happy marriage or financial security. The term itself is not often used now. It is a content oriented prediction or forecast.

Semantics teach that words are power. Those who are against predictive astrology, or simply cannot do it through conscience or inability, are in full possession of a linguistic arsenal.

Fortune telling is now a pejorative implying that the teller is not spiritually or scientifically up to par in his astrological outlook. This is unfortunate for the pejorative fortune telling bleeds through onto predictive, a term used by such astrologer as Frances Sakoian.

While there are abuses and faults in the predictive levels of astrology, they also abound among its analytical, scientific and spiritual levels.

I believe the fifth house covers prediction. It is a house of the future. Every fifth house matter involves a future element of risk; love, children, ego extension, gambling, creativity, with the outcome unknown. Thus it might be said that the laws of probability, and a noting of success/failure, would better cover the predictive process than statistical analysis, which is simply a carpenter's tool in a fisherman's tackle box.

Astrology is not scientific, nor can it be, as neither planetary position or earthly consideration (e.g. people and event) are equal or constant. In fact nothing stays the same and everything is constantly changing.

The correct term is empirical astrology. When A is with B in C, X often happens. A with B in C often appears in the chart of X. A with B in C often indicates X conditions. We are actually talking about observed reality, that is the correlation of earth and sky. Good astrologers have figured it out for millennia.

Scientific astrology and statistical analysis are the 20th century Trojan horse of astrology, due in part to the highly publicized statistical work of Michel Gauquelin.

Pure analytical astrology, by its name implying no future work, may be said to be two dimensional and fails to test itself.

Not all events are yes/no, win/lose, but some that are include contests, elections, divorces, wars, lost and found, and matters that represent the outcome of an event in progress. Note that divorce is included. The forced decision of one party is easier to predict than the free choice of two (marriage); also, divorce is the outcome of an event in progress.

Some events that do not yield simple yes/no answers are often ongoing or long lasting, involving many parts and parties. These require a general direction (probably yes/no), a less structured period of time and a description of content closely stated as probable. Events in the former Soviet Union and elsewhere relating to the Uranus/Neptune conjunction are examples.

It is harder to predict an event that has not happened, than to predict the outcome of one in progress. An event does not have to happen. In natal work it can be illustrated with the transits of Mars. Not every transit will bring anger or injury, but when it does come, a transit of Mars will be there. The fact that an event does not have to happen is seldom dealt with in prediction nor is there a proper or uniform way to integrate it into the success/failure score of one's predictions. Some mundane astrologer and earthquake forecasters are grappling with the problem under the term probable times.

You can't predict what you're not looking for.

Generally speaking, exact predictive scores can only be kept on a)binary events or b)a specific event related to an exact time frame. Correct prediction of the outcome of 23 of 30 ball games, and three of five lost jewelry questions, and the outbreak of a client's migraine headaches three months in a row are a good record, but I never can find the missing cats.

An event must be in a relevant time frame. Calling for rain when the clouds are in sight is not prediction. When there is annual rainfall, to say it will rain within nine months is not a prediction. As often stated, you must be able to see around the ben din the river. Predictive abilities are not always constant relative to events. Moon 0° to 3°, Moon void-of-course, Saturn in seventh, etc. are known horary strictures (Saturn in seventh relates to the astrologer re the event).

Predictive abilities are not constant for the prediction. Jut plain off-days and periods, as well as frames of mind, alter ability. So does tiredness. Mercury retrograde, Mars-Jupiter aspect and Saturn-Sun aspects damage ability.

Snatching defeat from the jaws of victory, twice in one week, makes a good example. Centering on September 16, 1992, there was a triple conjunction of Sun, Mercury, Jupiter in Virgo. I felt that there would be some seismic activity in or around Japan, for in fact most major Japanese quakes have something in Virgo. This was a strong energy complex and certain other planetary conditions were in order. Nothing happened.

Being so sure of the quake, I didn't pay much attention to the volcano potential and thus missed an opportunity. it was present in the chart and Mt. Spurr, 80 miles west of Anchorage, Alaska, went off. I lost the opportunity for a successful call by not looking for volcanoes. You can't predict what you're not looking for.

But what about that quake. Once again in stating my position too surely, I ended up wrong. The proper way to have stated this was a strong possibility of an occurrence at this time. While that looks like going from overconfidence to waffling, when one is dealing with predicting specific new events, in specific times frames, it is important to remember that an event does not have to happen.

I fell into the well again four days later by predicting a no vote in the September 20, 1992 French referendum on the Maastricht treaty. Instead, a 51-49 yes vote prevailed and the prediction was wrong.

In fact it might have been right. I am on record as predicting that the EC won't fly. On September 21, 1992, television newscasts stated that the narrow margin of victory in the yes vote may have irreparably damaged the hopes for the treaty and the EC as such, for the lynch pin of the EC is the common currency delineated in the treaty.

Had I simply stated that the referendum would not bode well for Maastricht, I might have claimed a successful call. I snatched defeat from the jaws of victory by the phrasing of the prediction, and by not thinking of other ways the negative planetary indicators might have worked, e.g. damage to the treaty as opposed to a ``no'' vote call. I still maintain both Maastricht and the EC are in trouble, but again my call as stated was wrong.

We have heard the following prediction on the morning news: "John Doe of XYZ predicts that within the next 50 years there will be a 75 percent chance of an earthquake of 7 Richter in Southern Bogonia." Having read this far, I hope you recognize an example of semantic and predictive gibberish.

This is only an observation that says a large quake may or may not come at any time. Seventy-five percent, 7 Richter, and 50 years are in fact unprovable or arbitrary and are meant to imply predictive content, ability and timing. None of these are present.

Appendix VIII

Full Circle

This text was written three times, nothing unusual, but changes and additions were substantial. I'm sure the rewriting also resulted in a few omissions, but I'm pleased with the overall lucidity. I was interested in communication among several parties as well as indicating new approaches to EM forecasting.

Please read the text through as the hypotheses, assertions and arguments often appear or are reintroduced as related to other matters. This is true in the section on signatures and in the appendices, some themselves dynamic chapters instead of the usual list or expanded footnotes.

I was especially pleased to cross corroborate the concept of lunar enhancement through *The Catalog of Significant Earthquakes 2150 BC-1991 AD*.

I am responsible for the ideas and errors of this work. I have also given acknowledgements where due, especially regarding Churchward's gas belts. While I wrote this alone, usually sitting at the kitchen table, by the end of it I realized that I was indebted to a higher power and to numerous individuals from the various fields who had derived the parts of the puzzle which I attempted to cobble together. I am also indebted to those friends who encouraged me, and to those skeptics whose outright scorn provided a useful spur. The loyal opposition often provided energy and concentration.

January 17, 1994, 4:31 a.m. PST, epicenter San Fernando Valley, California, major damage area Los Angeles, California, a 6.6 Richter quake threw people form their beds. The event, which will be the most covered by television to date, caused damage of $10 to $60 billion according to the speaker at hand. A mid-figure seems reasonable, along with the fact that whatever the cost, it will be greater than either Hurricane Hugo or Hurricane Andrew, and probably greater than both together.

It was not a great quake, only marginally large at 6.6R. But it was a direct hit and its vibrational direction, along with the geology, provided significant damage over a large area. It rose through the earth like a dum-dum shell, tearing out a wide area of damage, not with the clean piercing of a steel-jacketed bullet. It was more like a small New Madrid (there was uplift in areas) than a slip-fault event. It was shallow, some nine or 10 miles deep and geologists were quick to point out that it came from an ``unknown fault.''

Rest assured that there are many unknown faults. Since vulcanism is involved, the actual fault map itself changes deep within the earth, as well as the part of area under stress. When the magma hardens as a plug, new hard stone is formed. The surrounding area is softened and cracked. The next onset of magma would carve this adjacent weakened area. This may be seen in quarries. Like the tributary system of a river near the sea, faults change. A relatively minor change below fans as its rises, like a shot gun blast.

It is not primarily a matter of good or bad construction at this magnitude, but precise vibrational intensity. Geologists infer that the energy dispersal field is uniform, X Richter over an outspreading circle as if the ripples are even in strength or perfectly circular. Not so. When they actually reach the earth's surface I would illustrate the matter with a cropped hedge. All energy is greatest near these branch tips. It rose up from below. Buildings immediately above a branch tip, to continue the analogy, were destroyed, knocked off their foundations, etc. Meanwhile nearby buildings seemed relatively unscathed. They were between the branch tips. Impact (Richter magnitude) is not the same thing as vibrational or impact diffusion.

In breaking stones with a sledge hammer, technique wins over power. The stone splits when struck on the plane of the fault. If one sliced a piece of bread, the blow would be in line with the slice line. The hammer is swung like a knife, set to graze the plane of slice, If the stone is truck at right angles to this plane, energy is diffused and damage varies. This right angle blow also shatters.

Energy and vibration distribution through the affected area are not uniform. This is the real explanation behind damage variation.

A similar situation exists in hurricanes. I've only seen it mentioned twice in print. These are the hurricane tornadoes with winds of more than 200 miles per hour. In Hugo they were about 35 to 50 feet in diameter and bounced like a ball. Direction changes slightly with the bounce and I suspect they are reabsorbed into the main mass of the storm after a fraction of a mile or hundreds of feet.

The Mercalli type table of their damage is as follows:

- Buildings explode.
- Roofs fly.
- 4"x8" beams, 24 feet long, can fly with concrete blocks attached for 100 feet or more. These same beams are snapped and flung like spears.
- Century plant (agave) leaves are peeled off like artichoke leaves and dropped in place. Winds at 140 miles per hour do no damage to them. Some leaf fraying is probably the abrasions of other flying plants and matter.
- Trees fall in direction (parallel) as in Helen or Tugunska.
- Mangrove trees hit by these are killed. While not toppled, the life force is sucked out.

I saw all this with Hugo, as did others. Some roof, tree and mangrove damage is still evident after four years.

Astrologically, Los Angeles January 17, 1994 followed the California signature for major quakes. Shown here are the full Ascendant event chart and the 0° Aries analysis chart as used for forecasting.

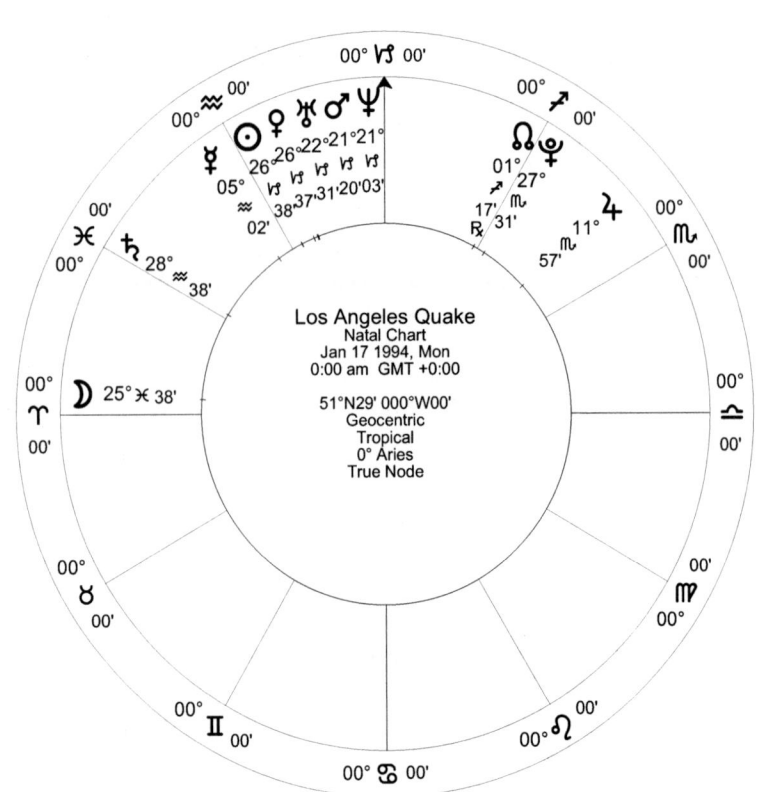

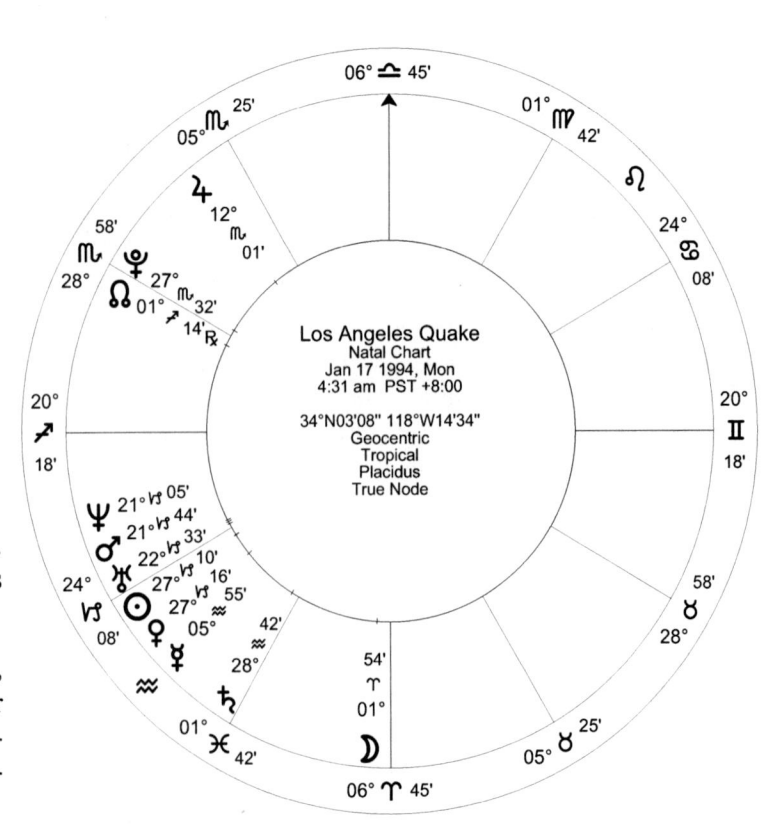

Interestingly enough the Ascendant and Nadir might be said to supply needed fire, a point the serious reader will note I haven't made before. Nevertheless, the chart angles as points should probably be considered in a passive context, receiving planetary energy.

The Moon, just into Aries, enhances fire and cardinality. Cardinality is already quite strong by the stellium, a compensatory aspect.

Blessedly, Uranus or other slow planets were not on the angles.

Three of the fixed planets are in early or late fixed degrees. These are quake degrees.

The Moon has passed over all trigger planets, Mars, Uranus, Mercury and sometimes Saturn by conjunction.

Mercury is not in the same degree as another planet, but following the rules, their collective midpoint or energy center at 21° Sagittarius 47' is right on the degree of Mars and Neptune. In the signature section on California I note the affinity of Mercury to choose the degree of Neptune in major California events.

The quake came without warning, the so-called Uranian event. The immediate and recent influence of the fast planets on Uranus and Uranus on them is so obvious that I'll refer the readers to the charts.

Venus separation is fair. It had not really separated form Saturn or Pluto. Note the exact 75° (15° type aspect, partile) to Jupiter.

Venus and Mars, Venus separated in recent conjunction and still in same sign, again common to major California events.

Venus conjunct Mars, separating, and Venus 75° Jupiter partile (exact) fulfill the Venus-Mars-Jupiter energy triad specifications.

A stellium intensifies the energy. The Moon into Aries gave that final touch to the planetary tumblers by enhancing fire and cardinal. The massive infusion of energy into the fault system by the stellium was too much and the quake occurred. It was like pouring hot water into a glass too fast.

Regarding the slow planet dance, Uranus here conjunct Neptune (San Francisco 1906 opposition), in both Jupiter and Pluto were in the same sign.

An important question remains. To what extent is Los Angeles in danger from another major quake in the near future?

I'll answer briefly in terms of contents within the text.

- I believe this was a major release event and odds are the next major Los Angeles quake lies some years into the future.
- Joker is wild is the rule for quakes and their forecasting. Very occasionally a location will be subjected to major events over several years. Tblisi is the most recent example.
- If a period of cataclysm is involved, all bets are off. Obviously such periods have occurred before and just as obviously the much vaunted millennium events are behind schedule. But remember psychics are notoriously poor on timing.
- Saturn in Pisces gives two and a half years of intensified grand trine water activity. Any fast planets in Cancer complete the circuit. Just the Sun in Cancer more than doubles GTW time . . . this without other planets or duration considered. I am considering this from the two and a half days per month of the Moon in Cancer.

Moving to another matter, it took only a glance to note that the quake conformed to the California signature, but to forecast that is another matter and I did not forecast this event at all.

To forecast Los Angeles in this instance would have required the ingress lunation group of charts as well as working the midpoints of the primary triad Sun-Mercury-Jupiter. Probable cause would have been a recent eclipse path or tremors. As in other Uranian events, warning tremors were notably absent.

The process of evaluation and forecasting for a general area would involve the nearest volcanoes and belts, both geologically and astrologically.

While not an impossible or even very difficult task for a location with or without a computer, it does involve more than hobby time. It is this that has severely limited the number of weather astrologers as well.

The historical facts as noted in other locations are that Los Angeles will be hit again. It is simply the cost of living and, as the saying goes, doing business. Death and damage are greater for the simple reason that there are more people.

Once again I am drawn to the ultimate in quake damage, heavy damage to a nuclear power plant. Charleston, New Madrid, New York State, California and Washington State. Where are the faults and where are the nuclear power plants? Bear in mind a simple fact. America east of the Mississippi and western Europe other than Italy (Iberian Peninsula, France, Germany) have major faults that cover a large area. No major quake has occurred in any of these places since the advent of nuclear power plants.

May all readers find something useful and beneficial in this book.

Bibliography

The American Ephemeris for the 20th Century, 1900 to 2000 at Midnight; compiled and programmed by Neil F Michelsen, 1980;

Astro Computing Services, PO Box 16430, San Diego, CA 92116 USA.

The Rosicrucian Ephemeris, 1900-2000, Midnight International Edition (Eng, Fr, Ger, Span, Ital); The Rosicrucian Fellowship International Headquarters, 2222 Mission Ave, Oceanside, CA 92054 USA.(This ephemeris also contains declinations and daily aspectarian.)

The Encyclopedia of Astrology, Nicholas DeVore, 1977, Littlefield Adams and Company, Totowa, NJ. (If you know no astrologers, this is all you need, and it includes an eclipse table.)

Dell Horoscope (monthly magazine) contains a monthly ephemeris, declinations, astronomical events, aspectarian and key to astrological symbols and aspects. (For beginner and professional.)

Earthquake Prediction, Ann E Parker, Aries Press; (temporarily out of print) this uses heliocentric points, eclipses, and geodetic equivalents. (Sepharial's) Her work constitutes a system in itself and creates a system of natal geodetic degrees for location and transiting degrees, eclipse degrees and others for event timing.

The Geodetic World Map, I I Chris McRae, 1988, American Federation of Astrologers Inc.O Box 22040, Tempe, AZ 85285-2040 USA. (This is a geodetic mapping system based on Sepharial's geodetic equivalents.)

Geodetic Equivalents, Sepharial, American Federation of Astrologers Inc., PO Box 22040, Tempe, AZ 85285-2040 USA. (Used by Ann E Parker and Chris McRae.(This is the most accepted geodetic system. A comparison study of geodetic equivalents systems exists in Mundane Astrology, Baigent/Campion/Harvey, Aquarian Press, Wellingborough Northamptonshire, England.)

The Astrologer's Handbook, Frances Sakoian and Louis S Acker, Harper and Row, New York, NY USA. (Perhaps the greatest aspectarian ever written, it will give ``feel'' to the work of a newcomer or geologist.)

Dictionary of Geological Terms, Revised Edition, Anchor Books, Anchor Press/Doubleday, Garden City, NY USA. (And you too can read geologese.)

The Catalog of Significant Earthquakes, 2150 BC-1991 AD, Report #SE-49, Sept 1992, Dunbar, Lockridge, and Whiteside, US Department of Commerce, National Oceanic and Atmospheric Administration (NOAA) National Environmental Satellite, Data and Information Service. National Geophysical Data Center, Boulder, CO 80303-3328 USA. (An excellent work, catalogued by time and country, with maps and bibliography.)

Earthquakes, Don DeNevi, Celestial Arts, Millbrae CA USA.

Earthquakes, Bruce A Bolt, 1978. 1988, Freeman.

1001 Questions Answered About Earthquakes, Avalanches, Floods, and Other Natural Disasters, Barbara Tufty, Dover Publications, 180 Varick Street, New York, NY 10014 USA.

Earthquake Country: How, Why and Where Earthquakes Strike in California, Robert Iacopi, Lane Publishing Co., Menlo Park, CA 94025 USA. (An excellent text, it details the California faults. As noted, I believe there are several location signatures for California.)

"Mount St. Helens," *National Geographic Magazine*, Jan. 1981.

"Inside the Earth," Stephen G Brush, *Natural History*, Feb 1984; PO Box 4300, Bernenfeld, NJ 07621 USA.

(While updating concepts on the earth's core, Brush inadvertently de-mythologizes geology and its unity.)

We Are The Earthquake Generation, Jeffrey Goodman Ph.D, 1979, Berkley Publishing Corp. 200 Madison Ave, New York, NY 10016, USA.

(The psychics Dr Goodman interviewed are late, their forecasts overdue. Nevertheless this remains a text fascinating for its geological insights and hypotheses.)

Edgar Cayce On Atlantis, Edgar Cayce, Warner Books, PO Box 690, New York, NY 10019 USA. (This history provides some provocative geological assertions.)

The Children of Mu, Volume II in a series, James Churchward, BE Books, c/o The Brotherhood of Life, INCl, 110 Dartmouth SE, Albuquerque, NM 87106, USA. (In this volume is the gas belt theory. His maps are crudely hand drawn.)

The Pole Shift, John White, 1980, ARE Press, Virginia Beach, VA. (An Anthology of ``tilt'' theory. White comments on the work of its great theorists, while allowing their positions to pervade. Probably the definitive overview on tilt.)

The Nuclear Waste Primer, League of Women Voters Education Foundation, Nick Lyons Books, 31 W. 21st St., New York, NY 10010, USA.

Poisoned Power-The Case Against Nuclear Power Plants Before and After 3-Mile Island, 1971, 1979, John W Gofman, Ph.D, MD, Arthur R Tamplin, Ph.D; Rodale Press, Emmans, PA, USA.

I repeat, the ultimate earthquake tragedy will not be the demolition of a Tokyo or New York, or millions of lives lost, but the perfect hit, epicenter and vibrational conduction, of a 6+R event on a nuclear power plant or a Hanford type nuclear dump. For the first time in history, land would not be reusable after the quake. Like Chernobyl, eventual loss of life might be inestimable.

The above of course also applies to a super volcanic eruption, a future Krakatoa. This also a less likely scenario while the quake remains almost an eventuality.